The Economics and Financing of Media Companies

SECOND EDITION

The Economics and Financing of Media Companies

SECOND EDITION

Robert G. Picard

FORDHAM UNIVERSITY PRESS • NEW YORK • 2011

Fordham University Press has no responsibility for the
persistence or accuracy of URLs for external or third-party
Internet websites referred to in this publication and does not
guarantee that any content on such websites is, or will remain,
accurate or appropriate.

Fordham University Press also publishes its books in a variety
of electronic formats. Some content that appears in print may
not be available in electronic books.

Library of Congress Cataloging-in-Publication Data

Picard, Robert G.
The economics and financing of media companies / Robert
G. Picard.—2nd ed.
    p. cm.
  Includes bibliographical references and index.
  ISBN 978-0-8232-3256-7 (cloth : alk. paper)
  ISBN 978-0-8232-3257-4 (pbk. : alk. paper)
  1. Mass media—Economic aspects.   2. Mass
media—Finance. I. Title.
P96.E25P528 2011
338.4′730223—dc22

               2010033993

Printed in the United States of America

14   5 4 3 2

Second edition

CONTENTS

PREFACE

This book is intended to help the reader to develop better understanding of how economic and financial forces influence the operations and developments of media and communications firms. It is designed to improve the knowledge of those who work or will work in such firms so that they can better cope with the increasing complexity of the environment in which their firms operate.

The book is designed to make new, junior and mid-level managers, and future managers, more effective in confronting the demands of the increasingly competitive communications industries by improving their abilities to respond to the ever-changing problems and issues that arise in the course of managing such firms. It is also intended to give those who observe media a broader context in which to consider the operations and decisions made by media managers.

This book strives to provide concepts for understanding and analyzing communications companies and their situations, to increase readers' abilities to identify and evaluate alternative strategies and courses of action, and to allow them to work more effectively with specialists with deeper expertise in finance and economics.

This second edition updates and expands the first edition. It contains updated examples of concepts and issues faced by actual firms. It includes a new chapter on media distribution mechanisms, discussions of how many differ from other industries and differences among media and how they are produced, more material on intellectual property rights and management, and more information on Internet and other digital media whose significance has increased since the first edition.

The approach employed by this book is not theoretical. It uses a managerial economics approach that involves the use of economic theories and various tools to help managers make knowledgeable decisions and to help others understand why managers make those choices. The approach to financing is also practical and is based on the practices of contemporary capital sources and media firms.

The economics and financing of media companies are the foundations upon which all media activity takes place. Regardless of cultural, political, and social roles and expectations for media, media must cover their costs and create returns, just as any other business, or they will wither and disappear. The forces that require effective operation are the same for both private commercial media and noncommercial media such as public service broadcasting.

Since the beginning of the study of communications, attention has primarily been focused upon the roles, functions, and effects of communications. When media and other communications enterprises were studied, they were explored as social institutions and much of the focus was on the social, political, legal, and technological influences on the enterprises and their operations. Scholars ignored, or only lightly attended to, the effects of economic forces. This should not come as a surprise to anyone familiar with the history of communications inquiry, because communications scholars initially came from the disciplines of sociology, psychology, political science, history, and literary criticism and then passed on their approaches to studying media to new generations of communications scholars that were produced during the second half of the twentieth century.

In the 1970s, an increasing number of economics and business scholars began exploring media, as the result of technical and policy changes leading to the development of cable television and problematic trends in audience uses appearing in the newspaper industry. It was not until the 1980s, however, that communications scholars themselves began to accord economic and financial forces and issues the significant attention they were due. Since then, a coherent and growing body of knowledge about economic issues and problems and the financial strategies and behavior of communications enterprises has developed to help explain how economic and financial forces and strategies affect media developments and operations.

Several significant economic texts have emerged in the field, revealing how basic economic laws and principles can be applied to the study and operation of media, exploring the economic structure and organization of various communication industries, and focusing on economic issues in specific communication industries. Excellent analyses have considered the political economy of communications enterprises and its effects on society and vice versa.

This book expands upon those works concerned with how economic and financial pressures affect a variety of communications activities, systems, organizations, and enterprises across all media sectors and telecommunications. It builds upon those works and then introduces business concepts and their application in media firms to reveal how these factors influence choices and how they can be used to improve and understand industry decisions and practices.

The Economics and Financing of Media Companies

SECOND EDITION

CHAPTER 1

Media Firms as Economic and Business Entities

To understand media industries, one must understand what drives media companies, how their markets work, and the pressures that lead executives to make choices about the ways their companies will be structured, the activities they will undertake, and the performance they require. Companies raise capital, create facilities, employ personnel, create media products and services, and sell these products and services in the market. Some companies are successful and survive in the market, some that were once highly successful cease to be successful, and some are never successful and disappear. In the aggregate, these companies create the broader media and communications industries, but they operate individually—facing individual economic and managerial challenges, making individual choices, pursuing individual strategies, and achieving different outcomes.

Whether a media company is a commercial or a noncommercial operation, it faces a variety of economic and financial forces and must be operated as a business entity in order to respond to and manage those forces effectively.

The forms of media companies include the range of types of firms that exist in any industry. At the simplest level are sole proprietorships and partnerships. Sole proprietorships are firms owned and operated by one person. This form is found primarily among smaller newspapers and magazines, Internet firms, and advertising firms. Partnerships are similar but, as the name suggests, involve ownership by more than one person. This business form, used when one person alone has insufficient capital or skills to operate independently, is most often found in small publications, design firms, and advertising agencies.

More complex company forms involve incorporation—that is, the creation of a firm as a legal entity independent of its owners. This reduces the legal responsibility of individual owners for the performance or actions of the firm. Simple corporations can be sole proprietorships or partnerships of any size. Most media companies are incorporated as private corporations and tend to be small and midsized enterprises, but privately owned media firms include larger companies such as the Bertelsmann AG, Tribune Company, and Hearst Corporation.

A number of larger firms have chosen to become public corporations—firms whose shares are publicly traded on stock markets—typically to gain additional capital. Examples of public media firms are News Corporation, the New York Times Company, Pearson, and Viacom.

Another form of ownership found in media involves noncommercial firms that are typically created as not-for-profit corporations. These include public service broadcasters worldwide such as the British Broadcasting Corporation (BBC) and the Australian Broadcasting Corporation (ABC) as well as publishers (or media firms) of such periodicals as the *Christian Science Monitor* and *The Nation* and online news sites such as MinnPost and ProPublica.

All of these forms of media enterprises carry out the functions of acquiring and organizing resources to produce goods and services, just as firms in other industries do. The organizational forms of businesses exist because they are an efficient means of carrying out the various steps in the production and distribution of goods and services. Companies have evolved into their current forms because they create organizations that can enter into structured relationships with owners of capital, workers, and suppliers, and because the firm can provide the facilities, equipment, and management necessary to produce and distribute products effectively.

In public service and other not-for-profit media, producing information and programming useful and interesting to audiences is the primary function. In commercial media, however, the primary function shifts to producing audiences for advertisers or making sales of media products to customers to obtain financial revenue for continued operation and profits.

The differences in primary functions do not mean that commercial media necessarily must produce content of poorer quality, although some may in fact do so. The differences mean that commercial media managers' content choices are based on the need to produce audiences desirable to specific advertisers or categories of advertisers and to maximize the profitability of the firm. Managers of public service and not-for-profit media, obviously, are not subject to these same pressures; however, they must make content choices based on the need to provide optimal service based on the goals outlined for their operations and to maximize their services to different audience segments.

Social and cultural observers regularly argue about the desirability of commercial operations, particularly in broadcasting, because of such operations' additional pressures and functions. This book does not debate the desirability of commercial media, recognizing that the decision of whether to have commercial operations—and the extent to which commercial operations are permitted—is primarily a question of domestic public policy and media regulation.

The requirements of the varying types of media operations affect the forms and structures of media firms, as do the scale and scope of those operations. Because the needs of media differ and because the organizational requirements to create media goods and services vary depending upon their markets, the sizes of media organizations run the gamut from small to large.

These differences create disparate problems and issues among media. There are, however, underlying economic and financial forces that affect all media and certain economic and financial factors that are unique to specific media. This book explores those factors and their implications in a way designed to provide information and understanding that can be used in making choices within media firms and in better analyzing media industries and companies.

THE CHANGING MEDIA ENVIRONMENT

Five decisive trends are altering the media environment and forcing media companies to change their thinking and operations: media abundance, audience fragmentation and polarization, product portfolio development, the eroding strength of media companies, and an overall power shift in the communications process.

Abundance is seen in the dramatic rise in media types and units of media. The growth of media supply is far exceeding the growth of consumption in both temporal and monetary terms. The average number of pages in newspapers tripled in the twentieth century; the number of over-the-air television channels has quadrupled since the 1960s—supplemented by an average of about fifty-six cable channels in the average home; there are four times as many magazines available as in the 1970s; 1.5 million new Web pages are created daily; and created and stored knowledge (as measured by information scientists) is growing at a rate of 30 percent per year. We used to think of competition among newspapers or competition among television channels, but this media abundance has created competition not only among media but also competition for time expenditures between media and other leisure-time activities such as sports, concerts, and socializing at cafés and bars.

This abundance has created fragmentation and polarization of the audience because people are spreading their media use across more channels, books, magazines, and Web sites. This produces extremes of use and nonuse among available channels and titles. For example, individuals tend to focus on three or four television channels. Increasing channel availability does not create an equal amount of increased use. Advertisers understand this development and have responded by spreading their expenditures and paying less for smaller audiences. The audience-use changes mean that competition is no longer institutionally and structurally defined, but is being driven by the time and money audiences/consumers spend with media, and the competitive focus is now on the attention economy and the experience economy. The attention economy recognizes the scarcity of attention that people can give to communications and that media, marketers, politicians, and others vie for the limited amount of time consumers have available. The experience economy is based on the idea that enterprises need to organize satisfying and memorable interactions (that is, experiences) for their customers in order to generate loyalty and repeated engagement.

The difficulties faced by individual units of media have led media companies to create and operate portfolios of media products. This response occurs because declining average return per unit makes owning a single media product problematic. The creation and operation of the portfolios are efforts to reduce risk and obtain economies of scale and scope. These portfolios can increase return if they result in efficient operations and joint cost savings.

Despite the growth of portfolios and large media companies, the strength of the companies is eroding. Today no established content-producing media companies are in the top one hundred companies in the United States or in the top five hundred worldwide. Moreover, the reach of media companies is declining, even though such companies have grown bigger. Each has less of the viewers', readers', and listeners' attention than in the past, and their difficult strategic position is of concern to many investors. As a result, media companies are struggling with their major investors, and all major media companies fear becoming takeover targets.

Underscoring all of this is a fundamental power shift in communications. The media space used to be controlled by media companies; today, however, consumers are gaining control of what has become a demand rather than a supply market. And media consumers are no longer satisfied being merely passive receivers; many are now participating in production through the variety of forms of interactive and user-generated content such as rating and adding comments to articles and creating their own blogs and Web sites. This shift is apparent in the financing of contemporary initiatives in cable and satellite, TV and radio, audio and video downloading, digital television, and mobile media, which are primarily based on a consumer payment model, where most income comes from purchasers rather than advertisers. Today, for every dollar advertisers spend on media worldwide, consumers spend three. Major advertisers are cutting back on traditional types of advertising—already only about one-third of their total marketing expenditures—and spending their money on personal marketing, direct marketing, sponsorships, and cross-promotion.

This shift has been promoted by the development of software that makes it easier for individual to produce effective videos, audio recordings, and online presentations without the help of professionals. In addition, technology is promoting peer-to-peer file sharing, social networking, and collaborative games that are creating new distribution networks. The fixed location application of these technologies is now also moving to mobile platforms, empowering individuals even further.

Media companies worldwide are struggling to understand and adjust to wide-ranging external and internal changes that are altering modes of production, rapidly increasing competition, eroding their traditional audience and advertiser bases, altering established market dominance patterns, and changing the potential of the firms. The need for media managers to understand and adjust to the new conditions increases daily because such changes can lead to failure of both existing and new products as well as, ultimately, to the loss of value or the collapse of firms.

Today, media markets are far more complex and turbulent than they were in the past. The greater complexity is evident in the challenges that firms encounter as the number of competitors increases, as they strive to produce multiple products or services, and as they operate in multiple markets simultaneously. Market turbulence is seen in the instability and lack of clear direction in markets. This raises uncertainty, makes it difficult to reduce risk, and creates the need for rapid innovation. However, it concurrently forces managers to make quick investment decisions, to rapidly introduce new products and new markets, and to alter existing products—all of which carry significant risks.

These factors make it crucial that media managers and personnel, and those who want to understand media, clearly understand their business operations and the economic and financial forces that affect their choices and structures.

HOW MEDIA DIFFER FROM OTHER PRODUCTS AND SERVICES

Media differ from other products in that their benefits are not measured solely in economic terms. The gains from media are also measured in terms

Implications of the Changing Media World

The characteristics of media, combined with the changing environment in which they operate, produce unstable conditions and great challenges for media managers.

Digitalization has made the underlying technologies of media production, storage, and distribution more alike. This has caused many boundaries among media and adjacent communication industries to blur or to disappear altogether, creating opportunities to move content across communication platforms and deliver it to consumers in multiple ways. Media companies today contend with many more competitors driven by a wider array of interests and opportunities than in the past.

In this setting, content (whether entertainment, news, or general information) is relatively expensive to produce, yet relatively inexpensive to reproduce and distribute because of digitalization and information and communication technologies. Those factors combine with the excess in supply of content to create markets in which prices for content are declining or suppressed. This is, of course, good for consumers but bad for producers.

The volatility of prices and general instability in media markets are removing the stability that produced predictable consumption, income, and employment in media during the second half of the twentieth century. Today, newspapers, television, radio, Internet services, and telecommunications firms are all facing riskier situations than in the past. In order to control that risk, media companies are altering their means of operation, changing their workforces, acquiring rivals and new firms that offer strategic opportunities, and seeking greater enforcement of copyrights and related rights so they can increase prices, revenue, and profits.

As one looks to the future, it appears that the main challenges will involve not production of media content itself but the monetization of that content. The principal contests between competitors will be over control of highly desirable content and access to and control of distribution channels that reach both aggregate audiences and individual consumers and create direct-sales mechanisms.

of social, cultural, and political benefits. Although media products involve significant social welfare gains and are often artistic endeavors, they are still subject to basic economic, financial, and managerial laws and pressures. However, there are some differences in supply and demand characteristics, the nature of the industries, and activities required that affect the business dynamics of media industries. They differ from other industries in a number of respects.

At a basic level, they differ from other firms and industries because media products result from creative work that is based on information, ideas, and literary and artistic endeavor. Media products accrue special benefits from copyrights and related rights that are not extended to other types of products. Media companies also tend to be more visible to consumers than other businesses because they are a noticeable part of day-to-day life and because often the individuals involved have celebrity status and consequently attract great attention. Further, media are highly influenced by public policy and regulation because social, political, and cultural goals are pursued through media policies, and media rely upon publicly controlled spaces such as radio spectrum and public rights-of-way to a greater degree than most other industries.

On more specific levels, media are differentiated from many other products and services because of both supply- and demand-side differences.

SUPPLY-SIDE DIFFERENCES

Although operating in competitive environments, when compared to other industries, media companies tend to face less direct competition than other types of companies. First, the number of newspapers and radio channels in markets tends to be far lower than the number of shoe stores or kebab restaurants, for example. Similarly, the number of television channels is far lower than the number of types of candy available.

Second, many decisions in media industries are based on noneconomic criteria and rely upon public service, artistic, and cultural factors, established relationships, the intuition of creative decision makers, and—sometimes—whimsy and hubris. Although not all producers of other products always act with economic rationality, the extent of the economic irrationality in media industries tends to be higher and more widespread than that found in other industries.

Third, many people will create content even without compensation because of expressive and artistic motives, public service motives, and desire to achieve fame and celebrity. The media industry thus differs significantly from automobile manufacturing, fast-food industries, and good retailing, where it is unheard of for people to work without compensation. People do not volunteer to work on automobile assembly lines, but often are very willing to write books, record audio content, and make films without assurance of payment.

A fourth difference involves the methods of production. Because media products are based on creative and artistic elements, the processes of production are not as straightforward and controllable as in other industries, and production often involves employees with a good deal of professional autonomy because of their knowledge and artistic abilities and because employers acquiesce to professional norms and standards. As a result, organizational conflict is ingrained in media businesses, and content creators and managers often differ on goals to an extent uncommon in most industries.

Fifth, many media products have nonphysical properties, resulting in very different distribution mechanisms and costs than those associated with physical products. The "virtual" nature of these products has significant advantages. For example, the current conversion of motion picture theaters in the United States from film projection to digital exhibition technologies is expected to save about $1 billion annually in distribution costs because of the switch from a physical product (film stock) to a nonphysical (digital) medium.

Finally, many media products are vulnerable to piracy and counterfeiting in ways other general consumer products are not. Because of the technologies required, an individual cannot easily counterfeit a Porsche Cayenne in his garage, but that individual can easily create unauthorized copies of digital content (for example, audio recordings) in that same garage with relatively inexpensive and accessible technologies. The ease and ability with which one can make unauthorized duplicates of media products can interfere with legitimate supply and affect both its costs and revenues. Not surprisingly, media companies aggressively promote action against what they consider to be piracy and counterfeiting to protect their ability to receive revenue from their products.

DEMAND-SIDE DIFFERENCES

The most important characteristic of media compared with that of other products and services is the high unpredictability of success of a product. This occurs because of difficulties in forecasting product quality and consumer demand. Because of their characteristics, one cannot produce test units for most media products to determine market demand before full production. Consequently, product failure rates are high, especially among books, audio recordings, and films.

Another unique property of media are multiple reuses for media products and the reuses may be more valuable than the original use. Motion pictures, for example, have multiple uses after theatrical exhibition—cable license sales, DVD sales and rentals, television license sales, and so on—and audio recordings can be secondarily sold for various types of audio collections and soundtracks.

A third demand characteristic is a large oversupply of content from which consumers can choose. Because it is impossible to consume all products, consumers have significant power in media markets in determining the success, failure, and pricing of media products.

Fourth, much of the economic value of media products results from a small number of products and services. Although failure rates are high, successes are well rewarded financially. In Hollywood, for example, 10 percent of the top two hundred films typically account for 50 percent of industry revenue.

Fifth, media products tend to be consumed more often than other products, and the time devoted to their consumption—especially that for television and radio programs and audio recordings—is far beyond that for other products. These factors create unique relationships between consumers and suppliers that are beyond those experienced in other industries.

Sixth, demand is influenced by the dual product (two-sided platform characteristic in economic terms) nature of commercial media, a factor that influences demand for only a few other products. Two-sided markets are markets in which more than one set of consumers must be addressed and there is an interaction between strategies and choices for each set of customers. Prices for one group of consumers affect their consumption quantity and this, in turn, affects the prices for and consumption by the other groups. Optimal revenue can only be achieved by dealing with all groups of consumers simultaneously.

Revenue for products in which advertising is carried is not determined by the time and attention given by audiences alone, but involves separate demand functions that exist for advertiser expenditures. As a result, media products that appeal to audiences but not to advertisers fail if audiences are unable or unwilling to provide the revenue necessary for the product's survival.

Today, however, product and price choices are getting much more complex because media are shifting from two-sided to multi-sided platforms in which relationships among consumers are compounded. Newspapers, for example, have paid and free print editions, paid and free online content, and paid and free content available through e-readers and mobile telephone-based services.

Finally, it must also be recognized that consumption patterns differ because many expenditures for acquisition are sunk costs (that is, previously made expenditures that cannot be recovered and tend not to affect current choices), and direct and immediate expenditures for consumption are not made. Because of subscriptions (a form of sunk costs) and advertiser financial support for many media, demand functions for much content do not follow traditional patterns. Instead, consumers tend to acquire large quantities of content that is not consumed and consume a good deal of content that is only minimally satisfying.

Thus, media products differ among themselves and between themselves and other products in terms of their market, financial, and operational characteristics. These characteristics create differences in business dynamics and managerial issues faced by media managers. Because experience in one media type does not necessarily lead to understanding of the conditions and environment of other media types, managers of one type of media who assume managerial responsibilities over another type often struggle to understand the second type's business dynamics. Similarly, managers from other industries who are brought into media firms typically have a long learning curve in attempting to apply their knowledge to media industries.

Appreciating the differences among media products and between media products and other products helps managers and those analyzing the industries to determine factors and interactions on which to focus their attention, identify the most important aspects in creating and distributing the products, and understand their dependencies and vulnerabilities.

THE THEORY OF THE FIRM

Mere effective organization of resources and processes alone is not sufficient reason for the creation of commercial business organizations. Underlying these structural elements are the fundamental goals of companies which are explained by *the theory of the firm*. The theory asserts that the development and operation of firms are guided by the primary goal of maximizing both profit and the value of the firm. The purpose of the creation and operation of commercial media firms is thus to produce the most profit and highest value for the firm. The former tends to be a short-term annual goal and the latter is a longer-term goal. If resources and the processes by which they are transformed into goods and services are efficiently and effectively organized and managed, the ability to achieve both of these goals becomes possible.

This neoclassical view of the theory of the firm conceptualizes companies as rational decision makers operating in a market system that seeks optimal allocation of resources under conditions of perfect competition or with a minimum of market imperfections. In this view, firms are created to organize activity more efficiently and to reduce costs of constantly negotiating for materials and independent labor. According to this conceptualization, firms that are better organized and more efficient than others become more successful.

In recent years, a structural evolutionary view of the firm has taken hold, accepting that firms are profit-seeking but asserting that they are not always profit-maximizing enterprises. It holds that firms will forgo short-term profit for long-term gain and may forgo profit for social or other purposes such as research and development, product differentiation, and growth. This view recognizes that markets are rarely perfect, that information needed for rational decision making is imperfect, and that government intervention produces market and firm behaviors contrary to the tenets of the neoclassical theory of the firm.

The resource-based theory of the firm comes from this new theoretical perspective and posits that firms are a collection of resources necessary to carry out their activities and that those with better resources and capabilities can achieve better results vis-à-vis competitors. Both tangible and intangible resources such as specialized equipment, highly skilled personnel, intellectual property rights, and superior knowledge can provide inimitable sources of value.

Another modern behavioral theory of the firm argues that enterprises are affected by their environments as well as by internal structures and activities, and that they must often make choices with insufficient knowledge. It asserts that rationality is bounded by constraints on information and knowledge because of needs to make decisions before better clarity exists in markets.

These modern conceptualizations of the theory of the firm reveal that, with the rise of modern corporations and the separation of management and ownership, the goals may sometimes be maximization of sales rather than profit or enhanced firm value. Sales maximization proponents argue that once shareholders' basic needs for profit have been satisfied, the goal of some managers of modern corporations becomes maximization of sales to increase cash flow that can be used for growth, and thus the measurement and ranking of firms by revenue has become a significant factor in executive compensation.

In the modern conceptualizations, not all firms can be expected to behave similarly because they have varying goals, differing expectations of owners and managers, and dissimilar risk preferences that will lead them to react differently when faced with the same conditions. When one considers media companies, one must be cognizant of these differences and wary about generalizing from what is observed in a few enterprises.

MEDIA FIRMS AND RISK

Because the future is unknown, all firms—including media firms—and their investors face risk when they make choices about current and future activities. Risk is a concept that results from uncertainty about the future and about the results of choices that must be made today. Not everything can be known, the future is not fully predictable, and unforeseen events and factors may arise, because many things are conditional and tentative, and because the environment is constantly changing.

Companies and managers are constantly struggling with uncertainty. Behavioral economics has shown that individuals and firms are affected by psychology and social psychology and that decisions are often made using existing frames of reference and groupthink. Choices are often made with limited knowledge and based on experiences and rules of thumb. In these situations, people tend to try to remove ambiguity by asserting superior knowledge and may act to avert or minimize risk and loss potential. These actions, however, can lead to difficulties when industries, markets, and products are in rapid change, because they tend to produce behavior that limits innovation and entrepreneurial responses.

All business decisions ultimately involve an estimation of their outcome and the risk that the outcome may vary from the expectation. Any decision in which the probability of results cannot be estimated with reasonable certainty carries greater risk. This uncertainty is particularly important in communications industries today, because managers are simultaneously making decisions on how they will respond to changing technologies, changing audience use of communication products and services, and changing patterns of advertising expenditures.

Even on a daily basis, certain media firms face greater risks than others. Newspapers, magazines, and broadcasters face relatively less risk than book publishers and filmmakers because reading, viewing, and listening patterns tend to be relatively stable in the near term and serve the same functions from day to day. The risks of these firms are even lower if their revenues have been stabilized by audience subscriptions.

Book publishers, audio recording companies, multimedia producers, and motion picture producers, however, have higher risks each time they introduce a new book, recording, production, or film. This occurs because the content is not stable from product to product, because consumption patterns vary, and because it is difficult to determine how audiences will receive the combination of elements in each new product.

Managers usually try to diminish risk by spreading it across income-generating activities to reduce the effect of negative outcomes from some choices, but to nonetheless allow firms to take advantage of potentially rewarding opportunities. This is sought by firms through ownership of multiple magazines, newspapers, or broadcasting outlets, and through the production of multiple books, recordings, TV programs, films, or Internet sites.

Although risks can and should be ameliorated, avoiding risk is dangerous to firms. Managers who try to avoid all additional risk place their firms in jeopardy by allowing other firms to achieve the rewards of profit from those risks and to gain competitive advantages that reduce the competitiveness of the risk-avoiding firm.

THE ROLES OF PROFIT AND RETURN

From a basic accounting perspective, profit is the money that remains after expenses are subtracted from income. From a managerial perspective, however, profit is a broader and essential element for the development of both

How Media Companies Spread Their Risk

The risk of failure of media products is high where individual titles or productions are involved because their producers make production decisions based on their estimates and beliefs about market demand.

It is difficult, however, for producers to anticipate changes in audience tastes and expectations and the extent to which audiences' interest in specific genres will continue. Predicting the continuing success of currently popular performers, directors, or writers is also problematic. Producers are also unable to foretell the success of marketing efforts or what competing products may be offered by competitors. These factors make it difficult for producers to estimate with any certainty demand for specific films, books, and audio recordings. The result is that there are very few successful titles each year and many more unsuccessful or less profitable media products.

In responding to the risks created by this uncertainty, media firms attempt to spread the risk among different titles. A recording company may produce fifty recordings with different artists recorded in several genres or a motion picture company may fund ten widely different motion pictures. In 2010, for example, EMI Group issued Cypress Hill's "Rise Up" for hip hop music fans through its Capitol Records subsidiary, "Mwaliko" by jazz guitarist Lionel Loueke on its Blue Notes Records label, and Beethoven's String Quartets performed by the Artemis Quartet through its EMI Classics label. That same year, Universal Pictures distributed the comedy *Get Him to the Greek*, the action film *Robin Hood*, and the animated feature *Despicable Me*, in an effort to attract a range of audiences and thus reduce its vulnerability to a flop in any one genre.

Some firms will attempt to spread their risk by operating in different media industries in hopes that lower performance of, for example, its magazines during an unsuccessful year in the magazine industry will be offset by better performance of its television programming subsidiary.

Companies also seek to reduce the risks of rapid price increases and problems in the availability of necessary resources by entering into long-term contracts, becoming shareholders in suppliers' firms, or entering into joint ventures to own resource firms with competitors that face similar risks.

commercial and noncommercial media. Profit is needed to provide opportunities to finance improvements in equipment and facilities, to experiment with new methods, and to develop new products and services that may or may not be successful.

Profit creates the money available to pay the owners or investors of commercial firms, to make capital expenditures, and to pay debts. Owners or investors of noncommercial media do not receive the profit, but it provides funds to improve the company through capital investments, to make additional expenditures on content and other items, and to pay debts.

Many business theorists and managers argue that profit should be considered a cost of operation, not the result of operations. In this view, the division of profits among company owners or investors and the internal reinvestment or uses of profit are expenses required to ensure the continued availability of capital and the viability of the firm.

Firms operating under this view construct budgets based on achieving a specific monetary or percentage return from their operations. They build into the budget profitability requirements or *costs* for their activities each year.

Monetary profit alone does not indicate the efficiency with which a firm produces the monetary result, however. To gain the broader picture one can use the concept of return, which indicates profitability of a firm in nonmonetary terms, to maximize the effectiveness of a firm's activities.

Planning for Profit

Media and other companies can plan a specified level of profit in their budgeting processes. When a level of return is specified, it is essentially entered into financial calculations as a cost so that operating expenses, plus the desired return, are covered by operating income. In practice, this means that expenses are limited to a level at which the specified return can be achieved.

Profit planning is exemplified in Bertelsmann—owner of book publisher Random House, magazine publisher Gruner + Jahr, broadcaster RTL Group, and the recording firm BMG Music—which set out to achieve an 8 percent return on invested capital beginning in 2008. To achieve this target would require sales growth and divestment of unprofitable enterprises. "You're not going to turn a lamb into a lion," CEO Hartmut Ostrowski told company executives when announcing the plan. "We have to evaluate our business areas and—if necessary—make tough decisions."

During a budget year in which profit levels have been planned, the desired return can be met only if projections of income and expenses are met or if expenses are reduced proportionally if income falls below projections.

This is especially important for publicly traded companies, because investors follow the performance of public companies in meeting profitability targets during the year by reviewing monthly and quarterly performance figures. Share prices and ratings typically rise or fall depending upon the extent to which a firm is meeting its projections for or market expectations of profitability.

Worries about future profitability also affect share prices and trading. When the New York Times Co. announced a decline of 3.2 percent in revenue and a 6 percent decline in advertising during the first quarter of 2010, for example, share prices dropped from $12.74 to $11.61, a 9 percent decline. Conversely, when good performance is expected, prices and trading are also affected. Before Morgan Stanley analysts raised their price target on Time Warner Cable to $54 on April 21, 2010, for example, shares were trading at $52.18. The following day share prices rose to $54.54, a 4.5 percent increase.

A manager who considers only a monetary figure counts only money that is left after expenses are paid. A manager who employs the concept of return combines the ideas of overall revenue, the effort that took place to generate that revenue, and the profit produced.

The latter method produces an indicator of profitability that incorporates efficiency of the internal operations, which is useful because profit creation is affected by the extent to which management is able to promote efficiency by holding down the costs of resources and increasing revenue from sales. When there is above-average performance in this regard, above-average profit or return can be achieved.

The achievement of above-average performance, or at least the avoidance of below-average performance, is necessary to achieve adequate returns, to make the firm attractive when additional capital is required, or to reduce significant fluctuations in the share prices of publicly traded firms.

The role of profit in capital investment decisions is explained by the *risk theory of profit*. It argues that the potential for high economic profits is necessary to induce investment, especially in industries involving greater levels of risk. As a result, firms operating in these sectors or industries require above-average returns or the capital will move to other, more profitable investments.

Profits also rise as a premium paid by consumers for innovative products and services. Those returns tend to diminish rapidly, however, because other firms imitate successful goods and services. In order to promote innovation, governments provide incentives in the form of limited monopolies on innovation provided by copyrights and patents. These extend the time in which better returns can be achieved by innovative firms and are justified on the basis that they promote research and development, investment, and other activities that promote social goals.

Questions of what factors promote and create above-average profitability are a concern of management and economic researchers and theorists because profit is a fundamental necessity and goal of firms.

MARKET, FINANCIAL, AND OPERATIONAL CHARACTERISTICS OF MEDIA

The nature of media products and services, production and distribution necessities, and economic forces affect media and influence decisions of media managers. The effects of these factors are not common across all media but produce significant differences in the characteristics of media products and services. The differences affect the environments in which

The Importance of Profitability to Media Firms

Profitability is crucial to all media companies because it allows firms to produce their own financial resources and makes them more attractive to lenders and other capital sources when they require additional financing to support their strategies and activities.

Even noncommercial and not-for-profit media need to produce profit that can then be used to develop their content and organizations. Media firms that are not able to operate profitably fall into a spiral of decline that makes it difficult to sustain their operations and to offer quality content. As illustrated in Figure 1-1, a firm that does not operate profitably falls into a spiral of decreasing financial resources that continually reduces its ability to produce or acquire quality content, to invest in personnel, to upgrade equipment, or to engage in marketing to attract audiences and advertisers.

Conversely, profitable media firms are able to reinvest in their operations to improve their content, making them more attractive to audiences and advertisers and ultimately making themselves more profitable.

If allowed to continue, the spiral makes it impossible for the firm to continue operating because it can no longer meet its expenses, much less invest internally to improve its operations. This spiral of decline combines with the increasing strength of profitable competitors to heavily disadvantage the less profitable or unprofitable firm. It ultimately leads to the death of weak commercial firms or dooms unprofitable noncommercial and not-for-profit media to precarious existences dependent upon outside funding.

they operate, force managers to respond differently than managers in other industries to market and cost forces, and significantly affect market structures and operating choices.

The characteristics of major media products and services are shown in Table 1-1. Although there are commonalities among the characteristics, such as the intensity of labor required, the products and services are most notable for wide differences in capital requirements, fixed costs, barriers to entry, levels of competition, complexity of logistics, and product and market strategies that can be employed. The nature and importance of these factors will be explored in later chapters.

Awareness of the limitations and opportunities afforded by the characteristics of the media products and services that a firm offers, as well as those offered by other firms, helps managers better understand their business environment in developing effective company and competitive strategies. The context or environment in which firms in different media industries and sectors operate varies significantly. Understanding these differences is important in understanding the contemporary situation of various types of media.

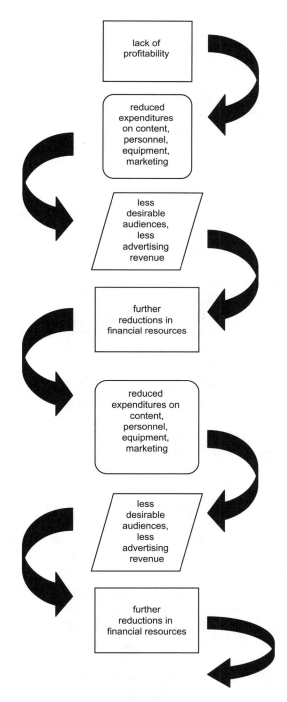

FIGURE I-I   Spiral of decline created by lack of profitability

Publishing industries (book, magazines, and newspapers) are mature industries throughout the developed world. They have traditionally been locally and nationally based but are increasingly operating at regional and global levels. The book and magazine publishing industries have the potential for moderate growth in both the short- and mid-term. The ability to significantly increase revenue from advertising or circulation is generally limited, as is the ability to achieve significant growth through market expansion. Newspaper publishers in North America and Europe face limited growth potential as well as the potential for decline, although publishers in Asia are enjoying growth as a result of improved economies and literacy. Opportunities for electronic publishing are starting to be used in all three sectors; these opportunities are generating products and services based on the Internet and multimedia. The growth of revenue from these initiatives is slow, but the potential for growth is strong.

The broadcasting industries exist at different levels of development in higher income nations, depending upon when privatization and commercial operations were authorized. In the United States both commercial and noncommercial radio and television are well developed and mature. In most other developed nations, noncommercial/public broadcasting is mature and well developed, but private broadcasting is still maturing because it was authorized only since the last quarter of the twentieth century. In markets in which commercial broadcasting is well established, the ability to increase advertising revenue is limited. In markets in which commercial broadcasting is still developing, advertising expenditures can be expected to grow only to levels approximating the average share of advertising expenditures for television in other nations with mature broadcasting industries. Increasing opportunities for analog and digital channels, as well as for market expansion via cable and satellite, are presenting significant new possibilities for growth of well-established broadcasters with regionally and globally recognized broadcasting brands.

The prospects for many new digital media are clouded by a good deal of uncertainty because they are in early stages of development. Nevertheless, digital television, Internet Protocol TV (IPTV), and video and audio on-demand services have strong potential for growth. This potential is dependent upon the willingness of audiences to acquire the necessary equipment—hardware as well as software—to access and use content. It is also dependent upon the development of methods of financing that are broadly acceptable to audiences, advertisers, or both. Despite the uncertainty, there is high interest in online and digital media activities among media and communications firms, capital sources, advertisers, and audiences. That interest is spurring a great deal of online, mobile, and advanced television

TABLE 1-1 · CHARACTERISTICS OF SELECTED MEDIA

	Books	Magazines	Newspapers	Radio Stations
Market Characteristics	Language-based market Long product lifespan Low barriers to entry High level of direct competition Most sales through retailers Low public sector involvement Threats from new technologies are low	Strong link to special interest or topic Mature markets with limited growth potential Relatively short product lifespan Low barriers to entry Moderate level of direct competition Increasing number of titles Declining average circulation per title Moderate to high elasticity of demand for circulation Direct consumer sales through subscriptions and single copy sales through retailers Moderate elasticity of demand for circulation Moderate elasticity of demand for advertising Low public sector involvement Threats from new technologies are moderately high Strong link to specific geographic market	Mature markets with limited growth potential Short product lifespan High barriers to entry Relatively low level of direct competition in most markets Stable circulation Declining market penetration Direct consumer sales through subscription and single copies through retailers and company sales Low/No elasticity of demand for circulation Advertiser preference for largest circulation paper Moderate/Low elasticity of demand for advertising Low public sector involvement (in developed nations) Threats from new technologies are high	Strong format and geographic market link No product lifespan Regulatory barriers to entry High level of direct competition Unstable audience High elasticity of demand for advertising High public sector involvement

TABLE 1-1 · (CONTINUED)

	Books	Magazines	Newspapers	Radio Stations
Financial/Cost Characteristics	Low capital requirements	Low capital requirements	High capital requirements	Low capital requirements
	Low fixed costs	Low fixed costs	High fixed costs	Low fixed costs
	High production costs	Moderate production costs	High production costs	Low production costs
	High distribution costs	High distribution costs	High distribution costs	Low distribution costs
	Moderate marketing costs	Moderate marketing costs	Low marketing costs	Moderate marketing costs
	High first copy costs	High first copy costs	High first copy costs	
	Moderate variable costs	Moderate variable costs	Moderate variable costs	
	Rapidly declining average total costs	Rapidly declining average total costs	Rapidly declining average total costs	
Operational Characteristics	Most firms are SMEs, a few large multinational firms	Low labor intensity	Most firms are SMEs, a few large firms	Most firms are SMEs, a few large firms
	Labor intensive	Complex logistics	Labor and equipment intensive	Labor and moderately equipment intensive
	Reliance on contract labor	Most costs are not related to core business	Complex logistics	Most costs are for core business
	Most content is acquired	Moderate dependence on advertising revenue	Most costs are not related to core business	Most content is acquired
	External production is typical	Advertising purchases stabilized with long-term contracts	High dependence on advertising revenue	High dependence on advertising revenue
	Moderately complex logistics	Circulation purchases stabilized with subscriptions	Advertising purchases stabilized with long-term contracts	Advertising purchases stabilized with long-term contracts
	Most costs are not related to core business	High cyclical financial performance	Circulation purchases stabilized with subscriptions	Moderate cyclical financial performance
	Moderate to high cyclical financial performance	A wide range of product and market strategies	High cyclical financial performance	Many product and market strategies possible
	Many product strategies possible	High paper waste creation, moderate chemical waste creation	Product and market strategies limited	Low waste creation
	High paper waste creation, moderate chemical waste creation		High paper waste creation, moderate chemical waste creation, high vehicle emission creation	

	Television Stations	Cable Systems	Motion Pictures	Online Media
Market Characteristics	Geographic market link	Geographic market link	National and global markets	Low entry barriers
	No product lifespan except through recording	No product lifespan	Strong secondary markets (cable-video/DVDTV)	High level of direct competition
	Regulatory barriers to entry	Regulatory barriers to entry	Moderate entry barriers	Growing market
	Other entry barriers moderately high	Other entry barriers high	High level of direct competition	Short- to long-term product lifespan
	Moderate level of direct competition	Low direct competition	Much substitution possible	Unstable audience
	Unstable audience	Direct sales to consumers through subscription	Genres and performers influence demand	Free and direct sales to consumers
	High elasticity of demand for advertising	Moderate elasticity of consumer demand		High elasticity of demand for advertising
	High public sector involvement	Threats from new technologies are high, particularly satellite and IPTV		Low public sector involvement
	Threats from new technologies are moderate to high			Threats from new technologies are low
Financial/Cost Characteristics	Moderate capital requirements	High capital requirements	High capital requirements	Low capital requirements
	Moderate fixed costs	High fixed costs	Low fixed costs	Low fixed costs
	High production costs	High distribution costs	High production costs	Low production costs
	Low distribution costs	Moderate marketing costs	Low distribution costs	Low distribution costs
	Moderate marketing costs		High marketing costs	High marketing costs
	No variable costs		High first copy cost	No variable costs
			Low variable costs	Rapid decline in average total cost
Operational Characteristics	Most firms are medium to large sized	Most firms are medium to large sized	Labor intensive	Labor intensive
	Most costs are for core business	Most costs are for core business	Most costs are for core business	Most costs are for core business
	Most content is acquired	Most content is acquired	Moderate cyclical financial performance	Dependence on advertising revenue and e-commerce
	High dependence on advertising revenue	High dependence on consumer revenue	Market strategies are limited	Many product and market strategies possible
	Advertising purchases stabilized with long-term contracts	Consumer sales stabilized with subscriptions	Dependence on limited number of theatrical distribution channels	Low waste creation
	Low cyclical financial performance	Moderate cyclical financial performance		
	Product and market strategies limited	A number of product strategies possible		
	Low waste creation	Low waste creation		

activity by media firms and some capital sources, but the movement of audiences and advertisers varies widely by nation and location.

Because the publishing industries are mature industries, and the same is true of broadcasting industries that are well established, they do not face developmental and resource problems on the scale of those encountered by communications firms in industries such as audiovisual production, multimedia, information technologies, and telecommunications.

Media companies are affected by their ownership structures, their need to produce adequate returns, the risks they encounter, and the overall contexts in which they operate. The extent to which these economic and financial forces affect individual firms and firms within different media industries determines the constraints and requirements that managers encounter and the choices that are available to them.

The following chapters will explore these economic and financial forces in greater depth. They will focus on the nature and creation of media products and services; the market, cost, and regulatory milieus that affect operations; and the effects on performance of business cycles, inflation, interest rates, and exchange rates. Attention will be directed to the needs and choices of audiences and advertisers, and to how different levels of competition affect media, finance requirements, and sources of capital including venture capital, equity markets, and debt.

The development of large media firms and the economic and financial pressures that play significant roles in the strategies and initiatives of their managers will be considered, as well as issues of how global trade in media products and services affects operations and choices. Ultimately, the focus will turn to questions of how to understand and monitor the economic and financial health of media firms.

The Context of Publishing Industries

A number of specifics of publishing industries are important in understanding their contexts and the contemporary issues they face.

Most publishing firms fall into the small and mid-sized enterprise (SME) category. Only a few large publishers exist and these typically operate both regionally and globally.

Barriers to entry are relatively low in the magazine, directory, and book publishing industries but higher in the newspaper industry.

Most published products, with the exception of books, have relatively short life spans. Some of the content and data generated through these products, however, has residual value for additional uses.

Economic fluctuations influence the amount of advertising support available.

Economic fluctuations influence consumers' decisions to purchase publications.

Consumption patterns for published materials and for advertising in published materials vary widely among nations.

Wide differences in the patterns of subscription versus single-copy sales create varying marketing strategies and financial dependency of newspapers and magazines on these revenue sources.

Publishing is labor intensive, requiring skilled content creators and processors, information processing specialists, skilled printing craft workers, and distribution workers.

Sophisticated logistics and transportation systems specifically designed for the publishing industry play important roles in the distribution of products to customers.

Large amounts of material waste are created by the disposable nature of many published products. The primary waste results from newspapers and magazines that are discarded after use. Recycling programs and use of recycled paper in production is being undertaken to address this issue.

Production processes result in a variety of environmentally damaging solvents, wash residues, and other chemicals. Governments are addressing this issue by requiring investments in new equipment and developing processes for recovery and safe disposition of this waste.

Traditional publishers are facing increasing threats and opportunities from the development of electronic publishing. The threats result mainly from not responding to (that is, taking advantage of) the opportunities.

Trade in published products has tended to face minimal levels of regulation.

Publishing industries are not research-intensive industries in comparison with pharmaceutical, high-technology, and consumer goods industries.

Basic intellectual property protections are in place and generally protect published works in printed form within developed countries, but problems with property rights protections still exist in other regions and nations.

Protection of intellectual property and rights collection in the areas of electronic data, information, and knowledge production and distribution is not as well developed and impedes growth of the electronic publishing sector.

SUGGESTED READINGS

Albarran, Alan B. 2002. *Media Economics: Understanding Markets, Industries and Concepts.* 2nd ed. Ames: Iowa State University Press.

Barney, Jay, and Delwyn Clark. 2007. *Resource-Based Theory: Creating and Sustaining Competitive Advantage.* New York: Oxford University Press.

Caves, R. E. 2004. *Creative Industries: Contracts between Art and Commerce.* Cambridge, Mass.: Harvard University Press.

Cyert, Richard, and James March. 1992. *Behavioral Theory of the Firm.* New York: John Wiley & Sons.

Demsetz, Harold. 1997. *The Economics of the Business Firm: Seven Critical Commentaries.* Cambridge: Cambridge University Press.

Doyle, Gillian. 2002. *Understanding Media Economics.* London: Sage Publications.

Jensen, Michael C. 2001. *A Theory of the Firm: Governance, Residual Claims, and Organizational Forms.* Cambridge, Mass.: Harvard University Press.

Picard, Robert G., ed. 2002. *Media Firms: Structures, Operations, and Performance.* Mahwah, N.J.: Lawrence Erlbaum Publishers.

Williamson, Oliver E., and Sidney G. Winter, eds. 1993. *The Nature of the Firm: Origins, Evolution and Development.* Oxford: Oxford University Press.

CHAPTER 2

Business Models, Workflows, and Value Chains in Media Firms

Media companies are producers that acquire and combine resources to create a product or service that is purchased by others. The characteristics of media products and services, the ways they are intended to be provided in the marketplace, the methods by which they are produced and distributed, and the value created by these processes are central concerns in understanding commercial and competitive issues.

This chapter focuses on the work of media firms by exploring the nature of media products and services, the business models upon which different media are based, copyright protections for the content products, the type of work that takes place in media firms, and the value chains of media firms.

MEDIA PRODUCTS AND SERVICES

Although one often hears about media products and services and the industries that supply them, particular attributes of the products and services are typically assumed or ignored. This presents problems in discussions of industry issues and trends because it permits broad, sweeping generalizations to be made about media. These sweeping generalizations ignore important elements that distinguish the abilities of media and communications firms to serve the wants and needs of various audiences and advertisers.

As shown in Chapter 1, the market, financial, and operational characteristics of media differ significantly. However, there are also significant differences among media in terms of the ways they convey content that are dependent upon the human senses by which the content is perceived. These differences affect the context in which messages are received and the attention given to content. For example, print media rely upon the sense of sight; radio and other forms of audio content upon the sense of hearing; and television, motion pictures, and other forms of video content on both of those senses.

Most of us have had the experience of viewing a motion picture in a theater and later on television. Although both communicate using audio and visual stimuli, the experience of viewing is different—because televisions have traditionally been unable to present films in widescreen format; because one does not typically view television in a darkened, quiet environment that reduces distracting stimuli; and because the audio systems of television tend not to surround the viewer with sound and vibration as they do in motion picture theaters.

Print media tend to be used in different contexts as well. People reading books tend to seek solitude or focus senses more heavily on the activity than most magazine readers. Newspaper readers focus more directly on its content than readers of outdoor advertising.

The differences in formats and use produce significant differences in the ability of media to convey different types of content most effectively. Print media tend to be better for carrying significant amounts of information and sparking the imagination. Audio and audio-visual media tend to be best at providing diversion and work most effectively when they carry only basic levels of information.

These differences in ability to better serve different needs make specific types of media products and services better at responding to the needs of audiences and advertisers. Although all media serve the needs of general or specialized audiences, only some media products and services serve the needs of advertisers, as shown in Table 2-1.

Because the capabilities of certain media products and services can better provide diversion, general information, and specific information and because they serve audience and advertiser needs differently, media products and services do not serve the same purposes and are used in varying ways by audiences and advertisers.

Although similarities may make some media interchangeable in limited ways for limited purposes, the differences are significant and do not permit complete substitution for all situations and uses. This is why newer media have not had a history of completely replacing more established media. They have altered industry structures, content, and use patterns of existing media, but their primary impact has been to bring new methods for communication as additional types of media rather than as replacement media. Radio, for example, did not bring an end to print media or audio recordings. Television did not destroy the motion picture industry. Cable did not

Entertainment	General Information	Topic or Search-specific Information	Focus
Audio recordings			Audience needs
Books		Books	Audience needs
Film			Audience needs
Video/DVD		Video/DVD	Audience needs
Public service broadcasting	Public service broadcasting		Audience needs
Commercial radio			Audience and advertiser needs
Commercial television			Audience and advertiser needs
Consumer magazines	General magazines	Specialty magazines	Audience and advertiser needs
	Newspapers	Specialty newspapers	Audience and advertiser needs
Online services	Online data and services	Online data and services	Audience and advertiser needs
Video on demand			Audience needs

end local television broadcasting. Although it is still too early to determine their full effects, multimedia and online media seem to be seeking to serve functions that parallel or complement those of existing media and there seems to be some substitutability among them for some people.

Studies of the introduction of additional media have produced little evidence of reduction in nonmedia time use or change in consumer expenditures for existing media—with the exception of heavy at-home Internet users and game players, who tend to reduce the time they devote to television. Instead, it appears that additional media produce specialization and permit greater choice by individual consumers rather than wholesale changes in media consumer behavior.

DIFFERENCES IN MEDIA TYPES AND ENVIRONMENTS

Because media product characteristics vary considerably, they experience significantly different business environments. At a fundamental level, two major categories of media products and services can be seen: single-creation products and continuous-creation products.

Single-creation products are creative and idea-driven products that are based on unique media content. Typical examples of single-creation products are books, motion pictures, audio recordings, and games. Because of the single-creation nature of these products, the conditions of their creation are project oriented. Managers of enterprises therefore must cope with project management challenges. The core competence of firms producing single-creation products is by nature content creation. Because each product is unique, companies must expend significant marketing and sales costs to gain the attention of consumers, inform them about the content of the product, and induce them to consume it. The market for the products is fickle, so single-creation products are very risky and experience high failure rates.

In contrast, continuous-creation media products are concept-driven products that involve ongoing creation of changing content provided within a package that exhibits continuity. They differ from idea-driven products because they involve multiple creations built on multiple ideas Examples of these types of products are magazines, newspapers, television series, and television networks. Whereas a film is an idea-driven single-creation product, a television series is a continuous-creation product based on a concept—for example, a situation comedy involving workers in a meat packing plant in which individual episodes incorporate different individual story ideas. Enterprises involved in these types of products operate somewhat like those in packaged goods industries, relying upon strongly structured and coordinated processes that tend to be time constrained and require that managers cope with process management issues. The core competence of firms producing continuous-creation products is not content creation per se but the selection, processing, and packaging of content. Managers of these products focus on the look and feel of the concept, the experiences delivered, and processes of content creation and content selected for inclusion within their packages. Issues of branding are crucial for continuous-creation products. These products tend to require lower marketing and sales costs because they are able to create habitual use patterns and are available as subscriptions. Once these patterns have been established, the failure rates in continuous-creation products are relatively low.

The separate characteristics and business dynamics of the two media types produce different underlying business logics and strategies. The primary business logic for established media firms producing single-creation products fundamentally focuses on managing failure, whereas the companies with continuous-creation products focus on maintaining and improving their products and processes and building upon success already achieved.

Companies producing single-creation products typically create portfolios of projects to spread the risk and to allow them to employ "hit" strategies in which income from popular products compensates for losses from unappreciated products. In the music industry, for example, only one in ten recordings makes money for the major record labels, with six recordings losing money and only three managing to break even. The characteristics of products in single creation are such that investments in the failed individual media products are sunk costs, that is, costs that cannot be recovered. Consequently they must be covered by profits from the small number of products that are successful. As a result, managers in this environment must focus on managing the failures and creating conditions in the company so it can sustain itself despite the inevitable failures.

In addition to portfolios, companies producing single-creation products typically seek to increase the probability of success by strategies involving previously successful writers, actors, directors, and artists. But even previously successful performers are not a guarantee of success. The example of Mariah Carey, the bestselling female recording performer of all time, is illustrative. During the 1990s Carey was the winner of two Grammy awards, had fourteen number one hits, and released ten platinum albums (one million copies sold); and many of her recordings sold between four and eight million copies. Altogether she has sold more than 140 million recordings. In 2001 Virgin Records (part of EMI) signed her to a four-album deal for $81 million, with a $21 million upfront signing payment. The first album produced for the deal was *Glitter*, which sold 500,000 copies making it a gold record, a success by general recording industry standards. However, because it was part of an $81 million package designed to produce profits as well as cover expenses for unsuccessful recordings, *Glitter* was deemed a failure and sent shockwaves through EMI/Virgin. In 2002, the company paid Carey $28 million not to make any more albums, and she walked away with a total of $49 million for one album because the company believed it was less risky to pay out the money than to continue recording, releasing, and promoting three additional albums that might not sell the requisite millions of copies.

In making the decision to avoid more risk, the company gave up the opportunity to benefit from possible future success. Later, executives probably regretted the decision because Carey signed with Universal Music Group and her subsequent recordings did very well. *Charmbracelet* sold more than six million copies; a compilation disc, *The Remixes*, sold more than one million copies; and *The Emancipation of Mimi* won three Grammys and sold more than ten million copies. In 2008, $E = MC2$ sold a half million copies in its first week and has now sold more than 2.5 million copies

Strategies for Failure

For established firms in creative enterprises, the primary business logic is often based on managing failure rather than achieving success. Motion picture companies, audio recording companies, book publishers, and—to a lesser extent—broadcasting companies face the challenges of constant failure.

Managing failure is necessary because in the audio recording industry, for example, only one in ten recordings makes money for the major record labels, with six recordings losing money and only three managing to break even. In Hollywood, 10 percent of the top two hundred films account for 50 percent of industry revenue. In television programming, new shows have a 5 percent success rate.

The economics of the industries are such that investments in the failed individual media products are sunk costs that cannot be recovered and must be covered by the small number of products that are successful. The reasons for failure of individual creative products vary, but common ones are because audience tastes are uncertain, because the quality of the final production is uncertain, because direct competition from similar genres or topics is produced by other creators, and because reviews affect demand.

The primary strategy for managing the built-in failure of creative industries is for companies to offer a portfolio of titles and programs and to make money off the products that are successful in the market. This fundamental logic is the reason why national and international trade organizations such as the Motion Picture Association of America and the International Federation of the Phonographic Industry are so active in seeking out and prosecuting violations of copyright and related rights. Because popular materials are the most pirated, counterfeited, or illicitly traded, industry organizations and copyright owners seek enforcement to protect the income from success.

Another strategy employed because of the high failure rates is the "hit model," in which companies invest heavily in content that has a high potential for success in order to compound the potential reward. This includes heavy marketing before and during release, production of related media products, and merchandising. In the hit strategy the producers receive not only income from the film but also profit participation or licensing payments for related products, including merchandise, games, books, and spinoff productions.

Producers of continuous-creation products do not put the same focus on managing risks and failures once their products are in the market. Instead, they are able to focus on improving the content within the packaged ongoing products by research on the preferences of audiences revealed by the success of those products, by alterations in creative personnel, and by repositioning the products vis-à-vis any similar and substitutable products. Managers of these types of products operate as product or brand managers rather than as portfolio managers, perfecting and improving the product and the experience it delivers, promoting additional consumption, and improving relations with those who consume the product.

Differences in the forms and production characteristics of media produce differences in the basic economic environments and economic forces they encounter. Media can be differentiated as operating in production environments primarily affected by either unit cost economics or fixed cost economics. Unit cost economies are ones in which the costs of a single unit—one book, one CD, or one copy of a paper—are influenced by the total number manufactured, but this does not happen in fixed-cost economies. Thus the cost for a television broadcaster is not affected by the number of people tuned to the channel.

Those operating in unit cost economies are media whose activities are based in physical production and whose success is affected by economies of scale, transaction costs, and similar factors. Media in this environment tend to engage in production cost and price management activities. Media types most affected by the unit cost environment include books, magazines, newspapers, and recorded media in physical form, such as CDs and DVDs. Because products in these industries have physical form, they must be distributed directly or indirectly to consumers, and that process has logistical requirements which result in significant additional costs such as those for warehousing, transportation, and retail distribution mechanisms.

In fixed cost economies, variable costs for additional production are not significant factors, and basic production costs for competitors tend to be similar. As a result, competition in this environment is typically based on experience delivered, product and service quality, and brand. The media types most involved in the fixed cost economies are broadcasting, motion picture, television programming, and Internet media. Distribution in this environment generally does not require physical distribution to audiences but can involve some limited distribution requirements of finished products to intermediary firms, but they are relatively inconsequential by comparison to those found for products in the unit cost economies.

The differences produced by these two factors create significant variation in the cost structures and cost pressures felt by managers in media firms. Newspapers, for example, operate in unit cost economies, and printing and distribution costs make up half or more of all costs and have significant implications for the enterprises. Transmission costs for television broadcasters, however, are often only less than 15 percent of total costs, and they face different financial challenges.

LIFE CYCLES OF MEDIA

Industries, as well as specific products and services associated with industries, have their own life cycles that progress through stages of introduction, growth, maturity, and decline. As the industry progresses through the life periods, changes in sales, costs per customer, profits, customers, and competitors occur that are common across industries.

As shown in Table 2-2, sales rise in the introductory and growth periods and peak during the maturation period before entering the decline period. The costs of the industry relative to the customer begin high and decline until the maturation period. Profits begin to appear in the growth period, and rise to a high level during the maturation period before dropping in the decline period. The types of customers across the periods are represented by the different types of individuals who adopt products and services at different rates. In the initial stages, competition is low but as an industry becomes profitable more firms enter the market. By the maturation period, the number stabilizes before declining.

The life cycle stage in which media are operating is important to managers because it determines the types of challenges and issues with which they must contend and the opportunities and threats encountered. Media exist at different stages of industry life as shown in Table 2-3. All the major traditional media industries are in the maturation period in developed countries. Print media (books, magazines, and newspapers) are in the late stages of maturity, close to the edge of the decline period because audiences and advertisers are becoming increasingly familiar and comfortable with newer information and communications technology. The print media have enjoyed one of the longest known cycles of any manufacturing industry.

BUSINESS MODELS IN MEDIA

Business models provide an understanding of how a firm conducts commerce. The term *business model* is often confused with *strategy*, such as

TABLE 2-2 · BUSINESS DEVELOPMENTS IN DIFFERENT PERIODS OF INDUSTRY LIFE CYCLES

	Introductory Period	*Growth Period*	*Maturation Period*	*Decline Period*
Sales	Low	Rapidly rising	Peak	Declining
Costs/Customer	High	Medium	Low	Low
Profits	Negative	Rising	High	Declining
Customers	Innovators	Early adopters	Majority	Laggards
Competitors	Few	Growing	Stable	Declining

TABLE 2-3 · LOCATION OF MEDIA INDUSTRIES IN PERIODS OF INDUSTRY LIFE CYCLES

Introductory Period	Growth Period	Maturation Period
IPTV	Satellite television	Audio recordings
Mobile TV	Online media	Books
	Multimedia	Magazines
	HDTV	Motion pictures
	Mobile Web and games	Newspapers
	Streaming or online video	Radio
		Recorded video
		Television
		Cable television

company strategies, product strategies, marketing strategies, or pricing strategies. These strategies are the means employed by firms to guide activities toward goals but they are not models of the business.

A business model is much more fundamental. Business models are created and understood by stepping back from the business activity itself to look at its bases and the underlying characteristics that make commerce in the product or service possible. A business model involves the conception of how the business operates, its underlying foundations, and the exchange activities and financial flows upon which it can be successful.

Business models can be described as the architecture for product, service, and information flows. They include a description of various business activities and their roles as well as a description of the potential benefits for the various business actors and the sources of revenues. In terms of modern communications, business models need to account for the vital resources of production and distribution technologies, content creation or acquisition, and recovery of costs for creating, assembling, and presenting the content.

Business models clarify the product segment (or segments) in which a firm operates. Although most people would indicate that Twentieth Century Fox is a studio that produces motion picture and television programs, the firm's business model is based upon both the production and the distribution of films and programs, including those of other producers.

A business model also pays attention to the involvement of intermediaries, that is, firms or infrastructures that exist between the provider and the customer. It considers the incentives for wholesalers, distributors, and service providers to carry the product or service.

Business models outline how a firm makes or will make its money. Media business models can have up to four basic revenue sources: consumers, advertisers, sponsorships, and business-to-business payments. Consumer payment models include pay-for-use forms built on single purchases or subscriptions and up-sell models in which the cost for basic access and use is low, but extended or premium access and content use comes with a price. These consumer models allow for various bundling and versioning strategies that permit some price discrimination. Advertising payment models include payments for space or time and payment for action such as leads generated or click-through. Sponsorship is a form of marketing related to advertising in which companies and brands make payments in order to be associated with the media brand or product and thus make the content available for free. Business-to-business payments involve syndication and licensing content for use by other firms. Some media operations rely on only one type of revenue in their business models, whereas other employ hybrid models that combine more than one revenue stream.

Understanding the business model under which a firm or product operates or will operate is especially important when new products or services are developed or when the industry in which one operates is undergoing significant changes.

As the environment in which a firm or industry changes, so do the factors that support a business model. As a result, business models that may once have been successful may become less successful and be abandoned. Previous models may have to be changed if a product or service is changed or product extension takes place. Business models that seem appropriate for new products or services may not produce the support and structures necessary as the business milieu changes and may then be altered or abandoned in favor of other models.

Some individuals make the mistake of assuming that failed or abandoned business models can never again be successful. This is not always the case if the conditions under which they failed are no longer present or if resistance to some elements disappears. A situation may then arise in which such a model may be reintroduced successfully for the same or a different product or service.

BUSINESS PROTECTION THROUGH COPYRIGHT AND RELATED RIGHTS

One of the special traits of the media business is that the production effort involves creating a first copy of a work, a single original work that can be reproduced and distributed via print, recorded media, broadcasting or in virtual form. Because the business models of media involve investment in

The Changing Business Models of Online Content Services

The business models of online content service providers have changed rapidly as firms have attempted to find a model that can support their operations. These firms, such as aol.com (America Online), Yahoo!, and MSN organize and provide users access to content of interest including news, information and entertainment, leisure activity, and other materials.

These companies are broad service portals that also provide free e-mail, messaging services, voice mail, user customization, online shopping, notification services, software downloads, chat lines, and access to a wide variety of online communities and content.

The history of online content service providers includes four abandoned business models, a model in current use, and an emerging model evolving from the existing model. Each was made possible by particular developments in technology, had different financial bases, and produced different results.

The Videotext Model

This model was used in initial attempts to use television screens to convey text-based content. Efforts to create videotext as a commercially viable activity were led primarily by newspaper companies in the 1970s. The impetus for this new content service was the change to information and communications technology for phototypesetting, which allowed newspapers to reuse or easily alter content prepared for newspapers in a videotext operation. The concept was particularly attractive because it allowed publishers to update materials and convey breaking news between printed newspaper editions.

Because most of the infrastructure and content creation and formatting costs were already covered by revenue from the newspaper operations, the financial costs of this secondary use and distribution of the content were relatively low. This permitted publishers to offer videotext at a low price or to provide it free as promotional costs for the newspaper itself.

Although the producers of videotext had strong cost advantages in producing and distributing the material, the consumers—either as audiences receiving it for free or purchasers of the service—were generally uninterested. As a result, most content providers abandoned the videotext model.

The Paid Internet Mode

When videotext did not produce results desirable to content providers, they began to seek other methods through which costs could be recovered from individual users. The pre-existing infrastructure of the Internet became an attractive alternative for distribution.

The Internet and the software required for its operation had been funded originally by the United States government to support military research communications. Wider access to the system created the potential for commercial use and in the 1980s content producers discovered that they could make their materials accessible through the Internet and charge a fee for access to the content.

The market, however, did not look kindly on the development. General audiences did not embrace the payment idea, and complicated processes were required to gain access to information. As a result, general content providers soon abandoned the model based on providing content through the Internet and recovering costs from audiences.

The Free Web Model

The World Wide Web and the associated browser and server software made it a lot easier to access the Internet. The development costs for these improvements had been carried by the European nuclear science community, who wanted to improve their ability to convey data, graphic displays, and other materials to researchers. The widespread distribution of browsers in standard software packages for new computers rapidly made the Web the primary online use of general consumers.

Many new types of content providers began moving rapidly onto the Web and generally provided materials free of charge as promotional materials for commercial firms or as special interest materials provided by individuals or organizations. Traditional media content providers grasped the utility of the Web and began operations to reuse existing materials again—as they had under the videotext model—but this time with the advantages of true graphic capabilities. Other firms developed means to organize materials in a way that reduced the frustrations of users seeking content.

Content users found this arrangement quite workable and the lack of cost for use made it the equivalent of obtaining material from free television or radio. The model, however, did not provide means for commercial firms to recover costs for providing or organizing content from users and they soon rejected the model.

The Internet/Web Ad Push Model

In an effort to create a nonuser revenue stream, some content providers, Internet service providers, and content organizers attempted to use lists of subscribers and users, combined with demographic, lifestyle, and other profile information obtained through registration, as a means of attracting advertising. In other cases they attempted to find advertisers for products and services related to Web pages on which particular content was organized. In both cases, the firms *pushed* advertising toward audiences that would be most interested in the products or services offered.

The process based on user information was an advertising system based on direct-mail models. Although the model created a revenue stream, audiences often were unhappy with the intrusiveness of the content or the number of advertisements. Many Internet service providers and content organizers did not want advertisers who were not associated with them to use their systems. Additionally, many advertisers soon questioned the intrusiveness and effectiveness of the model, which led many online content providers to look for another model.

The Portal and Personal Portal Model

Content organizers wanting an advertising revenue stream and control of advertising exposure moved to the current business model based on portals. In this system, users of Web browsers are brought to an organizing interface and advertisements. As users move to information of interest, additional or related advertising appears. The current revenue model is based on newspaper- and magazine-style advertising in which readers are brought into contact with advertisers' messages while making other use of the pages.

In most portals, only a single ad appears on each page, and it is designed to *pull* or attract users to click through the ad to gain additional information from the advertiser.

The current model is attractive because user resistance is not strong and a regular advertising stream is being produced. In this model, portals create value by organizing access to content created by others in a way that creates a brand for the portal that attracts returning users. Despite its improvement over other business models, however, the current model is still not producing profits for most portal operators.

The Digital Portal Model

The current hope for portal providers, backed by significant investments and new competition from telecommunications firms, is the success of multipurpose digital portals. With improvements in bandwidth and compression, the model is allowing the combination of current content portals with streaming video and audio.

A user of this system is able to view broadcast channels worldwide, to obtain pay-per-view services, to view potential nonbroadcast channels, to search video clip archives, to use a variety of multimedia materials, to seek additional information about the content, to chat with others while viewing a program, and to determine the language in which the content is received. Many of these services are now being provided by cable systems linking television and Internet activities and online by portals linked to Internet Protocol Television (IPTV).

Costs are recouped by revenue from an advertising stream and from users through pay-per-view and premium services subscriptions such as those currently offered by cable and satellite service providers. Major content organizers in operation today are hoping to use this new environment and business model to capitalize on strong online portal brands created during operations under the general portal model.

the production of the first copy and recouping the investment in distribution, and because content has social value, governments have created special property rights for media content.

Until the creation of these copyright laws, it was unclear who owned the work or how it could be used because copyright is not a natural right. Instead, it is a form of property rights that is defined in national legislation

The Changing Newspaper Business Model

The contemporary newspaper business model developed in the mid- to late-nineteenth century, replacing a very different model that was based on a specialized audience rather than a mass audience.

During their first 100 to 150 years of publication, U.S. newspapers served a relatively small audience—about 15 to 25 percent of the population depending upon location, literacy, degree of economic development, and other social factors. The audience represented the politically, socially, and economically active members of the community. Papers were highly dependent upon circulation sales for their income and the price of papers and subscriptions was very high. The business model was dependent upon circulation sales to this group and the little advertising that existed was primarily for raw materials and imports available to merchants and manufacturers rather than retail advertising.

In the last half of the nineteenth century the market began to change as urbanization, the industrial revolution, wage earning, and literacy created social changes that resulted in discretionary income and leisure time among an increasing amount of the population. Newspapers began changing to serve this larger audience. New sections to serve diversionary interests and attract more readers were added to newspapers (including entertainment, sports, and comics). Papers were sold at a very low price. This altered the business model to put more emphasis on advertising revenue and to produce a large mass audience of interest to retail advertisers.

The magnitude of this change in the business model can be seen in the fact that advertising provided one-half of the revenue of newspapers in the United States by 1880. That amount rose to two-thirds by 1910 and to about 80 percent in the year 2000.

The growth of readership and advertising support continued rather stead-

and international treaties. It is *given* by government, *defined* by government, and *protected* by government. Copyright gives exclusive rights to the owner of the copyrighted material and the owner can exchange ownership, partial ownership, and various use rights for the material.

Copyright and related rights are relatively modern constructions. There was a time in which a printer could republish a book that was originally printed by another printer. This allowed them to sell copies that reaped benefits created by the author and initial publisher. Because of this practice, governments began to understand that media are creators of economic and social value and policymakers began enacting laws that made content a form of property, thus creating benefits for the copyright owner and creating an incentive for increased production.

Under modern copyright law a variety of original works are protected: literary and dramatic works, musical works, artistic works, maps and technical drawings, pantomime and choreography, sound recordings, motion pictures, computer programs, and applied arts. Copyright and related rights ily until the years after World War II. When television appeared, it began to provide diversion and other information in forms increasingly attractive to those parts of the mass audience who were not part of the politically, socially, and economically active members of their communities. As a result, a portion of the reading audience began leaving newspapers behind and many readers began spending less time with newspapers. That problem has been exacerbated with the rise of multiple networks and stations, cable, and other electronic information and diversion opportunities that have developed in recent years. A free newspaper model has emerged that is successfully offering a light amount of advertising-supported news in many locations by appealing to those for whom general papers are less interesting.

As the changes continue in the twenty-first century, audiences and use patterns for newspapers will continue to alter newspaper use. The time is fast approaching when paid newspaper readership will look much more like its initial position rather than the position at its mid-twentieth-century height. Given the facts of greater income, literacy, and world outlook, it will probably not decline to the 15 percent level of the early nineteenth century. However, somewhere in the range of one-quarter to one-third of the population seems realistic. As this change takes place a new business model will evolve. It may look less like the current model and more like the model of the early history of the industry.

In addition, many publishers are beginning to offer a portfolio of print publications—including a general circulation paid daily, a free daily, a daily aimed at young people, weekly city papers, free advertising sheets—and are also offering online publications and mobile services in an effort to aggregate audiences and advertising income across the products. It remains to be seen if this business model will be successful.

give owners control over reproduction, translation, adaptation, arrangement, alteration, public performance, broadcasting, distribution, and rental of content.

There are some limited exceptions to copyright that vary depending upon national legislation. These involve fair use for social commentary and education and nonvoluntary licenses in which governments have created preset rules and prices for certain uses of content. The U.S. government, for example, sets rates for redissemination of copyright materials on cable systems and for Internet radio.

National copyright laws only apply to the specific nation in which they are enacted, but media content is traded internationally so international copyright treaties have been created to oblige signatory nations to use their domestic law to enforce agreed upon principles. The World Intellectual Property Organization (WIPO) is a specialized UN organization that works to enforce twenty international treaties and agreements on copyright and intellectual property, and in recent years provisions of treaties overseen by the World Trade Organization (WTO) have also provided protection for content.

Central to copyright and related rights is the idea that owners exclude others from receiving or using the material until after an economic exchange takes place in the market. Without an exchange, persons are excluded from its use. It is easier to enforce excludability when physical products such as books, CDs, and DVDs are involved, but much more difficult when virtually available digitalized content is involved. Efforts to increase excludability of virtual products through technological measures have been only somewhat successful.

Because of the increasing economic importance of media, copyright duration in the United States was extended to ninety-five years for works created before 1978 and to the life of the author plus seventy years under legislation sponsored by Congressman Sonny Bono, a former entertainer. Much recent legislation and enforcement efforts have been undertaken to halt uncompensated uses of material, particularly file sharing of audio and video content, and to address piracy and counterfeiting of content. The U.S. Digital Millennium Copyright Act and information society and copyright directives of the European Union provided punitive measures for appropriation or assisting appropriation of digital products and made it illegal to attempt to overcome encryption and other technical protection measures.

It is well recognized that these uncompensated uses create harm to rights owners and in recent years much of the focus has been on harm created for the recording and motion picture industries. Because of high failure rates in audio recording, piracy does not directly harm most artists; however, it has significant effects on recording companies. Because the most popular copyrighted products tend to be pirated, it denies recording companies compensation for their profitable recordings and reduces compensation to those artists. The losses of revenue and profitability make recording companies less willing and able to record as many artists, ultimately reducing the opportunities for new artists to receive the backing of major national and global recording enterprises. Similar problems occur in the motion picture industry, where piracy has little effect on theatrical exhibition or broadcast sales, but strongly affects the home video market.

TWO PRODUCTION ORIENTATIONS

Operations of media firms are highly influenced by their forms of production and the management of those activities. Media production takes place with two different operational contexts: process orientation and project orientation. These orientations require very different types of organizational structures that involve different economic and financial pressures and constraints.

PROCESS-ORIENTED PRODUCTION

Process orientation exists where there is continuous, ongoing production of goods. As the products become more complex and the number of component parts increase, production tends to become time constrained and strongly structured and coordinated processes are instituted to ensure efficiency. In such settings, activity takes place in a permanent organization, relying on employed labor, and facilities and equipment owned by the enterprise. There is an emphasis on work occurring in set order with relatively inflexible schedules and production activities are controlled by policies, checklists, or handbooks. This type of production depends on knowledge and skills resident in the organization itself and performance is measured by effectiveness of processes.

Product manufacturing or assembly can take place as flow production in which the same product is continuously produced using just-in-time supply flow. In these conditions, there is a dependency on suppliers and dedicated facilities, equipment, and personnel and firms endeavor to carefully match output with market demand. Manufacturing and assembly can also take the form of batch production in which a supply of the product is produced and production halted until more is needed. In the intervening time, the company produces other products in its portfolio. This situation can create difficulties matching supply with demand if consumption changes unexpectedly.

The process orientation and both flow and batch production methods exist in media. Newspapers and Web portals are clear examples of continuous production in using a process orientation with flow production. DVD production from a list of titles in a firm's film library is also process oriented but uses batch production to produce an ongoing and relatively constant production of different titles.

In such situations managing and innovating the processes employed are undertaken to gain efficiencies that make better use of resources, reduce the time and costs involved, and better serve customers. Process management involves planning and monitoring processes to improve performance. This is done by identifying the processes that take place, assigning responsibility for each part, and measuring performance of process activities individually and collectively. This management takes place in production process and business process management.

Production process management focuses on issues of workflow in manufacturing and assembly. It involves product design processes, creation and manufacturing processes, supply processes, and distribution processes.

These are managed by scheduling, job tracking, reducing downtime, collecting and employing production data, and analyzing and improving the process elements. Doing so requires understanding the coordination of technology, facilities people, finance, organization, logistics, and customers.

Issues of production are not merely applicable to industrial processes, but have significant importance to artistic and motion picture and television production and printing.

Business process management involves the procedures other than creation of the product itself. It involves activities such as marketing, sales, order fulfillment, accounting, distribution, service, and general management. Finding ways to improve, streamline, and reduce costs often involves use of business information systems and Web-based activities.

Process management activities typically face organizational challenges posed by significant fixed costs and overheads, organization-centered decision making, inflexibility in workforce and work methods, culture-limiting innovation and change, and difficulty maintaining employee enthusiasm for altering processes.

PROJECT-ORIENTED PRODUCTION

This type of production takes place primarily when there is a unique individual production, such as a film, new television program or series, or a book.

It occurs where there is one-at-a-time production, designed to produce a single or coordinated new unit of one content production, with the potential for high degree of customization. Thus a book publishing company such as HarperCollins takes on each new manuscript as an individual project to which an editor, designer, marketing person, and production supervisor are assigned. In many situations—such as filmmaking and television program production—work takes place within a temporary organization established for the project. There is greater flexibility in the order in which the work takes place and the schedule that is followed, and control over these and other factors rests more in project managers. Projects tend to rely upon professional knowledge and skills of project workers and employment can be temporary or in serial projects of an organization. In projects, investments in fixed assets tend to be limited and most facilities and equipment are rented or provided by a firm that funds serial projects.

In project-oriented production there is a clear beginning and end to the production, temporary forms of organization are employed, and performance is measured by success of the single project.

Production of single-creation content products tends to employ short-term financing arrangements and seeks content innovation in the short term by selecting new innovative content for each production. Technological and process innovations are not major concerns, except for organizations that sponsor serial projects.

For sponsoring organizations, issues of portfolio management come into play: project selection, multiproject scheduling, project reviews, and project lifecycles. For individual production, the primary concerns are planning, work breakdown, project design, budgeting, resource acquisition, scheduling, controlling, team leadership and management, and evaluation.

For organizations commissioning projects, issues of project economics are central and decisions are made based on issues of risk and potential return. These sometimes involve capital investment evaluation and risk analysis—particularly in film. Time value of money, rates of return, and benefit cost analysis are not unusual, using techniques developed from major engineering and construction projects. When there are choices between alternative projects similar types of investment decisions may also be employed.

In selecting media projects significant attention is paid to analysis and pre-selection of target audiences and advertisers,

WORKFLOWS IN MEDIA FIRMS

To understand the economics of a media firm, one needs to have a clear understanding of the work that takes place and the resources that are required to complete each stage. This can be aided by considering the workflow in a firm and the steps taken in the creation and distribution of the final product or service.

Differences in workflows and in the resources required for each media mean that managers need to be familiar with the entire process if they are to manage the entire operation or even parts of the process more effectively. Differences between broad workflows in media can be illustrated by considering the workflow for a motion picture (see Figure 2-1) and the workflow for a magazine (see Figure 2-2).

In reviewing the broad workflows, one can immediately see that magazine publishing involves more physical and mechanical processes than motion picture production. These workflow charts outline the major steps but each step can include dozens and even hundreds of activities that must take place in order to create and distribute media products and services.

Understanding the workflow characteristics of media are important because they result in significant differences in the structures and complexity of operations, investments required, and costs.

MEDIA VALUE CHAINS

Creating value is the central activity of successful companies. For any business to survive it must create value for customers by providing products or

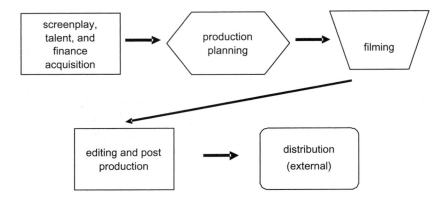

FIGURE 2-1 Production and distribution flow chart for motion pictures

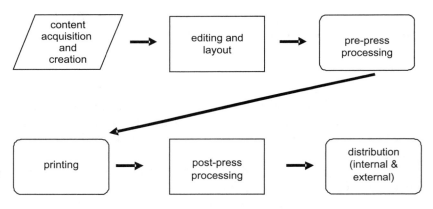

FIGURE 2-2 Magazine publishing flow chart

services that fulfill their wants and needs, and the company must do so more effectively than its competitors. The process through which this value creation takes place involves the entire range of activities within firms and is conceptualized as value chains.

The value chains show the value that is added to a product or service at each step of its acquisition, transformation, management, marketing and sales, and distribution. The value chain concept for products and services is now well established in business literature.

This value chain concept is particularly important in understanding market behavior because it places the emphasis on the value created for the *customer,* who ultimately makes consumption decisions. The concept is useful in considering those activities that are most central to the core activities of a firm and those that make the business operational. Although there are differences in the activities, creating the highest possible value in each activity is sought through the development of efficiency, quality, and service.

Several value chains are involved in any single firm's or industry's activities (see Figure 2-3). These include the value chain of resources purchased from suppliers to make production possible. In media firms these include materials such as paper, videotape or digital memory, editing stations, presses, and computer software.

The value chain of the producing firm involves the creation of value by using resources and processing them to create a product or service. A product or service is not worthwhile unless it is made available to purchasers, so another value chain involving distribution comes into play. Finally, there is a value chain created by use of the product or services by the purchaser.

The value in each of these chains is generated by the components purchased, the use of human resources and technology, the organizational structure, and the flow of information within the organization. In the end, however, it is the overall value of the activities that is valued by the customer.

If one focuses on the activities of media firms, one mostly considers the activities in the value chains of the producer and distribution (see Figure 2-4). Although there are slight differences among media industries and firms, the basic value chain involves content: that is, selecting, organizing, packaging, and processing content; followed by activities preparing it for distribution; and then distribution and related marketing activities for the product or service.

Magazine companies, for example, purchase and create text, photographs, and artwork that are to be the basis for a publication. The staff then selects, organizes, and packages this material in a way that gives the magazine its focus and personality. The processed materials are then sent for prepress preparation, printing, and binding and other postpress activities. The printed copies are then distributed to subscribers, wholesalers, and retailers

FIGURE 2-3　Value chains

FIGURE 2-4   Generic value chains of media firms

for single-copy sales. The distribution system is supported by marketing, advertising, and promotional activities.

If this process is considered in terms of the real value of media activities to customers, two links in the chain are especially important: the creation of content and the selection, organization, packaging, and processing of that content. These are important because the creation of content produces original material not available elsewhere and the selection, organization, and packaging of content are tasks that make the content easier to find, use, and digest. The other activities, although important to making the product distributable and useable in the physical magazine format, are not the central value-producing activities that make the magazine valuable to readers.

As discussed in Chapter 4, the extent to which the activities that create the most value contribute to the cost structures of media firms vary widely among media and make some more vulnerable to changes in technology than others.

CORE BUSINESS

Part of the examination of the value chain of a media business is based on establishing the nature of the firm's core business.

Many managers mistakenly define their core business as the activities generating the highest turnover, necessitating the highest capital investment, or requiring the largest number of employees. The core business, however, is better thought of as the central common activity of the firm. It is the fundamental activity of the firm that is supported by investment, company structure, personnel, and processes.

Are New Media New Products and Services?

The language surrounding industry and governmental discussion and decisions regarding new media tend to cast these technologies in terms of transforming lives and providing products and services previously unavailable. But are the changes really producing new communications products or services? Let's consider some examples.

First, consider digital television. The change from analog broadcasting to transmitting and receiving digital signals is underway worldwide and is increasing the number of channels available, improving reception quality, and increasing the width of television screens. Digital television is being implemented in many countries providing high-definition television, increased number of channels, and datacasting in which text, images, sound, and video can provide a variety of interactive content.

Television digitalization is making many more hours of television programming available from more sources. And, in its integrated form, it permits viewers such options as viewing a newscast at any time of the day or selecting a single story for viewing. It allows one to watch television dramas and comedies outside the time slot in which they aired. It provides opportunities to view and print a recipe at the same time it is being illustrated on a cooking show, as well to purchase and order ingredients from online shops.

But does digital television really produce a new product or service? The answer is no. It still transmits broadcast programming, but does so with better reception and more choices. It uses the convergence possible through digitalization to view television and simultaneously access materials that would previously be available through or used in the forms of print media, telephone, video/DVD players, Internet, and other communications. Consequently digital television really cannot be considered to produce new products or services but rather just new ways of accessing, receiving, and using existing products or services. The supply and demand for the new possibilities created by digital television, then, will be interrelated to the supply and demand of existing products and services.

A second example can be seen in advances in mobile telephone capabilities. Mobile communications, which have existed in radiotelephone form for many years and in mobile telephone form for about two decades, has already been transformed into a platform that allows users to use the phone to send and receive faxes, text and multimedia messages, and e-mail, as well as operating as cameras and music and video players. Increasingly, it is allowing access to the Internet, global positioning, radio and television broadcasts, advertising reception, and other functions.

These functions, however, are not new. They represent convergence of products and services provided by mail, telephony, Internet, positioning and mapping, printed schedules and brochures, radio, and narrowcasting. There are advantages in being able to access and use these services in a mobile environment, but the ideas and concepts of the services are not new. As with digital television, the supply and demand for many of these services will be interrelated to their supply and demand in their original forms.

The reason such new technologies are not truly producing new products and services is because they provide no real new communications capabilities. They are not affecting communications in such fundamental ways as did the arrival of the printing press, telegraph and telephone, photography and motion pictures, and broadcasting, which provided the abilities to move text, sound, and images with or without terrestrial lines.

Their primary effects are increasing the speed and flexibility of communications, producing economies of scope and integration that change the economics of content production and distribution, and permitting the combination and integration of existing means of communications to allow readers, viewers, or listeners more control and choice and easier use of functions in an single integrated product.

These are important improvements to existing media products and services, but they are not truly new products and services. The combination of existing content modes, the flexibility of use, and the shift of control provide significant advantages to users. And where there are advantages, there are consumers willing to spend time and money.

However, the demand for the "new" products and services providing these advantages must be understood as a part of, and an extension of, demand for existing content products and services. That demand is primarily within those who communicate and receive communications using existing means. To be commercially successful, new methods of accessing, using, and combining products and services must increase value to their users and help simplify their search for and access to the content and communication ability.

New media are increasingly being thought of as means for increasing the functionality and benefits of traditional media use, not supplanting it altogether. Digitalization of television and linking it to the Internet may allow viewers to select television programming or motion pictures with video on demand, but its primary use will be to increase the number of programmed channels or to add new features to that programming. A viewer of a televised automotive program, for example, will be able to use the digital features of interactive television to receive written directions on how to carry out a repair being shown or to order the parts needed to do it.

Those who adopt this view in media firms quickly come to the conclusion that content is the core business, the central activity, and the competency of their firms. The development of information and entertainment and its packaging and programming for use are the essential activities that take place in the value chain and the activities that provide the highest true value added in the process.

The production and distribution methods employed, and the business models used to gain compensation for the firm's activities, are structural necessities for the development and continuation of the core activity. Media managers differentiate their core activity by creating particular methods and types of presentation that create a personality for their publications or programs that become the brand of the companies. It is these activities that

The Value of Content Organization

Technological and policy changes have increased the ability of individuals to select single motion pictures, television programs, recordings, and other materials for their personal use. Some observers argue that choice in acquiring such materials will render traditional television, cable, radio, and Internet content providers unnecessary and result in their demise.

These arguments are based on the view that the emerging free and pay choices offered through cable, satellite, and Internet provide value to audiences. It is believed that the new offerings will supplant existing providers of services because audiences will find them more attractive. This is a tacit argument that there is less value in the current methods of presentation of that content.

This view, however, ignores the fact that the value created by the core business of television, cable, satellite, radio, newspapers, magazines, and Internet content providers is not distribution of that material but the selection, organization, and contextualization of that content.

The value is created for audiences because content organizers expend the time to consider the enormous amount of available or potentially available materials and make hundreds and even thousands of decisions about its quality, usefulness, importance, and entertainment value. Although individuals could make these choices for themselves and are sometimes willing to make the choices, individuals in audiences are not willing and do not have the time to do so on a daily basis.

This occurs because, although making individual choices is valuable to individuals, it is not perceived as having the same value all the time. As the amount of available information and content increases, the value of that additional communication to individuals is diminished and they seek to escape content and the necessity of making decisions regarding it. As a result, there is a growing demand for blocking, avoidance, and filtering systems and the services of content-organizing media.

The most successful new media firms of the past two decades are based on content organization. They aggregate content and help users search through their materials as well as the billions of Web pages available on the Internet, thus organizing content for use by individuals with different interests and needs.

---

make *Elle* different from *Vogue*, *The Times of London* different from *The Daily Mirror*, Facebook different from MySpace, and the Discovery Channel different from the Disney Channel. The core activity of these media, however, is the creation, acquisition, and packaging that transfers information and creates individual brands that serve consumer needs.

VALUE CHAINS AND CONVERGENCE IN PUBLISHING INDUSTRIES

Publishing industries today tend to be led by large national and international publishing firms who engage in information service strategies in which printed products are a base used for expansion into a wide range of information products and services. They are able to do this because the value produced in the creation, gathering, and presentation of content can be separated from the value of the production and distribution systems.

Many of the new products and services based on content creation, gathering, and presentation are electronic and Internet based. It is clear that publishing in the twenty-first century will increasingly be an information gathering, creating, packaging, and storage activity rather than a production or distribution activity based on a specific physical printed form. In adjusting to this new environment, publishing is moving farther away from its traditional position within the printing and paper industries to one under an emerging and not yet fully defined information and knowledge content industries umbrella.

Central to understanding the developments that are driving change is the distinction that must be drawn between publishing and printing. The difference involves the essential value-producing elements of the two activities. Publishing is the act of producing and issuing informative, educational, leisure, and cultural material. Printing is the act of placing that material on paper that can then be distributed.

Printing has always been important as a cost factor in publishing but it is not synonymous with publishing. Even in past decades, many publishers did not print the titles they published, especially publishers in the magazine, book, and directory publishing industries. Today this distinction is becoming even clearer as publishers who traditionally used printing as the medium for distribution are increasingly using electronic means for an expanding variety of published materials.

The development of information and communications technology is leading publishers to transform themselves into broader content creators rather than thinking of themselves as merely paper-based publishers. The basic processes of information gathering, journalistic and literary writing, editing, design, and dissemination have value in forms other than traditional publishing.

Content generated through traditional publishing can be reorganized, repackaged, and used in many different forms. In order to remain competitive in the long run, innovative publishers are exploring and exploiting opportunities presented by these technologies for electronic publishing, multimedia products, and other ICT products that enhance and operate parallel to the traditional publishing base that has made firms successful.

These changes have produced a new type of workflow in publishing and its use by audiences. In the new flow, the publisher not only gains flexibility, but audiences can become actively involved by using electronic information and reconstructing it in forms to their individual liking and by responding to that information and becoming part of the creation process as well (see Figure 2-5).

Although many firms are increasingly outsourcing portions of their activities, the opportunities for publishers and other media firms to use material in a number of ways is leading most firms in communications content to eschew large-scale outsourcing. Although outsourcing some functions can save costs, there is a loss of control over the form and quality of materials if it involves content. Many media firms, particularly those with time-sensitive content, are also reticent to outsource distribution functions upon which they depend.

The concepts of value chains and how and where in the chains media firms produce value make it difficult to continue considering publishing within traditional industry definitions. Publishing has traditionally been thought of as the activity of separate industries: for example, newspaper publishing, magazine publishing, book publishing, and directory publishing. However, it is becoming less relevant to use such definitions to describe the actual activities and modes of operations of many publishing companies today.

Publishing firms of all sizes that were traditionally based in only one of the publishing industries now engage in activities in other publishing industries. Operations are increasingly intertwined and dependent upon each other to the extent that their revenues and costs cannot be easily segmented. The changes in the operations of industries and the convergence of operations are creating a cluster of industries that are increasingly interrelated. Firms now simultaneously operate in different industries in the cluster by creating content that can be used by a variety of means and in a variety of physical and digital formats.

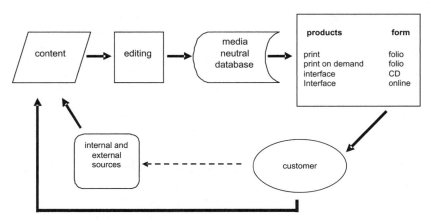

FIGURE 2-5   Electronic publishing flow chart

The Rise of the Concept

Media firms traditionally have produced discrete products or services that have dictated decision making about how choices of content should be made.

In media with continuing focused operations, such as newspapers or magazines, content has followed current events, persons, trends, and developments within the editorial scope of the publications. In radio broadcasting, content choices typically have been made within a format or content profile. In television and motion pictures, content choices have been made to provide a variety of types of programming.

Choices among content are typically made by considering the proposal of materials for use—editors make decisions on what stories to include, production companies and programmers make decisions on what music, programs, or films to produce or broadcast. These decisions are typically made at the media unit level.

In making these choices, managers typically attempt to maximize their audiences or—in the case of public service or not-for-profit media—to maximize their service to audiences. In commercial media, the choice to maximize audience also tends to maximize advertising, although specialized programming that maximizes a specific audience segment is also desirable to some advertisers.

Although these choice patterns continue today, the rise of media conglomerates operating a number of media has also led to content choice patterns that attempt to maximize performance across media.

Two patterns exist for this concept approach. In the first pattern, a successful product such as a book may become transformed into a concept for a motion picture or television program within the media conglomerate. Another example is a magazine that may be used as the basis for television programming. These activities thus extend and maximize the return from the concept of a media product or service already offered by the media conglomerate. In this pattern profitability is typically sought from all uses of the concept.

Thus, the magazine *Better Homes & Gardens* has used its success in the magazine industry to extend that well recognized and respected brand by creating BHG TV (Better Homes & Garden Television), providing a platform for similar types of content but with the advantages of audio and visual communications. The company publishes a range of books on home projects, decorating, and cooking, operates an extensive informational Web site, and markets garden and house planning software under the brand. The media platforms support each other with content and cross-marketing activ-

The nature of the cluster and its relationship to the printing industry and information technology industries are shown in Figure 2-6.

Perhaps the clearest example of problems with traditional definitions of publishing industries occurs in firms in the business information cluster because they are not specifically part of any one of the publishing industries.

ities. Although the uses of this type of cross-media content and activity are increasing, they do not produce economies of scale in production or distribution that significantly reduce the costs of operations of either firm.

In the second pattern, a content concept or story is selected with the intent that it is released simultaneously or progressively in different forms by media within a conglomerate. Thus a concept may produce a book, motion picture, television program, electronic game, and Web site. The result is that the marketing of each product or service supports the marketing and brand of the concept as a whole and vice versa. In this type of cross-media activity pattern, a company will want to make a profit on each media use of the concept, but it may sometimes cross-subsidize the activities so that the overall use and profitability is maximized. When it is not advantageous or possible to follow this pattern within a conglomerate, outside firms may be used for some portions through joint ventures or licensing arrangements.

This process was evident when James Cameron's film *Avatar* was released by Twentieth Century Fox in 2009. The release of the film was accompanied by the release of a similarly named video game published by Ubisoft Montreal, by the release of the motion picture's soundtrack by Atlantic Records, by merchandise including toy vehicles and action figures produced by Mattel, by the publication of a book on the art of Avatar published by Abrams Books, by a themed McDonald's Happy Meal, and other merchandise.

Despite the contentions in the late twentieth century that large media firms with holdings in different media would find ways to leverage that ownership into regular transformation of successful books into films, television programs, videos, and other products within the firm, that pattern has not successfully developed. Similarly, predictions that corporations owning motion picture and television programming firms along with television channels would work closely together on a regular basis have not been regularly borne out.

Although there are advantages in the development of concept media products, separate division managers and independent corporate evaluations of divisions have kept incentives from developing that promote full cooperation with other business units, and have typically not resulted in selling content or rights internally at a lower price than to other companies, and have not produced revenue sharing across divisions. As a result, the development and exploitation of many concept products has involved firms from media companies that are otherwise competitors rather than corporate sisters or cousins.

The firms in this cluster produce and distribute information that helps businesses understand and adjust to changing market conditions, follow trends in products and services, and locate potential new customers.

These firms are based less and less on single distribution channels, such as magazines or online services, but incorporate many methods of distribution,

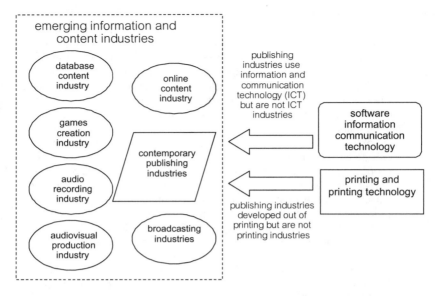

FIGURE 2-6   The information and knowledge content industries cluster

including periodicals, online services, radio and television broadcasts, books, and directories. Major firms in this cluster join multiple publishing associations and federations because their activities cross industries and many company executives are frustrated by the narrowness of the perspectives of individual organizations.

The changes occurring around and throughout publishing industries force managers to reconsider their strategies and operations or risk being left behind. The necessity to innovate, to question, and to alter past strategies is more critical in the publishing industries today than ever before. The new environment makes it possible for firms from other industries and new firms to enter publishing. Many are doing so without having existing print-based traditions or having to face the difficult choices of what do with existing operations, personnel, and facilities. These firms are able to change the foundations of the industry and become major companies in the industry through dramatic operational changes because that change does not threaten to their existing operations.

Managers of publishing firms today face the prospect of new firms taking away their business or pursuing internal innovation to remake their firms and industry. Otherwise they face the certainty of steady decline for their business if they do not innovate to counteract the pressures of the new firms.

One factor in the ability of media firms to successfully carry out their roles as creators of value for audiences and advertisers is the extent to which they evidence competitiveness.

There is a tendency to think that just because a firm competes it is competitive. But the concept of competitiveness runs much deeper. Competitiveness is a term that indicates the degree to which a firm or industry can survive, sustain itself, and remain a viable economic contributor. It also involves the degree to which a firm or national industry can respond to market opportunities or threats.

The degree of competitiveness is the result of a variety of factors within the firm or national industry, and in their general environments, that support the ability to grow, to expand markets, and to respond to increased competition from other firms or national industries.

Some firms and national industries have competitive advantages that make it easier for them to challenge other firms in competitive situations. Competitive advantages arise from constant efforts to improve the performance of firms and upgrade products and services. They result from internal atmospheres that support change and innovation.

The kinds of competitive advantages occurring from these factors include:

Lower costs

Differentiated products commanding a high price

Proprietary assets

Higher quality products and services

Efficient production

Rapid product development

Advanced features

Innovation

Publishers of multiple magazines, for example, have advantages in production and distribution that reduce the cost per copy and create efficiencies in production compared to companies that publish few titles. Online media companies have tended to have advantages over traditional media companies because they have business cultures and company structures that allow them to rapidly alter existing products and change directions quickly to respond to new market opportunities. This has been a particular advantage over traditional media companies whose cultures and structures have tended to create barriers to rapid change.

Advantages to some firms and consequent disadvantages to other firms can also result from:

Protectionist government policies

Subsidies

Monopolies

Actions designed to harm competition

For example, postal rates can create cost advantages for different classes of media and communications services. These might favor direct mail firms over newspapers or magazines. Similarly the provision of monopolies or preferences in cable services in a market through franchising can advantage and disadvantage firms.

Some firms and industries also have advantages because they operate in nations that have advantages such as strategic location, better infrastructures, financial stability, higher levels of economic development, policies supportive of business and economic development, and beneficial developments from the clustering of specific industrial sectors. Competitiveness, then, represents the degree to which a firm uses advantages and managerial competence to proportionally generate more wealth than its competitors.

At the national level, for example, the outdoor advertising industry in Germany operates in a country with significant advantages owing to its high level of economic development, advertisers with significant advertising budgets, and a well-established outdoor advertising industry. These provide firms in the German industry significant competitive advantages when compared to outdoor advertising firms operating in a country such as Algeria.

The degree of company and industry competitiveness is typically evidenced by factors such as turnover, productivity, lower cost and efficiency, profitability, investments, research and development expenditures, personnel skills levels, and trade balances. It is desirable for a magazine company or a national cable television industry, as examples, to perform above average on such measures—or at least in the average range—when compared to other magazine companies or to the cable television industry in another nation.

SUSTAINABILITY

Managers struggle between the need for short-term financial performance and the need for long-term sustainability of the firm. The goals of these choices are not contradictory, but they compete at the managerial level for attention, resources, and behavior. Attention to the issue of sustainability is

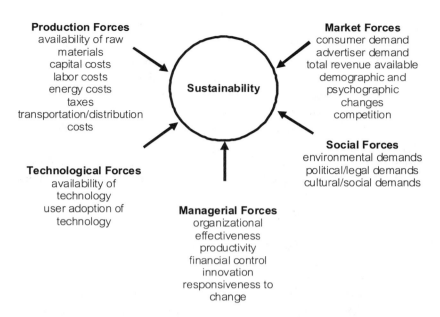

Production Forces
availability of raw
materials
capital costs
labor costs
energy costs
taxes
transportation/distribution
costs

Market Forces
consumer demand
advertiser demand
total revenue available
demographic and
psychographic
changes
competition

Sustainability

Social Forces
environmental demands
political/legal demands
cultural/social demands

Technological Forces
availability of
technology
user adoption of
technology

Managerial Forces
organizational
effectiveness
productivity
financial control
innovation
responsiveness to
change

FIGURE 2-7   Factors affecting the sustainability of media companies

critical to maintaining competitiveness because a firm that is competitive today can lose that competitiveness in future years.

Managers with a narrow view of their responsibilities focus primarily on short-term financial performance, seeking higher annual returns for owners, sometimes at the cost of reinvestment, by reducing resources for content quality or expenditures for labor.

Managers pursuing the longer-term goal of sustainability focus on broader issues that will affect the future development and value of the firm. Sustainability represents the viability of an industry or firm, its ability to maintain effectiveness and operations. Sustainability is affected by a variety of production, market, technological, social, and managerial forces (see Figure 2-7).

Managers thus seek to balance the needs of the short-term goal of financial performance with the longer-term goal of sustainability that requires attention and response to the variety of forces that affect firms or industries. Today, the most significant sustainability factor for most media involves the effectiveness of the managers in dealing with the managerial forces.

SUGGESTED READINGS

Afuah, Allan, Christopher L. Tucci, and Christopher Ticci. 2002. *Internet Business Models and Strategies.* Boston: McGraw-Hill/Irwin.

Aris, Anette, and Jacques Bughin. 2009. *Managing Media Companies: Harnessing Creative Value*. 2nd ed. Chichester: John Wiley & Sons.

Becker, Lee B., and Klaus Schoenbach, eds. 1989. *Audience Responses to Media Diversification: Coping with Plenty*. Hillsdale, N.J.: Lawrence Erlbaum Associates.

Chan-Olmsted, Sylvia. 2005. *Competitive Strategy for Media Firm: Strategic and Brand Management in Changing Media Markets*. Mahwah, N.J.: Lawrence Erlbaum.

Grieve Smith, John. 1990. *Business Strategy*. Cambridge, Mass.: Blackwell.

Karlöf, Bengt. 1989. *Business Strategy: A Guide to Concepts and Models*. London: Macmillan.

Küng, Lucy. 2008. *Strategic Management in the Media: Theory and Practice*. London: Sage Publications.

Lewis, James P. 2006. *Fundamentals of Project Management*. New York AMACOM/American Management Association.

Meredith, Jack R., and Samuel J. Mantel Jr. 2008. *Project Management: A Managerial Approach*. 7th ed. New York: John Wiley & Sons.

Porter, Michael E. 1985. *Competitive Advantage: Creating and Sustaining Superior Performance*. New York: Free Press.

CHAPTER 3

Distribution and Retail Sales of Media

Producing content is a fundamental activity of media firms, but that content must reach consumers before the firms can be considered as actually doing business. The processes of getting the content to customers are central and often-ignored aspects of media enterprises that are crucial to determining the success of the content. Media encounter differing degrees of distribution complexity because of dissimilarities in their nature, their geographical distribution areas, types of distributors involved, warehousing requirements for physical media products and the extent to which retail networks and retailers are involved.

Media distribution environments are determined by whether physical or nonphysical products are involved and whether sales are made on the basis of a single-product purchase or a subscription. Distribution systems can be internal or external to the producer and can involve business-to-consumer sales—such as those for newspaper or cable systems—or business-to-business sales such as motion picture distributors selling rights to show films to theatres or television producers selling broadcasters the rights to broadcast their programming. Some media are based in retail store distribution, such as audio recordings, DVDs, magazines, and books. These distribution activities involve warehousing, transportation, wholesalers, and retail stores themselves.

Physical distribution is highly influenced by unit cost economics whereas nonphysical distribution is influenced by transaction cost economics. Digitalization of content has made it possible for some products to change from physical to nonphysical distribution, to disintermediate the existing distribution system by removing or creating mechanisms to bypass some intermediary players, or to reintermediate the system by reconstructing the system with different intermediaries and different cost structures. These changes can reduce the cost of distribution in nonphysical systems but may have the simultaneous effect of increasing average cost of products remaining in physical distribution.

Nonphysical distribution includes broadcasts from a radio station, programming conveyed on a cable television system, content delivered over the Internet, and audio/video downloads. When nonphysical distribution is involved managers focus on fundamental activities such as ensuring system reliability and quality system capacity, ease of consumer use, and customer service.

INVENTORY AND DISTRIBUTION CHALLENGES

Multifaceted processes are involved in getting physical products from the production line to customers that involve warehousing, order fulfillment, and transportation to retail stores. But the processes do not merely involve getting the book, CD, or game from one point to the customer because multiple enterprises with different interests and different risks are involved. The media producer takes orders from retailers (or customers if direct sales are involved), coordinates these orders with accounting and payment systems, and then sends the orders to the fulfillment center to pull materials from inventory, package them, and ship them to retail shops or directly to customers. All these processes must also be coordinated with accounting and payment systems, inventory management systems, and production reordering systems. It is a dynamic process that must manage inventory on hand and the distribution activities themselves.

Inventory management issues involve ensuring adequate supply of product, producing rapid turnover of inventory, avoiding overstocking, and coordinating production to ensure that sufficient supply exists to fill orders. The biggest challenges result from an inability to forecast demand, from high levels of inventory, and because of differences in preferences for products in different markets. Inventory turnover is necessary; it is expensive to have product sitting on the shelf because of financing of manufacturing and the costs of warehouse space. These factors force companies to make sales at discount prices to clear warehouses when inventories are too high. These inventory challenges are compounded because the only thing worse for a business than overstocking is understocking that leads to lost sales when the company can't meet demand. Businesses attempt to overcome stocking challenges by constant monitoring of order and sales reports.

Distribution management concerns focus on speed in fulfilling and delivering orders, effective shipment scheduling and routing, and costs created by small orders from many retailers. Because of the fact that the number, size, and locations of markets may require multiple distribution centers, clarity of responsibility for markets and coordination among distribution centers is mandatory.

Media producers must be particularly concerned about their ability to gain access to markets and customers; the number of distribution points that must be served; market size, locations, and distances to markets; the amount of effort required; and cost effectiveness. The methods used for distribution create different issues. In some cases distribution involves media company intermediaries who have a business-to-business relationship with the producer. The television production company Worldwide Pants Inc., for example, has such a relationship with CBS to produce "Late Night with David Letterman." In other cases, there is direct-to-customer distribution in the form of a business-to-consumer relationship. This is seen in subscription sales of magazines, for example. Finally, distribution can serve retailers in a business-to-business wholesaler relationship. For producers the strategic challenge is to determine the degree of ownership and control needed in distribution processes. This—combined with cost, scale, and scope factors—influences decisions about the type of distribution system to employ.

Because of these issues, distribution costs vary among media, ranging from low costs for online and broadcast distribution to high costs for books, CDs, and DVDs.

A great deal of distribution and sales inefficiency in media results from excess product left unsold at points of availability. On average 15 to 20 percent of single-copy newspapers in newsracks and newsstands, 30 to 40 percent of books produced, and 60 percent of newsstand magazines are unsold. This excess creates uncompensated costs for production, distribution, and the return of unsold copies.

CHOICE OF DISTRIBUTION SYSTEM

An important strategic choice of media companies is whether distribution should be handled internally or externally. Internal distribution tends to be used when there is a need to control product customization, to control and adjust distribution time, or to participate in the retail network. External distribution tends to be used when specialized distribution service providers are available, when it is more cost effective, or when firms want to avoid investment costs necessary to establish a distribution system.

Distribution also tends to be internal when companies want more control over the process and more direct contact with consumers. The use of internal distribution, of course, increases company size, cost, and management

Solving Distribution Challenges at Netflix

Netflix, the world's largest online DVD rental service, has built an exemplary distribution system designed to deliver videos to U.S. customers' homes by mail. It is an IT-driven, Internet-based company, but its operations are grounded in brick-and-mortar facilities and physical logistics. The company ships more than 2.2 million DVDs each day from a network of fifty distribution centers that deliver to more than one hundred postal shipping points.

The distribution system operates behind a customer-friendly Web ordering operation. The business and order processing activities require significant centralized control abilities but customer service needs require a decentralized distribution system to ensure rapid order fulfillment. Because Netflix competes with many physical and digital providers of motion picture and television video, it required building a highly efficient and customer-oriented distribution system.

Netflix customers go online to select motion pictures and television programs among the nearly 100,000 titles currently available. A customer opens an account using a credit card and creates a list of DVDs he or she would like to receive. After the account is created, the computerized system checks the status of the customer's account, and sends an order for the customer's next requested DVDs to the distribution center that serves the customer's ZIP code. The desired DVDs are then pulled from the inventory, packed for shipment, and then sorted and delivered to the appropriate Post Office distribution and operations center which delivers it with other mail.

Although it would be possible to deliver across the United States from a single location, it would take several days for DVDs to arrive at distant locations. Because Netflix is committed to delivering within one business day, a high number of distribution centers located close to customers nationwide is necessary. This allows the company to currently deliver 95 percent of its DVDs within one day. The 5 percent that aren't delivered within one day tend to involve shipments to locations such as northern Alaska and Montana where postal service is slower. If a title is not available in the distribution center closest to the customer, the DVD will be shipped from the next-closest center and this may add some time to a delivery as well.

effort. External distribution reduces control, creates dependency on distributors and retailers, and reduces attention placed on the company's products; but those downsides are accompanied by benefits from distributors' specialization and transaction cost economies and reduced costs for the producer.

When choosing a distribution system, businesses have to decide whether to use a system specialized for a particular media type or a diversified distribution system carrying many products and whether the company will operate a distribution system in competition with its competitors or cooperate with competitors on distribution. The choices made affect the attention given to the individual company's media products, costs of distribution,

After a customer has viewed a DVD, he or she drops it in the mail in the provided, prepaid return envelope and the postal services delivers the DVD back to Netflix. The disc is then inspected, the customer's account is credited for the return, and the customer is sent an automated e-mail acknowledging the return, and an order for the next DVD on the customer's list is automatically generated and fulfilled.

The entire process is labor intensive; about 85 percent of the company's staff is employed in the distribution efforts, handling order fulfillment, mail sorting, return, and transportation activities. The company's distribution centers are typically located in industrial parks near major roadways. As the number of distribution centers has increased, their size has decreased. Basic distribution centers tend to be 5,000- to 10,000-square-feet facilities each with about 15 employees, who ship 10,000 DVDs daily. Mid-sized centers serve larger markets and range up to 50,000 square feet with about 100 employees and handle more than 50,000 DVDs daily. The company's central distribution center and warehouse in Sunnyvale, California, is an 112,000-square-feet facility. This central facility stores 45 million DVDs that are constantly circulated among distribution centers, allowing the centers to have only limited storage capacity. Smaller facilities have one to two vans or light trucks for pick-up and drop-off of shipments at postal centers; the number of vehicles rises with the size of the distribution center.

Recognizing the growth of broadband capabilities and opportunities in digital video streaming, in 2007 the company began offering digital distribution whereby customers can select a video and immediately stream it to a PC for viewing. In 2008 Netflix teamed up with electronics manufacturer LG to develop a system for streaming video of high-definition movies to television sets via a set-top box.

The company operates these digital activities from several locations and views them as complementary rather than in competition with its physical distribution. Titles available for digital streaming are fewer in numbers than for physical DVDs because studios make only a limited number of titles available at a time so that these titles will not compete directly with titles in packages made available to television stations.

and whether distribution is handled internally, in a subsidiary firm, or in a joint venture as shown in Figure 3-1.

Wholesalers and distributors serve different functions. Wholesalers provide warehousing, order fulfillment, and shipping of products to retailers. They have a service relationship with the producer of the product and keep about half of the retail price. Distributors provide the same services but also engage in sales and marketing and take part of the business risk because they essentially become partners with the producer. In these arrangements it is common for distributors to keep about two-thirds to three-quarters of the retail price. Distribution arrangements are governed by contractual

competitive
system

•dedicated system
•operated for advantages
over competitors
•most likely internal to a
media firm

•diverse products system
•operated for advantages
over competitors
•most likely subsidiary of
a media firm

specialized
distribution
system

diversified
distribution
system

• dedicated system
• operated for efficiency cost
effectiveness
• may be internal to a media
firm or a joint venture

•diverse products system
•operated for efficiency
and cost effectiveness
•most likely a joint
venture or subsidiary of
a media firm

cooperative
system

FIGURE 3-I   Distribution system choices and results

agreements regarding different aspects of intellectual property rights, as well as general commercial law.

Book and magazine distributors tend to be independent of major publishers or subsidiary companies and operate at both the national and international levels. When firms operate internationally they tend to serve continents or linguistic regions. Some act as general distributors focusing on serving retail outlets. These include firms such as Gardners, Ingram, Independent Publishers Group, National Magazine Distributors, and W. H. Smith. Specialized distributors focus on serving libraries and specialized retailers and include firms such as Baker & Taylor, Blackwell, Couts, Diamond Comics Distributor, Dawson, and Yankee Book Peddler.

Audio, film and video distribution, by contrast, is dominated by major producers. Major audio distributors are Universal Music Group, Sony BMG Music Entertainment, Warner Music Group, and EMI Recorded Music. Film and video/DVD distribution is concentrated in Sony Pictures, Warner Bros, Twentieth Century Fox, Disney/Buena Vista, Paramount, Columbia/Tri-Star, and Universal Pictures International.

Media distribution is strongly influenced by territoriality in which distributors or wholesalers are given exclusive distribution rights within their regional, national, or state/provincial territories. The rights to distribution can be quite complex. Even in a single geographic market, one firm may have the rights to distribute a motion picture to theaters, another firm may have the rights to distribute to television channels, and still another firm may have the rights to distribute DVDs. The territoriality issue has created problems for Apple's iTunes and other digital music providers because they must negotiate separately with music rights owners in each country and cannot sell globally under a single license from the recording companies. Consequently, an American interested in Italian music not available on the U.S. Web site cannot go the Italian Web site and buy it there because digital rights management software detects that the customer is in the United States and that the Italian site does not have rights to sell to U.S. customers.

Territoriality also allows producers to engage in price discrimination—that is, charging different prices to different groups of customers. Purchasers of a DVD of a motion picture in North America and Europe, for example, can be charged a higher price than customers for the same movie in Southeast Asia where incomes are lower. The use of territories also allows distribution of different product ranges. A music distributor in Latin America, for example, would find it undesirable to distribute the full range of recordings from North America, but would carry those most likely to be sold. Territoriality creates parallel import issues, of course, in which producers want to ensure that products from one territory do not reach other territories. This is the primary reason why DVDs are manufactured with zone protection technologies—DVDs purchased in Thailand will not play on DVD players or computers in Europe and DVDs purchased in Africa will not play on equipment in the United States.

Distributors not owned by producers are concerned about good returns on order fulfillment or marketing, sales, and fulfillment, so issues involving the number of retail outlets serviced, the degree of distribution exclusivity they receive, the length of distribution agreement, and cost recovery are central in their negotiations with producers. They often are interested in subsidiary rights for merchandise and secondary sales as well as guarantees of access to additional products from the producer in the future.

Ultimately, most media products reach customers through retailers that sell products to customers. These include cable systems, movie theaters, shops, rental stores, and newsstands. These retailers are served by the distributors.

CHALLENGES OF RETAIL ACTIVITIES

The size of the retail industry increases distribution complexity. In the United States, for example, more than 10,000 bookstores, about 2,000 newspaper shops, nearly 7,000 recorded music and video stores, 23,500 video/DVD rental stores, and thousands of general retailers carry media products. Media companies that reach customers through those outlets must have significant logistical capabilities, especially those operating in large nations or internationally.

LIMITATIONS ON DISPLAY SPACE

Even with such capabilities media companies face the challenge of ensuring that their product is selected to be carried by those retailers. Because retailers are interested only in products they believe will sell, they choose among media products and this selection process creates a bottleneck that media companies must overcome (see Figure 3-2).

Retailers' choices are based on the fact that their primary resource is shelf space and they must manage the return per square foot/meter that they receive for their activities. Retailers need rapid turnover or high return per space taken up by the products they stock and few media products provide high rates of return so these retailers typically are judged by the rapidity of the inventory turnover.

thousands of titles

consumer

Retailers' Selection Processes

FIGURE 3-2   Retailers are a bottleneck for abundant media products

These realities mean that media firms must be concerned about getting display space for media products and providing retailers incentives to do so. This is sometimes difficult because many retailers are provided standard title stocking lists by corporate parents or purchasing cooperatives and some firms receive shelf fees, extra payments to stock certain titles or to display them in prominent locations in their stores.

How media companies promote their products in stores varies depending upon whether purchases are considered impulse or deliberate. To help promote impulse purchases, point of sale marketing opportunities such as special displays or pricing are typically located near checkout lines.

The Power of Retailers: Deciding What to Carry

Wal-Mart is the world's largest retailer as well as the number-one music retailer in the United States. It sells more music than other brick-and-mortar businesses such as Best Buy and Target and more than online retailers such as iTunes and amazon.com. It offers both in-store and online sales of physical CDs and sells digital downloads online.

Because Wal-Mart accounts for about 20 percent of all music sales in the United States, it has enormous market power and uses that influence on recording companies and musicians. The retailer has a policy to carry family-oriented products, so it will not carry CDs with cover art or lyrics deemed sexual or controversial. This has induced record companies to create special versions for the company so they will not be banned from its shelves. A marijuana leaf on the cover of Willie Nelson's CD "Countrymen" was issued in a Wal-Mart version with a palm tree on the cover instead. Similarly images of the devil and Jesus in the background of John Mellencamp's "Mr. Happy-Go-Lucky" were removed for Wal-Mart release. The company does not stock audio recordings that have parental guidance stickers on them and some companies provide Wal-Mart with recordings that remove offensive words or lines to avoid losing sales.

The retailer pursues similar policies with DVDs, magazines, and books refusing to carry those whose topics or covers it believes contradicts its family-oriented policy.

One of the difficulties with media products is that some titles are more attractive to larger groups of consumers than others and some fail to sell altogether, creating the need for return systems and processes. To help mediate those issues, it is necessary to attract consumer attention amidst the abundance of media products, which can prove challenging, especially for single-title products and for creating impulse or nonplanned purchases. The result is that marketing costs for single-creation products are especially high.

Media companies recognize the need to attract attention at retail locations and that customer interests and preferences differ based on locations. To account for these differences magazine publishers sometimes vary cover designs for copies sent to subscribers and those sold as single copy at retail locations. To account for regional differences they may vary covers and some content in different parts of large nations. Media companies also find point of sale promotion necessary to support impulse buying and these are done through discounted prices, promotional tie-ins, shelf cards, and promotional display cases provided to retailers.

The needs of retailers differ as well, as do the ways in which retailers relate to media companies and products. Media specialty stores (audio stores, video stores, booksellers, newsstands), video and game rental stores, and general retailers that sell multiple goods, including media products, have different purposes and methods for stocking media products. Similarly full-price and discount retailers and chain stores and independent retailers have different incentives and are interested in varying types of media products.

Chain-store media retailers, for example, tend to be corporately owned, operate stores with an average of 100,000 titles in stock, and rely upon centralized buying and distribution services. Examples of these types of businesses include Barnes & Noble and the British retailer HMV. Independent media retailers on the other hand tend to be small and mid-sized enterprises that stock an average of 10,000 titles. They order individually or through cooperatives and shipping tends to be direct from distributor to shops.

Major media retailers tend to have multiple store locations and some operate multinationally. It is typically cheaper for media companies to serve these firms than to serve small, independent stores. The big media retailers want to sell volume at low price and carry a broad array of titles. They are unable to compete on price alone so they tend to compete on selection and store location. Because of their size they have market power to negotiate price, promotions, and artist appearances.

Specialty retailers can sell on volume or price, and most sell their specialized focus, knowledge, and service. In many cases they have stronger bonds with their customers than other retailers because of their shared avocations and values. Examples of specialty retailers include retailers focusing on jazz recordings, children's books, and foreign DVDs.

The Internet has produced many online retailers for media products ranging from giants such as amazon.com, which sells a range of products in addition to videos/DVDs, CDs, and books, to small specialty retailers such as The Madrigal, a purveyor of classical music. Online retailers want to sell volume at or near the price of major media retailers and their customer advantages is a nearly complete catalogue of available music. Their physical location is not a major issue because they use postal and parcel physical distribution, so they are able to locate warehouses and order fulfillment centers in cost-effective settings. They are increasingly offering not only physical copies of recordings but also digital downloads that overcome the time and space constraints on distribution of physical products.

A major advantage for online retailers is that, unlike brick-and-mortar retailers, shelf space is not an issue. And many online retailers do not even keep the majority of their offerings in stock, instead having them shipped directly from manufacturers or publishers. Online retailing is operated by sales companies who act as intermediaries for the producers; it also creates ways for direct sales by the producer. Thus companies such as the publisher Random House and the recording company Sony Music Entertainment operate their own online retail sites that serve promotional as well as sales functions. These sites also allow them to keep much of the purchase price that would have previously gone to distributors and retailers, thus boosting their revenues and profits.

Nonmedia retailers such as Wal-Mart, Target, and KMart and grocery stores are increasingly important distributors for media products and are becoming the primary outlet for popular, fast-moving books, audio, and video. These stores carry a limited number of titles and want to sell volume at the lowest possible price, so they focus on bestselling titles and heavily discounted back titles. Their practices exert strong downward price pressure on the wholesale and manufacturer's suggested retail prices, thus reducing profitability per unit but increasing overall sales.

A number of media companies have begun moving into retail sales to capture more value, to turn expenses into revenue streams, and to better manage customer contacts. These are being done through both physical and online retailing. Virgin Records, for example, now operates the Virgin Megastores and an online retail site and is increasingly closing less profitable brick-and-mortar stores. Universal Studios and CBS Television now offer streaming video/download sales of their products.

Successful retailing is more than selling products; it involves providing a comfortable experience. In recent years booksellers have been media leaders in this regard, creating stores designed to attract shoppers even though they do not contain all titles available from online competitors They have come to view their business activities as more than selling books and have developed stores that create a variety of book-related experiences. Bookstores have for many years marketed themselves as locations in which to spend leisure time, to take a break, to get a cup of coffee, and to meet friends. They act as cultural centers in which authors discuss their books and musicians can perform. They are designed to play a regular role in daily life and to bring customers to their shops more often. And, of course, they do so to sell more books and to accept orders for unstocked titles.

CUSTOMER CONTACT CHALLENGES

Retailers present strategic problems for producers of media products because they are placed between producers and their customers. It is optimal for media producers to have direct relationships with their customers because they can control customer service, get better information about their customers and their preferences, better tailor products to meet customer desires, and more easily create customer loyalty. When retailers independent of producers are involved, those benefits shift to retailers because the relationship is between the retailer and the customer and the retailer controls the experience delivered.

All activities of a media company need to create value and the distribution/retail chain is no exception. Effective value is created by delivering the media product to the consumer's home or to a nearby location, by the reliability of the delivery, by providing a wide selection of materials, through the convenience of the services offered, by providing satisfying customer service in the event of problems with the product, and by the overall user experience. The value produced by these activities creates exchange value above and beyond the price of the basic product. The ability to control and manage this value creation becomes crucial in a highly competitive environment, which is why some firms prefer to keep the activities in the distribution chain in-house.

The distribution of media products has traditionally been seen only as a requirement of doing business and as a cost center in the media firms. However, it can be an activity that adds value and generates revenue, if it provides better and customized services to customers or is turned into a profit center by providing services to other firms.

Regional newspapers across the United States have gained additional revenue by distributing national newspapers such as *The Wall Street Journal* or *USA Today* along with their own papers. Some papers have found additional ways to use their distribution fleets and personnel to obtain new revenue. *The Daily Sentinel* in Grand Junction, Colorado, for example, operates a next-day delivery service serving Western Colorado communities such as Grand Junction, Vail, Aspen, and Montrose in which it distributes parcels after making its newspaper deliveries.

SUGGESTED READINGS

Brae, C. Michael. 2002. *Music Distribution: Selling Music in the New Entertainment Marketplace*. BookSurge Publishing.

Gorchels, Linda, Edward Marien, and Chuck West. 2004. *The Manager's Guide to Distribution Channels*. New York: McGraw-Hill.

McCauley, David E. 1993. *Warehouse Distribution and Operations Handbook*. New York: McGraw-Hill Professional.

Özgun, Onur, Wolfgang Hörmann, and Mehper Cihangir. 2010. *Distribution Planning of Magazines: A Practical Approach*. Saarbrücken: Lambert Academic Publishing.

Parks, Stacey. 2007. *The Insider's Guide to Independent Film Distribution*. Boston: Focal Press.

Thorn, William, and Mary Pfeil. 1987. *Newspaper Circulation: Marketing the News*. New York: Longman.

Zylstra, Kirk D. 2005. *Lean Distribution: Applying Lean Manufacturing to Distribution, Logistics, and Supply Chain*. New York: John Wiley & Sons.

CHAPTER 4

Economic Forces Affecting Media

Four major categories of economic forces affect operations and choices of managers in media firms: market forces, cost forces, regulatory forces, and barriers to entry and mobility.

Market forces are external forces based upon structures and choices in the marketplace. Cost forces are internal pressures based upon the operating expenses of firms. Regulatory forces represent the legal, political, and self-regulatory forces that constrain and direct operations of media firms. Barriers represent factors that make it difficult for new firms to enter and successfully compete in a market.

MARKET FORCES

The ability of a media firm to be established, prosper, and grow is affected by a variety of external pressures that affect its ability to gain the financing and revenue it needs and to effectively compete in the marketplace.

These market forces include the availability and terms for obtaining capital, demand for the products and services offered, and the competitive situation.

CAPITAL AVAILABILITY AND COSTS

The availability of funds for the establishment and development of firms is a crucial element that determines whether and how many companies can exist. Without reasonable availability of funds, the number of media firms that will exist and the activities they can carry out will be limited. When capital is readily available at reasonable costs, existing firms can use those funds to further develop their activities and operations, and new partners or firms may be able to enter the media marketplace.

The problem of capital has been a factor in developing nations that tend to have less stable currencies and fewer mechanisms and institutions for capital accumulation, lending, and investment. This hampers the abilities of individuals and companies to acquire capital to establish private, commercial media. Even in developed nations, economic changes and political choices reduce or increase the availability of capital and the terms for its use at different times, affecting the ability of individuals and firms to acquire and use capital.

All capital comes with conditions. These conditions are not neutral because they direct and constrain choices in firms and ultimately have an impact on the products or services provided. In private ownership those who provide the capital have a high degree of control. In publicly owned firms, those that generate the capital often have limited control, but those who manage collective capital invested in the firm (for example, institutional investors such as pension funds) may have significant influence on the firm.

Capital is the fundamental, underlying asset that allows firms to operate, develop, and grow. Capital needs to be acquired, protected, used wisely, and increased if companies are to prosper. Capital is created and increased when financial resources are not consumed and saved for use in the future creation of goods and services. Firms wishing to carry out productive activities must have access to capital in order to procure goods, services, and labor necessary for that process. If they have previously accumulated capital by consuming less income than they receive, the self-generated capital can be used for this purpose. Otherwise, it must be obtained from other sources. If it comes from investors, they will have profit motives and expect beneficial dividends. If the capital is borrowed, those lending the capital will expect a reasonable return given the risk involved and other potential uses of the funds.

The significance of capital to companies is seen in the fact that the most important measures of the company stability and business performance use capital as a base factor. Measures of performance—returns on investment, capitalization ratios, price-earnings ratio, debt-to-equity ratio, and liquidity ratio—are linked to issues of capital, equity, and related assets. Sources of capital review these measures when deciding whether to invest or provide loans and other financing to firms.

AUDIENCE/CONSUMER DEMAND

The willingness and ability of audiences to use media or to acquire media products and services is another significant economic force that determines the success of media firms and the materials that they produce and disseminate.

The acquisition and use of media products and services requires individuals to spend time, money, or both on media. Because time and money are scarce resources, the decision to expend them for media is subject to the economic force of audience/consumer demand.

Given a twenty-four-hour day, of which two-thirds is typically devoted to sleep, work, education, and household maintenance, individuals have roughly eight hours per day for leisure and other activities, including media use. If individuals use three hours watching television, they cannot use those three hours to attend a concert. If individuals use one hour for online activities, they cannot use that hour to read a book. If individuals use two hours playing football, they cannot use that time to view a film in a theater. The activity choices made individually and collectively thus affect the demand for media products and services even when price is not involved.

When a price for the media product or service is involved, consumer choices take place within the entire available income. If individuals spend 35 percent of their income on shelter, they cannot use that income for cable subscriptions. If 2 percent of their income is spent on telecommunications, they cannot use that income to purchase food. If individuals spend 20 percent of their income on automobiles, they cannot use that income to purchase books. Similarly, if an individual spends 5 percent of her money purchasing a DVD player, she cannot spend that money on DVD recordings.

The amount of money available to consumers, and the choices made for the use of that money among a range of products and services, affects demand for media products and services that are available at a price. Audience/consumer demand is also affected by a variety of other factors including the size of the population, tastes and preferences of individuals, and consumer expectations in a given market.

Demand is also affected by the amount of media already available. Each additional unit of a medium and each additional medium available reduces demand for individual units of a medium. As the number of channels of communications increase, the number of choices rise and individuals' behaviors diverge, thus reducing demand for specific media units. This audience fragmentation is the inevitable and unstoppable consequence of the increase in channels available to audiences. It is true whether one is discussing publishing, broadcasting, Internet, or other forms of communications involving multiple individuals.

The result of fragmentation can clearly be seen in the decline of average television audience share when the number of available channels increases (see Figure 4-1). The average share of the total television audience drops dramatically with the addition of each new channel. Whereas the share of

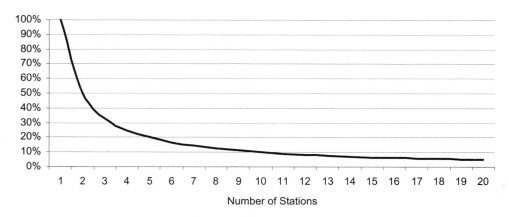

FIGURE 4-1   Diminishing demand for each new television station as seen in average audience share

the total audience is 100 percent with one channel, it plummets to an average share of 20 percent of the total audience with only five channels and then to 5 percent at twenty channels.

When one looks beyond averages at actual television and cable markets, one finds that some channels must struggle to survive with only 1 or 2 percent shares after about a dozen channels are available, because they fall below the average share of the total television audience. This occurs because it is rare that audiences devote equal attention to each of the channels.

This audience demand constraint is seen in the figures for multichannel television use where many channels go unviewed despite their availability. Research has shown that when eleven to twenty channels are received in a home, members of the family on average watch only six channels. When twenty to thirty channels are available, they view only seven channels. If thirty to forty channels are available the average family tunes in to only ten channels. When one hundred channels are received, only sixteen are ever watched. Thus, there is an oversupply of programming and audience use does not increase proportionally with supply. This, of course, increases competition among the providers for audiences.

ADVERTISER DEMAND

Advertiser demand for media products and services is primarily dependent upon the needs of advertisers to reach audiences, the sizes or types of audiences attracted to certain media content, and the prices for access to audiences.

Most media advertising is a part of the broader marketing efforts of manufacturers and retailers to draw attention to their products, to increase sales, and to build product loyalty. As a result, the extent to which advertisers require advertising to serve those needs may vary with season, the state of the economy, the number of competitors they face, and so on.

Demand for media advertising is also affected by the choices of advertisers among a range of marketing communications activities, including direct marketing (catalogs, advertising sheets, personalized mail) and sales promotion (point of sale displays, exhibitions, sponsorships). Different types of advertisers have different needs to communicate with audiences, and various types of advertising and marketing communications do not equally serve all needs.

COMPETITION

The amount and degree of competition among media and media units are another economic factor that affects the development and success of media firms. When a market is divided among multiple competitors, no one firm will control the market and each will take part in a continuing struggle to improve or maintain their market share.

Situations in which there are multiple media units help to produce benefits for audiences and advertisers. The competition process is one in which one competitor takes an action, and then other competitors in the market respond, inducing a reaction by the initial competitor, which results in responses by other competitors (see Figure 4-2). It is this process that produces lower prices, innovations, new features, and other changes in products and services that benefit consumers.

The leadership in this process may be evident as quality leadership, low-cost/low price leadership (in which the firm finds ways to decrease its costs and price), technical leadership, or innovation.

However, there are winners and losers in this process. Firms cannot remain in a position in which they are always responding to the actions of a competitor. If they are to survive and develop they must at some point break the cycle by taking some action that cannot be copied by competitors or cannot be done as well by competitors. This makes one the leader rather than the follower.

Taking leadership may be accomplished by changing the market though expansion or increased penetration, by introducing new products or services, or by operating in a desirable and specialized niche. Firms that set their own courses become market drivers that actively change the dynamics of the markets in which they operate. These firms are in more advantageous positions than companies whose strategies and activities are market driven and merely responses to changes induced by the actions of other firms.

The issue of the nature and complexities of media competition are discussed in more detail in Chapter 8.

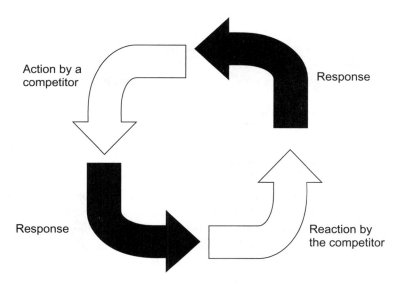

FIGURE 4-2   The competition process

SUBSTITUTABILITY

Substitutability refers to the degree to which competing products and services are equivalent and serve the same needs. The more substitutability between products and services the greater the degree of competition between them.

Although the magazine industry is a competitive industry involving thousands of titles, most titles are not substitutes. *Vogue* does not provide similar content and does not attract an audience similar to *Car and Driver*. The content and audience of *The New Yorker* and *Penthouse* are sufficiently dissimilar to keep them from being substitutes. Within niches of content there are substitutes, however. A subscriber to *Sailing*, for example, might be reasonably well served by *Cruising World* should the former be unavailable or the subscriber decide for some reason to change to another magazine devoted to sailboats.

In the newspaper industry, where local competing daily newspapers are scarce, a national newspaper may provide international and national coverage just as a local newspaper, but the national paper is rarely a substitute for the local newspaper because it cannot provide local news and advertising. Similarly, the local paper is rarely a substitute for the national paper because of its more parochial focus and because it carries far less international and national coverage than the national paper.

COST FORCES

A variety of forces related to the costs of operations play important roles in the economics of media firms. These include economies and diseconomies of scale, scope, and integration, and costs for content, production, distribution, and marketing.

ECONOMIES/DISECONOMIES OF SCALE

Costs for physical production activities in industries are typically affected by economies of scale and scope and this is especially true of media firms that engage in physical production.

Economies of scale result from increasing production that reaches a cost-effective point. Because the basic costs of operations must be met regardless of the amount of goods produced, manufacturing and selling more of the product allows basic costs to be spread further across the goods produced. Thus the basic operations of a newspaper may cost $25,000 per issue regardless of the number of copies printed. If one copy is printed the cost for that copy is $25,000, but if 25,000 copies are printed, the average copy cost is $1.

Thus, firms that are able to print and sell more copies than competitors have an advantage, created by economies of scale.

Diseconomies of scale result from the problems of both small and large size. A firm with a small production run may operate less effectively than a firm whose production is sufficient to achieve economies of scale. Similarly, as production grows, additional investments in equipment, staff, and management may not be fully recovered by the greater production costs and may ultimately produce diseconomies of scale.

ECONOMIES/DISECONOMIES OF SCOPE

These economies result through economies gained by joint activities—typically in manufacturing, distribution, and marketing—among separate products.

A recording and video distributor will have economies of scope over separate recording and video distributors because the distribution and retailing mechanisms for recordings and video are similar and overlapping. This permits the joint use of distribution systems and facilities in a cost-effective manner. Similarly, a magazine publisher will have advantages over independent publishers if it also produces a directory or yearbook. This occurs because of the advantages it has in terms of production, brand recognition, marketing, and distribution that make it less expensive to operate such secondary products.

Scope may also produce diseconomies if the operations are not, or cannot, be effectively integrated or if the scope produces administrative costs that are greater than any savings produced by expanding the firm's scope.

These economies result from shared platforms for multiple services that allow more efficient introduction of new products and the packaging of services in a cost-advantageous manner. For media companies, economies of integration have especially been made accessible by the widespread adoption of information and communications technologies (ICT).

ICT makes it possible to share resources and increase the value of production, particularly because products based on digital technologies can share information, facilities, and equipment and can be coordinated to create new services.

Digital technologies have made it possible to complement or end physical production and distribution of products and to make profitable information operations possible even if the basic product is provided free of charge. Because computer power and the costs of processing data and information are decreasing, economies can be sought from integrating operations using information and communications technology.

This development is primarily possible because marginal value rises whereas marginal cost declines as the audience size or number of users of ICT-based information products and services increase. As shown in Figure 4-3, this produces a wide area in which companies can work out different successful strategies.

Just as with scale and scope, it is theoretically possible for diseconomies of integration to occur if the integration is not effective or produces costs beyond those of separate operations.

FIGURE 4-3   Economies of integration

The structures of fixed and variable costs vary considerably among media and affect the operations and choices that can be made by media company managers.

Fixed costs represent those basic costs that must be incurred and met to support operation. They do not change in the short run based on amount of production. Television stations have basic expenses for facilities, studios, and transmitters that do not change significantly whether the stations broadcast sixteen hours per day or twenty-four hours per day.

Variable costs are expenses that relate to the amount of goods produced. A magazine that increases its press run from 100,000 to 125,000 will incur additional variable costs for paper, ink, production time, and distribution because of the added production. Conversely, if it reduces its press run, those costs will be reduced.

Fixed Costs for a Book Publisher

When books are sold, the revenue received is used to pay a variety of costs, including author compensation, overhead, marketing, manufacturing, ware-housing, distribution, retailer compensation, expenses for unsold copies, and profit.

Fixed costs do not change correspondingly with changes in the number of copies printed, so fixed costs in this environment include only marketing and overhead, which average about $3.50 on a hardback book priced at $25. All the remaining costs, except for profit and unsold copies, can be classified as variable costs and account for $20 of the book price.

This means that only about 14 percent of the income received from a sale is used to pay fixed costs (see Figure 4-4).

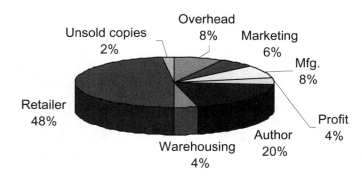

FIGURE 4-4　Distribution of revenue from an average-priced hardback book

Variable Costs as an Incentive to Online Music Sales

Variable costs in the recording industry include costs for manufacturing recordings, distribution, and retail expenses. These types of expenses make up the bulk of the price of a CD sold to consumers, accounting for more than half of the costs (see Figure 4-5). For every CD sold through the traditional manufacturing, distribution, and retail mechanism, 55 percent of the income from sales never reaches the recording companies, artists, and music publishers that create the underlying value of the product.

As a result, developments that can reduce the variable costs of operations are intriguing to recording firms, as they are for all physical goods producers. Assuming that the record company loses no benefits from economies of scale or scope, a recording firm using digital distribution, for example, would save approximately $7.15 in variable costs for each $13 CD sold outside the traditional physical production and distribution chain.

Thus, when a recording company reduces the amount of physical sales by digitally delivering some recordings via downloads sold through e-commerce, the firm can lower the price of the recording. If the recording company chooses not to lower the price of CDs by the amount saved, the amount retained from those variable costs savings could be used to increase return on sales for the recording company or to increase compensation for the artist, composer, or music publisher.

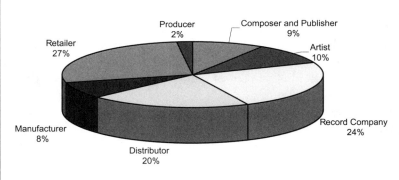

FIGURE 4-5   Cost centers and percentage of costs for normally priced CD recording

As media become increasingly digitalized they simultaneously operate in less of a variable cost environment, in which strategies of achieving lower unit costs by efficient production and pursuit of economies of scale, scope, and integration are critical to successful cost and price competition. This move into the fixed-cost realm has significant strategic and operational implications. In the fixed-cost environment, competitors soon operate with similar fixed costs because they use similar equipment and production techniques. As a result, they cannot compete effectively on the basis of prices for their media goods and services and must focus their activities to compete on the basis of quality, service, and brands.

COST STRUCTURES OF MEDIA RESULT FROM EFFECTS OF ECONOMIC FORCES

The cost structures of firms differ significantly among media, reflecting differences in operating processes and necessities and levels of competition experienced by the firms. These differences are seen in the number of employees, fixed assets required, distribution systems, and other factors required for operation.

If one considers cost structures in relative terms, comparing contributions of important and common elements of media, the most important differences occur in content, production and distribution, and marketing and advertising costs.

CONTENT COSTS

Major differences can clearly be seen in the contributions of content and production and distribution costs to overall costs (see Figures 4-6 and 4-7).

Content, which is the primary value-producing element in media value chains, is a higher contributor to overall costs for electronic media. It accounts for more than half of overall costs for average cable systems and one-quarter to one-third of all costs of radio and television stations. For print

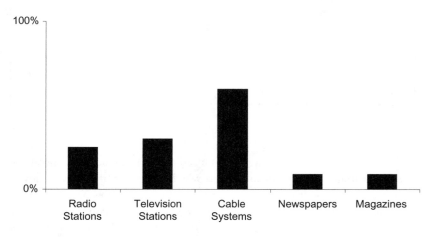

FIGURE 4-6   Differences in content costs among selected media

media, such as newspaper and magazines, content typically accounts for 10 percent or less of total costs.

PRODUCTION/DISTRIBUTION COSTS

The contributions of costs for preparation of materials for distribution (production) and distribution itself are reversed when compared to content costs (see Figure 4-7). Print media devote a far greater percentage of overall costs to these items, typically between 40 and 60 percent. This occurs, of course, because of the need for physical production and distribution of printed material.

Distribution costs represent the expenses for transferring the product or service from the producer to the consumer. In the case of tangible products such as CD-ROMs, books, and videotapes, these costs include transportation and costs associated with making materials available through retailers, such as self and display fees and return costs.

The Winner's Curse: The Problem of International and Major National Sports Rights

The rights to broadcast major international sporting events are an important programming resource for television, cable, and satellite channels.

There is little risk that major events such as the Olympic Games, World Cup, National Football League (U.S. football) and Premiere League Football (soccer) matches, Formula 1 racing, and others will not produce large and attractive audiences.

Because of the size of those audiences, and because managers of many television channels want to use such broadcasts to create or maintain their brand images, the rights to such events are hotly contested and significant bidding wars often ensue. Because of the high cost of acquiring rights, many program managers encounter what has been called "the winner's curse."

Although the channel may make the winning bid in the auction of the programming rights, it also wins the ability to lose a great deal of money. If advertisers are unwilling to pay the high prices upon which the managers predicated the bid, if the sporting events are not as interesting or prolonged (in the case of multiple final matches, for example) as expected, or if the audience produced is not as large and stable as expected, the channel may not be able to recoup its investment in the rights or may have to provide compensation to advertisers.

Analysts are closely watching to see how the joint $425 million deal between ABC/ESPN (Walt Disney Co.) and Univision for World Cup television, Internet, and mobile rights in the United States from 2007 to 2014 will fare. The deal, which is the largest purchase of soccer rights in the history of the sport, was based on $100 million for English-language broadcast rights and $325 million for Spanish-language rights. The networks will cooperate in content production to reduce costs.

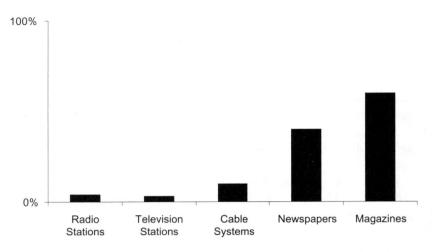

FIGURE 4-7   Differences in production/distribution costs among selected media

Distribution costs for content distributed through broadcasting, cable-casting, or satellite transmission include transmitters, cable system infra-structure, uplinks, satellites, and any uses of telecommunications services necessary to link those systems to the station or channel.

In online media the actual distribution costs are typically borne not by the media firm but by the customer who pays for telecommunications use and access to online services.

The costs of distribution are particularly problematic for tangible media and communication products, because costs rise as the distance to custom-ers increases (see Figure 4-8). This occurs because it takes more time and effort to reach customers, and the costs for transportation vehicles, operat-ing costs, personnel, and so on rise as distance from the production to the delivery point increases.

Distribution costs are a problem for newspapers that operate their own distribution systems because not only is distance a factor but distribution density as well. If a carrier is delivering a newspaper to one home on a street it is more expensive in terms of time and effort to make that one delivery than if the paper is delivered to 10 homes on that street. As illustrated in Figure 4-9, as the distribution density increases, the distribution cost de-clines. Distance and density issues can combine to create situations in which newspapers may have potential subscribers in some areas who want to re-ceive the paper, but the paper cannot serve them without making a loss on the transactions.

FIGURE 4-8   Distribution costs rise as delivery distance increases

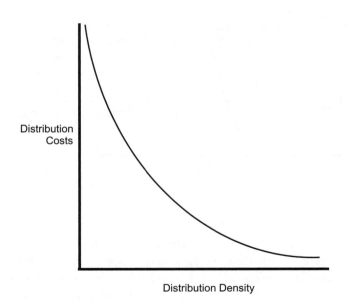

FIGURE 4-9   Distribution costs decline as distribution density increases

Savings from Moving a Newspaper Online

For several decades futurists have predicted the demise of printed newspapers, arguing that the costs of physical production and distribution and the increased speed of communications will induce publishers to give up traditional newspaper operations in favor of digital publication.

Setting aside issues of contemporary audience and advertiser acceptance, the potential of electronic operations is now nearly a reality. The compelling argument for online newspapers is the cost savings that would result from switching from printing and delivery of a physical product.

If one considers the financial operations using a model 38,000-circulation paper, typical of the average mid-sized newspaper market in the United States today, it has revenues of about $19.5 million, expenses of $17.1 million, and a return on sales of 13.3 percent. Moving such a paper from physical to online production and distribution would reduce expenses in production costs by about $4 million and in distribution by $1.9 million. Although moving to online delivery would eliminate the costs associated with the current physical delivery system, new expenses related to online delivery would replace some of those costs, which are estimated at $750,000 annually

Thus, the total cost savings from moving online would be $5.2 million, with online distribution reducing total costs by about two-thirds, and profits indicated by return on sales would triple (see Table 4-1). This would make the move to online newspapers a very attractive alternative from a cost perspective.

The problem with this scenario, however, is that it assumes circulation and advertising revenue would not be affected if the paper moved online. This is hardly an assumption that anyone who seriously considers the business model of newspapers could accept, especially because current data indicates that an online advertisement generates only 5 to 10 percent of the revenue of a print advertisement. Even if the paper were to convert all readers to paying online customers, it would still need to keep three-quarters of its advertising revenue to break even in online operations despite the production and distribution savings.

MARKETING AND ADVERTISING COSTS

Differences in marketing and advertising costs that must be borne to effectively operate a media firm are another economic factor affecting media companies. When competition is low and only a few media exist in a market, the costs that media firms must bear to gain the attention of audiences, consumers, and advertisers is lower than in a market with many outlets of the same medium and many media present.

Although this example does not make a case for moving newspapers online, it reveals the extent to which the noncore business aspects of production and distribution affect the operational costs of newspapers.

TABLE 4-1 · OPERATING STATEMENT FOR THE MODEL NEWSPAPER

	Printed Newspaper	Online Newspaper
Revenue		
Circulation	$3,800,000	$3,800,000
Advertising		
Classified	$6,600,000	$6,600,000
National	$350,000	$350,000
Retail/Display	$5,800,000	$5,800,000
Preprint	$3,000,000	$3,000,000
Total Revenue	$19,550,000	$19,550,000
Expenses		
Advertising	$2,065,000	$2,065,000
Circulation/Distribution	$1,920,000	$750,000
News-Editorial	$2,605,000	$2,605,000
Production (incl. newsprint & ink)	$4,000,000	$0
General/Admin. (incl. building)	$6,500,000	$6,500,000
Total Expenses	$17,090,000	$11,920,000
Operating Profit/Loss	$2,460,000	$7,630,000
Return on Sales	12.6%	39.0%

Because of the growing number of magazine and book titles, motion picture titles, television/cable channels, and other media and communications products and services, media and communications firms are now joining the list of the largest advertisers as they compete for attention and use.

In 2007, for example, Time Warner, Walt Disney Co., and News Corp. were among the top ten U.S. advertisers, spending a total of $4.4 billion to advertise their products and services to consumers (see Table 4-2).

The importance of such expenditures differs among media products and services as indicated in Figure 4-10, which shows the relative contributions

TABLE 4-2 · TOP TEN U.S. ADVERTISERS IN 2007

Advertiser	Expenditure (Billion)
Procter & Gamble	$3.5
AT&T	$2.2
Verizon Communications	$2.1
General Motors	$2.1
Time Warner	$1.7
Ford	$1.6
Walt Disney	$1.4
Johnson & Johnson	$1.3
Sprint Nextel	$1.3
News Corp.	$1.3

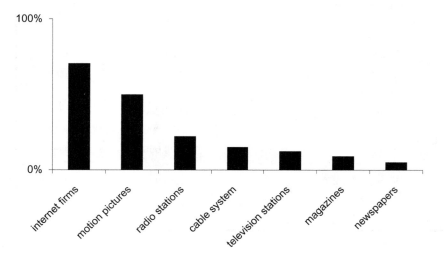

FIGURE 4-10   Average marketing costs as a percentage of total costs of media operations

of marketing costs to overall expenses. Because the expenditures are designed to capture attention, develop interest, and change or maintain use and purchasing behavior by audiences and advertisers, the amounts spent reflect the levels of competition encountered.

Because of their market structures and the amount of market power exercised, higher levels of competition occur in the Internet, motion pictures, and electronic media industries and lower levels in print media, such as magazines and newspapers. These levels of competition are mirrored in the percentage of total company expenditures devoted to marketing for these media.

In a broader context, advertising costs affect not only media firms but all firms that engage in advertising.

Advertising initially increases the costs of goods and services, as shown in Figure 4-11. Costs for products both with and without advertising decline as the amount of products or services sold increases. Because advertising is intended to increase sales, its costs may be covered by the additional sales generated as a result of the advertising, and the increased sales of the product may keep prices from raising or lowering the overall price to consumers.

TRANSACTION COSTS

An important economic factor in the operation of companies involves the need to rationalize the process and costs associated with each transaction

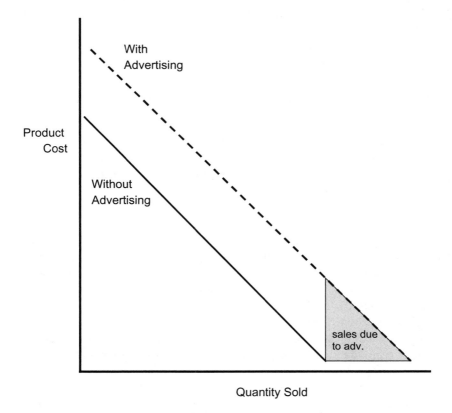

FIGURE 4-11 Cost of a good or service with and without advertising

that a firm makes. This approach to costs, articulated by Williamson (1985), examines the needs of firms to focus on the costs and efficiency of the transactions they make in order to create efficiency. This idea draws upon the work of R. H. Coase (1937) who argued that relational contracting, in which stabilized relations are created with suppliers, are useful in reducing activity and costs for firms.

The examination of transaction costs requires firms to seek economies in the transactions they make not only with suppliers but also with their own customers. They need to rationalize contracts and transactions to simplify and stabilize the information needed about products, services, and behavior in the market.

The result of the need to reduce transaction costs is seen in media firms in subscriptions for magazines, newspapers, and cable, satellite, and online services. On the supply side, contracts are made for important resources such as news and feature services provided by firms such as Associated Press and Universal Syndicate. Newspapers typically enter annual or multiyear contracts with newsprint suppliers. In television, broadcasters typically buy the rights to a number of episodes of series simultaneously, and successful television, motion picture, and audio stars and directors often enter into contracts with producers and studios for additional programs, films, or recordings that will be made in future years—processes that reduce the transaction costs for each of them.

NONMONETARY COSTS

Firms incur monetary costs (that is, expenses requiring direct payment) for labor, supplies, materials, rents, equipment, and so on as they produce goods and services for audiences and consumers. In addition, firms incur nonmonetary costs such as opportunity costs and costs for uncompensated use of labor and equipment, and so on.

These latter factors become significant when firms produce multiple media products. A magazine firm, for example, may choose to close or sell one of its magazines because it believes the financial investment and time spent by staff may produce better returns if another type of magazine is produced. This is because it incurs opportunity costs, that is, the cost of lower returns vis-à-vis the potential for higher returns elsewhere, if it continues operation of the poorly performing publication.

Uncompensated costs are expenses that are incurred but are not fully compensated by the product or service for which the expenses are incurred. These types of expenses are often found when a media company operates a secondary product.

A newspaper, for example, may choose to reuse portions of its current contents and archives, as well as the firm's information technology infrastructure, to produce an online newspaper site. By using these resources at no cost or below real cost, the firm does not require that the online operation actually pays true costs for the resources. Even if full costs are paid, the firm may nonetheless incur nonmonetary costs because of the additional supervision that top managers must give the operation and because of the additional workload the operation requires for the information technology managers and other personnel.

REGULATORY FORCES AND INTERVENTION

Regulatory forces involve approvals for media operations or requirements placed on media to avoid or to behave in certain manners. Despite rhetoric to the contrary, Western governments—even in nations practicing the highest degrees of *laissez-faire* capitalism such as the United States—have regularly intervened in markets. The roles that governments play in economic affairs are necessary to create and perpetuate markets.

At the broadest level, actions by governments make economic markets possible. Economies are not self-generating and perpetuating. They require coordination for production and distribution and for exchange to take place. Governments play significant political and legal roles in creating the framework in which enterprises can operate by creating and enforcing property, contract, corporate, and other rights necessary for markets to function. In addition governments create currency, implement tax activities, and affect and intervene in economies through various fiscal and monetary policies.

Governments also intervene at the level of specific industries. The rationales have typically been to promote activities or results beneficial to the public good, to limit or halt activities or results harmful to the public good, and to fulfill needs that markets cannot efficiently serve.

Although media tend to be given more latitude in liberal democratic states because of concerns over freedom of expression, governments regularly intervene in communications markets. The primary rationale for government intervention in communications is that it serves important social, political, and economic needs in democratic, capitalist societies and that governments need to promote and increase communications possibilities. Other reasons to promote intervention include to control behaviors of communications firms that harm social, political, and economic interests and to permit government to provide basic services or supplement services of commercial firms when they do not serve important social, political, and economic needs of society.

Regulations exist to facilitate communications as well as to promote or constrain certain types of communications activities.

Technical regulations exist when governments or nongovernmental organizations set and maintain standards or control technology to make some communications possible. For example, the International Telecommunications Union through the World Administrative Radio Conference assigns frequencies for use in nations so that users of radio waves for terrestrial and satellite broadcasting, mobile communications, and other communications using radio waves do not interfere with each other and make radio communications impossible. At the national level, government organizations such as the Federal Communications Commission then assign frequencies for use to operate radio stations, mobile telephones, radio-controlled toys, and so on.

Regulations also exist to standardize communications, creating the ability to link telephone systems worldwide and to ensure that television set manufacturers and television broadcasters are using similar standards so that reception is possible. Without such regulation, operations of both domestic and global media systems would be impossible.

Structural regulations also control the structure of media markets, such as limiting the number of radio stations to ensure profitable and stable operations or the establishment of limited monopolies in cable or television services. Controls also affect ownership structure. In the United States, for example, foreign owners may own no more than 25 percent of a radio or television broadcasting entity and no single owner may have a penetration of more than 35 percent in his or her market with multiple stations. The United Kingdom prohibits foreign ownership of broadcasting, except for owners from European Union nations.

Governments provide licenses (that is, the rights to operate) to media and communications systems. In democratic nations these tend in practice to be limited to licenses to use radio frequencies or rights to operate cable systems and telecommunications systems. In less democratic nations, licenses are sometimes required for print and other media as well.

Behavioral regulation either prohibits media firms from engaging in certain practices or requires them to engage in specified practices. These are economic factors when they affect market choices of media managers and require firms to forego certain revenue or to incur specific costs.

Proscriptive regulation regulates the carrying of pornography, offensive speech, violence and libelous expression, material damaging to national security, advertising for certain products, and other material deemed harmful to broad social interests. Proscriptive regulation is an economic force when it reduces the ability of a firm to benefit in the marketplace. This occurs, for example, if regulations prohibit the carrying of advertising for alcohol products and media firms are thus denied a source of income from sales to alcohol beverage firms.

Prescriptive regulation requires behavior such as broadcasters carrying a certain amount of public affairs or children's programming, the production of television receivers capable of receiving captions for the hearing impaired, or the use of a specified percentage of independent producers as sources of programming.

Regulations requiring specified behavior are an economic force because they require certain expenditures and limit the choices of managers to carry materials that might cost less or be more profitable to provide.

BARRIERS TO ENTRY AND MOBILITY IN MEDIA MARKETS

Barriers to entry are economic factors that halt or make it difficult for new competitors to successfully enter a market in which they have not previously competed. These barriers typically result from the market, cost, and regulatory forces discussed above.

These barriers affect two main types of entrants: New firms entering the market for the first time—such as a new business wanting to publish a magazine—and established firms seeking to expand their reach—such as a magazine publisher interested in internationalizing a title by establishing a subsidiary operation in another country, or a television network that is expanding its operations by beginning the operation of an online service.

New businesses encounter barriers to entry and established businesses encounter what are called barriers to mobility. Some of the barriers are the same in both cases.

Many factors can act as barriers to entry and mobility. Among the major barriers are capital requirements, economies of scale, product differentiation, switching costs, limited access to distribution channels, government policies, and competitive advantages.

CAPITAL REQUIREMENTS

These requirements involve the financing needed to establish operations and pay start-up losses. Capital becomes a barrier when insufficient capital is available or when it is available only to certain firms or at preferential rates to certain firms. For example, a firm or entrepreneur may have the knowledge and desire to establish and operate a cable television distribution system but may not have the capital required to purchase the equipment and optical fiber lines necessary to construct and operate the system.

As previously noted, economies of scale are created when unit costs decline as the volume used or produced increases. Existing firms with high volumes will thus operate at a lower cost per unit than a new firm entering the market. Large established firms also experience economies of scale in the cost of purchasing supplies because of bulk purchase discounts. Other economies are found in production costs and distribution costs, such as the costs of servicing newsstands. A firm serving newsstands or kiosks with 200 titles will most likely have economies of scale over a firm serving them with only 25 titles.

Firms with economics of scale can thus sell products and services at a lower price or retain greater profits than firms with lower economies of scale or diseconomies of scale.

PRODUCT DIFFERENTIATION

Differentiation creates consumer loyalties and identification with existing products. These loyalties are difficult for a new firm to overcome and induce customers to substitute the new product or service.

Product differentiation is a strategy used by firms to make their products unique and more desirable to a group of consumers than products of a similar type by other producers. Product differentiation in media occurs through a variety of techniques designed to vary the elements of media products and services as shown in Table 4-4.

The more differentiation among units of a medium and among media, the more difficult it is for others to enter the market because they will need to differentiate their new product or service and make larger marketing expenditures to try to create a successful entry.

SWITCHING COSTS

Switching costs are consumer costs associated with giving up use of one product and signing up for use of another product. Consumers who switch from cable TV subscriptions to satellite reception must typically make substantial investments in equipment. This makes it more difficult for new communications and media technology that offers substantially the same benefits as an existing technology to enter a market. Switching costs can also be psychological as well as financial. Consumers may express some discomfort when switching from a product they are familiar with to a new product.

LIMITED ACCESS TO DISTRIBUTION CHANNELS

If access is limited because of exclusive contracts or because a new product is not seen as important enough, obtaining good distribution becomes a

The Problem of Newspaper Market Entry

The trend toward local markets with one general circulation, paid daily news-paper has taken hold across the Western world since the middle of the twentieth century in response to advertiser preferences for the paper with the largest circulation and because of the cost structures inherent to news-paper operations.

Efforts to enter markets already served by a paid local daily have nearly always failed because of the barriers to entry created by capital require-ments and high fixed costs, and because of competitive advantages such as market dominance and economies of scale held by existing newspapers.

High first-copy costs require a newspaper to achieve significant sales to spread the costs across an adequate amount of circulation. In addition, the fixed costs of newspaper publishing limit the ability of managers of startup papers to substantially lower their cost-per-thousand for advertising and maintain unprofitably low rates over a long period of time.

These factors make it improbable for a successful entry to occur. The financial problems faced in entering a market are illustrated in a model of the entry of a newspaper into an average market in the United States. Using the most optimistic scenarios possible, the model shows that the firm would not operate profitably at any point (see Figure 4-12). It would incur an op-erating loss of $286.1 million and net loss of $540.5 million over a ten-year startup period (see Table 4-3).

The model assumes "success" in circulation (that is, parity with the preex-isting newspaper) in the tenth year of the startup period. Even with that assumption the enterprise would still incur an operating loss of $11.2 million and a net loss of $26.7 million for that year. Operating losses of that magni-tude would be expected to be incurred in subsequent years as well, but the net loss would be reduced, because the cost of capital would end unless additional capital was borrowed.

The model shows that entry, even if a firm could operate at losses for a long period of time, would not produce a commercially viable operation

FIGURE 4-12   Annual operating income (loss) and net income (loss) of the entering paper

TABLE 4-3 · FINANCIAL AND PERFORMANCE PROJECTIONS FOR THE ENTERING PAPER

	Year One	Year Two	Year Three	Year Four	Year Five
Market Revenue					
Circulation Revenue	$18,000,000	$18,000,000	$18,000,000	$18,000,000	$18,000,000
Advertising Revenue	$74,400,000	$74,400,000	$74,400,000	$74,400,000	$74,400,000
Total Revenue	$92,400,000	$92,400,000	$92,400,000	$92,400,000	$92,400,000
Entry Paper's Revenue					
Circulation Share of Entry Paper	15%	20%	25%	30%	35%
Circulation Revenue of Entry Paper	$2,700,000	$3,600,000	$4,500,000	$5,400,000	$6,300,000
Advertising Share of Entry Paper	10%	15%	20%	25%	27%
Advertising Revenue of Entry Paper	$7,440,000	$11,160,000	$14,880,000	$18,600,000	$20,088,000
Circ. & Ad Revenue of Entry Paper	$10,140,000	$14,760,000	$19,380,000	$24,000,000	$26,388,000
Competitive Increase (15%)*	$1,521,000	$2,214,000	$2,907,000	$3,600,000	$3,958,200
Operating Rev. of Entry Paper	$11,661,000	$16,974,000	$22,287,000	$27,600,000	$30,346,200
Operating Expenses					
Editorial	$9,282,000	$9,282,000	$9,282,000	$9,282,000	$9,282,000
Advertising	$6,188,000	$6,188,000	$6,188,000	$6,188,000	$6,188,000
Circulation	$9,282,000	$9,282,000	$9,282,000	$9,282,000	$9,282,000
Administration	$6,961,500	$6,961,500	$6,961,500	$6,961,500	$6,961,500
Marketing and Promotion**	$10,000,000	$10,000,000	$10,000,000	$10,000,000	$10,000,000
Capital Expenditures***	$2,000,000	$2,000,000	$2,000,000	$2,000,000	$2,000,000
Production	$11,602,500	$11,602,500	$11,602,500	$11,602,500	$11,602,500
Newsprint & Ink****	$2,107,500	$2,810,000	$3,512,500	$4,215,000	$4,917,500
Operating Exp. of Entry Paper	$57,423,500	$58,126,000	$58,828,500	$59,531,000	$60,233,500
Operating Income Of Entry Paper	$(45,762,500)	$(41,152,000)	$(36,541,500)	$(31,931,000)	$(29,887,300)
Non-Operating Expenses					
Capital Expenditures	$100,000,000				
Capital Costs*****	$15,441,630	$15,441,630	$15,441,630	$15,441,630	$15,441,630
Non-Operating Expenses	$115,441,630	$15,441,630	$15,441,630	$15,441,630	$15,441,630
Net Income Of Entry Paper	$(161,204,130)	$(56,593,630)	$(51,983,130)	$(47,372,630)	$(45,328,930)

*Due primarily to duplicative advertising and circulation

**Estimate includes direct marketing expenditures and the effects of sampling and discounts

***Used for expenditure for land, building, production equipment, vehicles, furnishings, etc., and first year operating costs.

****Variable cost increases proportionately with circulation and advertising market share

*****Assuming 9%, 10-year loan

Year Six	Year Seven	Year Eight	Year Nine	Year Ten	Ten-Year Total
$18,000,000	$18,000,000	$18,000,000	$18,000,000	$18,000,000	$180,000,000
$74,400,000	$74,400,000	$74,400,000	$74,400,000	$74,400,000	$744,000,000
$92,400,000	$92,400,000	$92,400,000	$92,400,000	$92,400,000	$924,000,000
38%	41%	44%	47%	50%	
$6,840,000	$7,380,000	$7,920,000	$8,460,000	$9,000,000	$62,100,000
30%	35%	40%	45%	50%	
$22,320,000	$26,040,000	$29,760,000	$33,480,000	$37,200,000	$220,968,000
$29,160,000	$33,420,000	$37,680,000	$41,940,000	$46,200,000	$283,068,000
$4,374,000	$5,013,000	$5,652,000	$6,291,000	$6,930,000	$42,460,200
$33,534,000	$38,433,000	$43,332,000	$48,231,000	$53,130,000	$325,528,200
$9,282,000	$9,282,000	$9,282,000	$9,282,000	$9,282,000	$92,820,000
$6,188,000	$6,188,000	$6,188,000	$6,188,000	$6,188,000	$61,880,000
$9,282,000	$9,282,000	$9,282,000	$9,282,000	$9,282,000	$92,820,000
$6,961,500	$6,961,500	$6,961,500	$6,961,500	$6,961,500	$69,615,000
$10,000,000	$10,000,000	$10,000,000	$10,000,000	$10,000,000	$100,000,000
$4,000,000	$4,000,000	$4,000,000	$4,000,000	$4,000,000	$30,000,000
$11,602,500	$11,602,500	$11,602,500	$11,602,500	$11,602,500	$116,025,000
$5,339,000	$5,760,500	$6,182,000	$6,603,500	$7,025,000	$48,472,500
$62,655,000	$63,076,500	$63,498,000	$63,919,500	$64,341,000	$611,632,500
$(29,121,000)	$(24,643,500)	$(20,166,000)	$(15,688,500)	$(11,211,000)	$(286,104,300)
					$100,000,000
$15,441,630	$15,441,630	$15,441,630	$15,441,630	$15,441,630	$154,416,300
$15,441,630	$15,441,630	$15,441,630	$15,441,630	$15,441,630	$254,416,300
$(44,562,630)	$(40,085,130)	$(35,607,630)	$(31,130,130)	$(26,652,630)	$(540,520,600)

	Newspapers	Magazines	Radio Stations	Television Stations	General Online Portals
Time Offered	Morning Evening All day		Time of specific programming Counter-programming	Time of specific programming	
Frequency	Daily Weekly	Weekly Monthly Quarterly			Rapidity of content updates
Content Choices	Coverage emphasis News focus Presentation tone Readability level	General interest Specialized interest	Music format Specialized format Mixed format		General interest focus Special interest focus Video focus Social network focus
Production Choices	Tabloid or broadsheet Paper quality Paper color Ink colors Binding	Size Paper quality Ink colors Binding	Analog Digital Live or taped broadcast Amount of self production	Analog Digital Life or taped broadcast Amount of self production	Complexity of design Degree of interactivity Number of graphics Audio Video
Sales Method	Subscription Single copy sales Free distribution	Subscription Single copy sales Free/controlled circulation			Subscription Free
Target Audience	General Target	General Target	General Target Segmentation by program	General Target Segmentation by program	Targeted by interests Targeted by behavior
Target Place of Use	Home Office Commuting	Home Office Other	Home Office Commuting	Home Office	Home Office

problem. Joint distribution systems may choose not to carry a new competitor, or it may be difficult for a new magazine to gain prominent display at newsstands and magazine racks. This access issue has been a particular problem for cable networks because cable channel capacity has not been high enough in many markets to make channels available to all companies interested in bringing their networks to new markets.

GOVERNMENT POLICIES

Licensing and franchising regulations may provide barriers to new broadcasters and cablecasters. If the government agency in charge of such issues has only twelve available frequencies, a company that is not granted use of one of those frequencies will not be able to operate a radio station.

Antitrust and other regulatory controls may limit some firms from entering specific markets in order to preserve competition or serve other social purposes. Thus, a newspaper firm may not be able to operate a television station in its hometown if regulations prohibit cross-ownership of media in the same locality.

COMPETITIVE ADVANTAGES

Certain firms have inherent advantages over other competitors. These arise from factors such as patents, trademarks, reputation, experience, preferred locations, better employees, or innovations. If two firms are considering entering a new market, the company with better brand recognition will be likely to have more success. Thus a programmer such as Canal + may be able to enter a new cable market more easily than a smaller, less internationalized firm with less experience in foreign markets.

OVERCOMING AND REDUCING BARRIERS

Barriers to entry and mobility can sometimes be overcome by the ability of existing firms to invest sufficient resources over a longer period of time. A well-funded firm may be able to bear negative or low returns in the short- to mid-term to achieve desirable long-term returns. Small and startup firms rarely have sufficient funds on their own to pursue this option.

Firms introducing new techniques and methods of operations that avoid traditional cost structures can sometimes overcome barriers to entry. They can also be overcome by the introduction of products that are sufficiently innovative to surmount the traditional barriers.

Another method of overcoming barriers is to engage in joint ventures with existing firms in the market or in related markets or with firms that have resources needed to overcome the barriers. Such tactics allow businesses to lessen the risk borne by a single company and to pool competencies in various firms. For example, a magazine with no online experience, or with personnel unfamiliar with the tasks needed to start an online magazine, might enter into a joint venture with a firm that provides online design and management services and telecommunications access.

Government policies can help reduce barriers as a means of increasing competition and the number of firms in an industry. One mechanism is guaranteed and subsidized loan funds that provide venture capital or capital for technology acquisition. Operation subsidies that provide another source of revenue and reduce operating losses in startup firms can also be provided in some settings. Preferential awarding of licenses and franchises so that small companies have advantages in entering broadcasting or telecommunications is another mechanism of overcoming barriers for new firms.

SUGGESTED READINGS

Albarran, Alan B. 2002. *Media Economics: Understanding Markets, Industries and Concepts.* 2nd ed. Ames: Iowa State University Press.

Alexander, Alison, James Owers, and Rodney Carveth, eds. 2004. *Media Economics Theory and Practice.* 3rd ed. Hillsdale, N.J.: Lawrence Erlbaum Associates.

Coase, R. H. 1937. "The Nature of the Firm," *Economica* NS4 (4):386–405.

Doyle, Gillian. 2002. *Understanding Media Economics.* London: Sage Publications.

Picard, Robert G. 1989. *Media Economics: Concepts and Issues.* Thousand Oaks, Calif.: Sage Publications, 1989.

Williamson, O. E. 1985. *The Economic Institutions of Capitalism: Firms, Markets, Relational Contracting.* New York: Free Press.

CHAPTER 5

The Influence of the General Economy on Media

General economic and financial forces are important to media and communications firms because these business enterprises are simultaneously consumers and producers. Changes in the economy and economic activity affect the consumption of goods and services by media and communications firms as well as the production and sales of media and communications goods and services.

A number of influences of the general economy are significant to financial developments of media firms and have impact on the well-being of companies and the choices available to managers. This chapter focuses on four economic factors that need to be well understood because of their effects on the operations and financial health of firms.

First, I consider the causes and effects of growth and contraction of the general economy and how these changes affect media and communications firms. Second, I look at the effect of inflation on these companies. Third, I review how interest rates constrain the choices of managers and affect budgets and operations. Finally, I consider the issue of exchange rates and why these rates are important in the globalized and increasingly internationalized environment of media and communication firms.

GROWTH AND CONTRACTION OF THE ECONOMY

Perhaps the most noticeable external influence on short-term performance of media companies results from directional changes in the general economy itself.

Regular growth and contraction in the general economy is often called the *business cycle*. Growth and contraction are significant to communications managers because business cycles affect revenue, cost and availability of supplies, profits, production, and employment.

Expansions and contractions of the economy have been recognized for three centuries. Adam Smith, David Ricardo, and John Stuart Mill explained them as the results of external disruptions to production or labor. In the early nineteenth century, business cycles were asserted to result from the under-consumption of goods in the economy. In the early twentieth century, they were explained by investment, cost price, and long-wave theories and then by John Maynard Keynes's argument that investment volatility creates self-generating pressures that lead to recession and recovery.

Today, many economists believe that business cycles are natural, self-perpetuating phenomena in which economic forces create prosperity and then other forces react to that prosperity in counteracting ways. The cycle works as illustrated in Figure 5-1.

This occurs because prosperity increases the costs of doing business by leading to expansion and increased capacity, increases in wages and benefits, and increases in costs for items such as supplies, rents, and interest rates on short-term loans. Ultimately, output increases and demand and investment

FIGURE 5-1 Economic forces and developments that create and perpetuate the business cycle

decline, which are greeted by tighter credit, declining growth, and then company reductions in production, workforces, and so on.

Although the processes of expansion and contraction are generally agreed upon, economists still debate whether there actually is a cycle per se because the periodicity and magnitude of vacillations are not always consistent. As a result, some economists prefer to describe these processes as *fluctuations in the economy*. Common language in business and economics still speaks of cycles, however, to indicate these upward and downward movements of the economy.

If a contraction of the business cycle is very strong it can result in a recession or a depression. A depression is a very deep and prolonged recession.

Recessions and depressions can also result from other shocks to the economic system, such as a decline in key resources, monetary or fiscal policies, and problems with key customers or trading regions.

As a general rule, companies and investors in companies suffer during recessions because of decline in income and profit. Depressions and recessions result in fewer sales, less production, lower employment. When the economy improves, this process is reversed. As demand increases and companies experience improvements in their financial performance, they begin investing more money into advertising and other marketing activities.

Media, then, are particularly sensitive to such changes in the economy for two reasons. First, sales of communications products and services are affected by general economic conditions. Second, advertising sales are strongly affected by changes in the general economy.

Sales of communications products and services are affected by fluctuations in the economy because consumers' expenditures overall and expenditures on media are affected by perceptions of their current and future economic situations (see Figure 5-2).

During downturns in the economy, consumers tend to postpone purchases of expensive communications hardware such as television sets, computers, satellite receivers, and stereo systems. Purchases of media such as

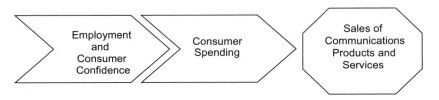

FIGURE 5-2 Consumer sales of communications products and services and the general economy

CDs and DVDs also decline as consumers tighten their belts. The use of subscribed media and communications services declines somewhat as well. For example, premium services offered by cable and satellite television systems show a decline when a significant number of households is most affected by the downturn. In such cases, the group of subscribers most affected tends to reduce or drop premium services and retain only basic services. Only during the most severe and prolonged downturns will a small number of households cut their subscriptions altogether.

Advertising sales are highly influenced by the business cycle and other factors that affect the businesses of major advertisers. The producers and retailers of automobiles, luxury goods, and major appliances are significantly affected because consumers tend to reduce purchases of such big-ticket items during poor economic times. These companies respond by reducing their advertising budgets and buying fewer advertisements in magazines, newspapers, and on broadcasts, as well as reducing outdoor, cinema, and other types of advertising and promotion. Additionally, advertising for real estate sales, travel services, and employment are significantly reduced (see Figure 5-3).

The effects of a recession vary depending upon the depth of the decline and the breadth of sectors of the economy involved. It is clear, however, that when the gross domestic product (GDP) declines into negative territory it produces a significant downward movement in advertising expenditures. The rate of decline is highest with a small amount of decline in GDP and then slows as the depth of the decline in GDP increases, as illustrated in Figure 5-4.

The degree to which expenditures are affected is also related to the timing of when advertisers change their purchasing behavior. In most cases it appears that major advertisers reduce expenditures concurrently with changes in the economy that may be the result of their own tracking of sales and the economy.

There is evidence that reductions of advertising in developed nations more strongly affect print media advertising expenditures than expenditures

FIGURE 5-3   Effects of changes in the economy on advertising sales

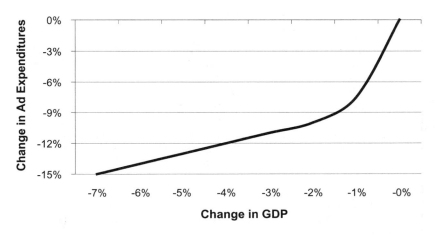

FIGURE 5-4   Change in advertising expenditures is greater than change in GDP

for electronic media, especially television. This may result from differences in the types of advertisers most carried by those media and the uses of media by the advertisers. Newspapers, for example, are the primary advertising medium for retail establishments, especially local retailers. Magazines are widely used by manufacturers and large service providers to advertise a wide range of consumer goods and to support brand images. Specialty magazines also receive a good deal of advertising from retailers serving their fields. Manufacturers and large service firms and a few larger multilocation retailers primarily use television. Manufacturers, large service firms, and local retailers use radio.

Because recessions affect retail sales, local and large multilocation retailers cut their expenditures, as do real estate firms and automobile dealers. Because such firms are prime advertisers for newspapers and radio, expenditures in these two media fall more noticeably. Television expenditures are apparently less affected because the manufacturers, large service providers, and larger multilocation retailers appear less willing to cut their expenditures in television than in other media.

INFLATION

Inflation is a sustained rise in the general price levels for goods and services that affects the buying power of producers and consumers by increasing the costs of goods and services. Inflation is caused by a number of factors, including rapid growth in the general economy, concerns over the value of a currency caused by economic turmoil, and war or other national crises.

Effects of Recent Recessions on Media

Examples from two recessions during the first decade of the twenty-first century clearly reveal the effects of economic downturns on media products and services.

In the United States during 2001 to 2003, for example, the newspaper industry experienced a serious recession following the dot-com bubble and the NASDAQ crash, and it was compounded by the 9/11 attacks. The newspaper industry suffered an overall decline in advertising revenue of 9.3 percent between 2000 and 2002 as a result of the downturn. After the banking crisis in 2008 created another recession, the industry experienced a dramatic drop of 44 percent of its revenue (see Figure 5-5). The extent to which revenues will recover following the recession are unknown.

Another example of the effects of a recession can be seen in total expenditures for total advertising in the United Kingdom. The United Kingdom and European economies were affected by the U.S. recession and rapid deflation of the European economy. During the period of 2000 to 2001 total advertising expenditures plummeted nearly 5 percent, as seen in Figure 5-6.

Declines in the economy also affect sales of media products to consumers, as illustrated in Figure 5-7, which shows the decline in consumer expenditures on video and computer games in the United States during the recession of the early twenty-first century. The strong growth of industry sales in the late 1990s was affected by the recession before regaining upward momentum as the recession neared its end.

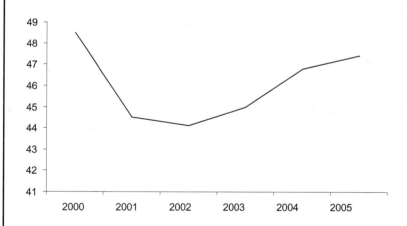

FIGURE 5-5   Advertising revenue of the U.S. newspaper industry during the recessions of the 2000s ($ billions)

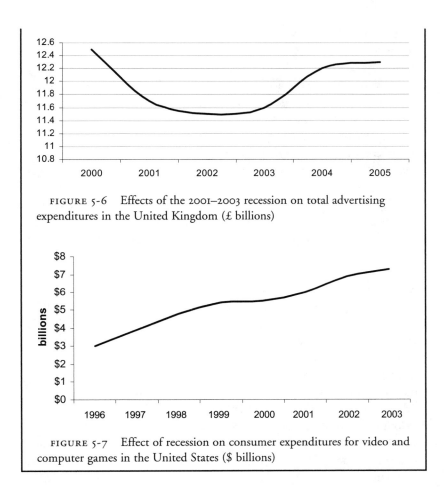

FIGURE 5-6 Effects of the 2001–2003 recession on total advertising expenditures in the United Kingdom (£ billions)

FIGURE 5-7 Effect of recession on consumer expenditures for video and computer games in the United States ($ billions)

A nominal level of inflation is normal and generally constant when the economy expands. It tends to diminish when the economy contracts. When inflation ranges between 1 and 3 percent per year it does not typically pose significant problems for businesses. If inflation rates rise higher, however, it is difficult for firms to increase their turnover and return rates to the higher levels required to achieve real growth rates. This occurs because high inflation rates slow the growth rate of the economy as a whole.

Economists measure inflation by collecting the prices of a sample of goods and services at regular intervals and comparing changes in the aggregate prices to previous periods. The primary measures used are producer price indexes that measure prices paid by producers for necessary resources and consumer price indexes that measure prices paid by consumers to purchase goods and services.

In the short term, inflation forces businesses to adjust their budgets to account for increased prices and most often requires them to pass on the costs to consumers in the form of price increases. If the increases are significant, however, they may affect consumer demand adversely and reduce income for firms, so managers must carefully monitor inflation and their businesses' reactions to it.

The ability of media managers to respond to inflation is sometimes limited by sales strategies employed to stabilize audiences and advertising. A magazine that relies primarily on subscribed circulation is unable to increase its prices and revenue until existing subscriptions are fulfilled, thus limiting its ability to respond to increased prices for printing and paper that may result during the subscription period. Similarly, a newspaper that has annual rate contracts with advertisers who purchase large amounts of advertising is unable to respond to inflation by increasing prices for that advertising.

Because businesses operate on fiscal years, the effects of inflation over time is sometimes ignored or seen as unimportant by some managers. This is problematic, however, because in the long term, inflation has the effects of decreasing the wealth of firms when the growth of the value of firms or their assets does not equal or surpass the inflation rates. As a result, some responses must be made to inflation through growth and reinvestment.

When comparing financial data from different time periods (usually years but sometimes quarterly if inflation rates are high), adjustments for inflation need to be made if one is to gain an accurate understanding of trends and developments. To do so data must be adjusted with a deflator that reduces successive values by the amount of inflation. When a deflator has been used, the data are reported as being in constant currencies (constant $, constant €, constant £, constant ¥, and so on).

A magazine that has been sold at a cover price of $3.50 for the past decade does not offset the costs of its production and distribution today at the same level as ten years ago. In the United States, for example, the purchasing power of that $3.50 in the year 2008 was about one-third lower than it was in 1998.

Some additional problems in analyzing data and correcting for inflation, particularly in cross-national settings, must be noted. This is important in comparing industries or the performance of divisions or subsidiaries operating in other nations. The products and services that make up the national producer and consumer price indexes differ at times due to differences in measures used. If these differences are significant, or if costs for only certain resources are being reviewed, one may have to make specific adjustments or take these into consideration when making comparisons among national media industries and companies.

Adjusting for Inflation Alters Perception of Financial Performance

The usefulness of adjusting for inflation can be seen in the financial performance of a sample media company. If the financial performance of the firm is considered using annual data for operating and net income, the firm appears to be strong and healthy, with both measures increasing each year (see Table 5-1). Its operating income (revenue) increased from $1.2 billion to $3.5 billion during the ten-year period, experiencing an average annual growth rate of nearly19 percent per year, and its net income or profit after taxes and adjustments grew an average of 16 percent annually.

If those figures are adjusted for inflation, one gets an additional perspective on the condition of the firm (see Table 5-2). Operating income increased from $1.2 billion to $2.1 billion, an average annual growth rate of 7 percent. Net income grew from $152 million to $233 million, an annual growth of 5 percent annually. These figures still indicate overall health but a closer look reveals that in constant currency the net income figures twice declined, including the current year (Year 10), because inflation rates were stronger than the growth rate for income.

The effects of inflation are quite explicit when current and constant currency figures are displayed in graphic form. This is illustrated in Figure 5-8 using advertising expenditure data for France, which reveals that although expenditures in 2006 were about 4 percent higher in 2006 than in 2001 in current currency, they were actually 6 percent lower in 2006 when viewed in constant currency.

Additionally, differences in national and regional inflation rates may require examination when making comparisons between media firms and national media industries. This occurs because the inflation rate in New Mexico may differ from that in Massachusetts, the inflation rate in the United Kingdom may differ from that in Germany, and the inflation rate in Japan may differ from that in South Africa.

It should also be noted that communications products and services are not equally affected because they depend on different resources. Broadcasting and telecommunications firms are not affected by increases in paper and ink and distribution costs to the extent that changes in costs for those resources affect print media. As a result, one may need to make distinctions about the effects of inflation rates when comparing the performance of media firms or industries.

When inflation rises to unhealthy levels, political pressures rise for governments to implement fiscal and monetary policies designed to slow or lower inflation rates. These general economic policies ultimately affect sales of media products and services and the short-term performance of media firms.

TABLE 5-1 · FINANCIAL PERFORMANCE FOR A SAMPLE MEDIA COMPANY ($ THOUSANDS)

	Year 1	Year 2	Year 3	Year 4	Year 5	Year 6	Year 7	Year 8	Year 9	Year 10
Operating Income	1,214,983	1,367,171	1,519,514	1,703,646	1,960,197	2,209,421	2,801,497	3,079,447	3,314,485	3,518,189
Net Income	151,985	172,506	180,507	191,665	223,934	253,277	276,404	319,395	364,460	398,509

TABLE 5-2 · FINANCIAL PERFORMANCE FOR A SAMPLE MEDIA COMPANY IN CONSTANT CURRENCY ($ THOUSANDS)

	Year 1	Year 2	Year 3	Year 4	Year 5	Year 6	Year 7	Year 8	Year 9	Year 10
Operating Income (Constant $)	1,214,983	1,250,961	1,320,458	1,410,619	1,538,755	1,652,647	2,039,490	2,118,660	2,124,585	2,054,622
Net Income (Constant $)	151,985	157,843	155,056	158,699	175,788	189,451	201,222	219,744	233,619	232,729

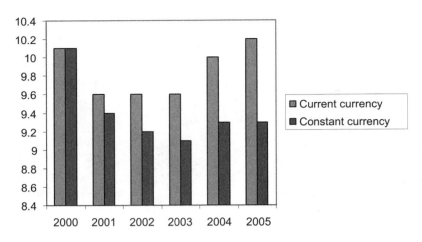

FIGURE 5-8 Total advertising expenditures in France, current and constant euro (billions)

INTEREST RATES

Interest rates represent the cost for borrowing capital. If interest rates increase, the cost of acquiring the capital increases. This affects the ability of managers to fund new initiatives, to expand, or to arrange cash-flow financing. If the cost rises too high, many firms cannot borrow and use the capital in an effective way to produce profit.

For example, a cable television network that has plans to purchase shares in satellites that will allow it to expand its operations into Asia may have based the budget for the operation on obtaining the capital at an interest rate of 6.25 percent. If the rate rises to 7 or 7.5 percent, the management could be forced to postpone or abandon the expansion because it may not be able to operate profitably or recoup the investment in an adequate period of time based on the higher rates.

Because higher interest rates reduce the growth and activities of firms, investment is reduced and general economic activity tends to slow when interest rates increase. Conversely, when interest rates are lower, firms have greater ability to use the capital effectively and tend to make investments and increase production in ways that help the general economy grow.

The link between interest rates and the general economy is used by central banks to help regulate the growth rate of the economy and inflation rates that move simultaneously with such growth. By deliberately increasing and decreasing interest rates, banks such as the Federal Reserve Bank and the European Central Bank can slow or spur economic activity and inflation.

The Effects of Interest Rates on Company Costs

The costs of borrowing capital are affected by interest rates and the length of loan terms. Even small changes in interest rates have significant effects on the costs of capital. For example, a one-half percent increase in the interest rate on a one million dollar loan will cost a firm an additional $12,985 over a five-year period. Similarly, as the length of the loan term increases, it costs more to borrow the capital. But the rate of increase declines annually because each additional year the principal remaining on the loan declines. The effects of these interest rate and time factors can be seen in the following examples.

Example 1

A newspaper publisher is borrowing $15 million on a fifteen-year loan to help finance the purchase of a new printing press. If the company is able to obtain financing at a 6.5 percent interest rate instead of 8.5 percent, it will save $3.1 million in the cost of the capital (see Table 5-3).

Example 2

A television station needs an additional $5 million to acquire digital studio equipment and remodel its facilities so that it can produce news and local programming in full digital format to be broadcast on its new digital transmitter.

If the management is able to select a five-year loan instead of a ten-year loan term, it will save $3.3 million in the cost of capital (see Table 5-4). The table indicates that the cost of capital increases with the length of the loan because the capital is tied up longer. However, the rate of cost increase from each of the previous years diminishes annually.

TABLE 5-3 · COST OF CAPITAL FOR A FIFTEEN-YEAR PRESS LOAN AT THREE DIFFERENT INTEREST RATES

Capital Borrowed	Interest Rate	Loan Term	Cost of Capital
$15,000,000	6.5 percent	15 years	$8,519,898
$15,000,000	7.5 percent	15 years	$10,029,334
$15,000,000	8.5 percent	15 years	$11,587,968

TABLE 5-4 · COST OF CAPITAL FOR A FIVE-, SEVEN-, AND TEN-YEAR LOAN FOR STUDIO DIGITALIZATION AT THE SAME INTEREST RATE

Capital Borrowed	Interest Rate	Loan Term	Cost of Capital	Change
$15,000,000	7.5 percent	5 years	$3,034,154	—
$15,000,000	7.5 percent	6 years	$3,673,321	$638,167 (21.1%)
$15,000,000	7.5 percent	7 years	$4,326,074	$652,753 (18.9%)
$15,000,000	7.5 percent	8 years	$4,992,772	$666,698 (15.4%)
$15,000,000	7.5 percent	8 years	$5,672,846	$680,074 (13.7%)
$15,000,000	7.5 percent	10 years	$6,366,518	$694,672 (12.2%)

When interest rates are increased, the result is typically a slowing of the economy, which lowers sales of goods and services, including media and communications goods and services. And, as noted previously, when retail sales decline, advertising expenditures by manufacturers, retailers, employers, and other advertisers also decline, reducing the revenue of media firms supported by advertising.

Interest rates are important to media and communications firms because nearly all firms are dependent upon loans to fund acquisitions, growth, and large capital expenditures. The largest media firms borrow billions of dollars of capital to carry out their strategies and operations and even small media firms often have millions of dollars in such debt. The cost of this capital is thus significant to many managerial decisions about whether to reinvest in equipment, whether to acquire or establish new operations, what levels of return will be required from subsidiaries or divisions, and how various departments will be budgeted.

Over time, interest rates force managers to make decisions about whether to borrow capital, how much to borrow, how long to borrow, whether to use additional financial resources to pay down debt more rapidly than planned, or whether to try to refinance existing borrowed capital.

EXCHANGE RATES

Exchange rates represent the value given to a currency when it is exchanged for another currency. These rates change not only daily but by the minute and few companies are completely unaffected by these changes.

If a company's entire operations and exchange relations take place within one country, exchange rates are a relatively unimportant economic factor. If purchases are made outside of the country, or involve products made outside of the country, or if the company has sales outside of the country, exchange rates will affect its costs and revenues.

Media companies typically have a number of direct or indirect activities that involve the flow of goods and services and money across borders. For example, a magazine publisher in the Netherlands may purchase coated paper from a German paper manufacturer. A Hollywood film studio rents and sells motion pictures and videos worldwide. A newspaper publisher in Brazil may purchase a printing press from a Japanese manufacturer. A Web portal operating in Australia may purchase rights to carry information from a news service in the United Kingdom. A publisher in New York may have books printed in Hong Kong.

Because of these operations and relationships, exchange rates for currencies are important factors in the profitability of firms as the amount of non-domestic activities increases. The effect of changes in exchange rates is to make imports and exports become more or less expensive. Ultimately, consumption and production will increase or decrease somewhat when significant changes in exchange rates occur.

Domestic accounting standards, such as Statement 52 of the Financial Accounting Standards Board in the United States, directs how the financial operations in foreign currencies should be converted and reported on income statements and balance sheets. Gains or losses in conversion are typically reported as adjustments after operating income on the operating statements and as adjustments to owner's equity on the balance sheet.

The importance of exchange rates on corporate performance is illustrated by their effects on the financial accounts of News Corp., which adjusts corporate earnings (EBITDA) for foreign currency gains and losses due to its extensive international operations. From 2005 to 2008 it incurred foreign currency gains of $92 million, $149 million, $870 million and $976 million respectively—a total of about $2 billion—because of the declining strength of the U.S. dollar against foreign currencies in which it does business. In 2009, however, it incurred losses of $1.7 billion.

PREPARING FOR ECONOMIC CHANGES

Media and communications firm managers who want to prepare for changes that will affect revenues and costs, and the concurrent problems these present for their companies' operations and performance, watch for changes in economic indicators that signal a downturn or upturn in the economy. Statistics on production and retail sales, inflation, interest rates, and exchange rates provide evidence of the changing state of the general economy and the situation of the firm.

Changes in the economy occur locally, nationally, regionally, and globally. Managers need be aware of changes in all locations in which products or services are purchased and sold and locations from which advertising is obtained because the economies of different geographic areas change in different ways and at different times.

Managers should have a clear understanding of their priorities and contingency plans of what their firms or divisions will do when the general economy changes. Otherwise they are doomed to riding out economic turbulence and hoping they will not sink in the storm. If one monitors economic changes, however, one can prepare and implement strategies before the storm fully arrives to avoid or reduce its effects.

PREPARING FOR FLUCTUATIONS IN THE ECONOMY

Because the business cycle is created by a group of changing events over time, the factors that create changes in the general economy that will affect

The Effects of Exchange Rates on Company Operations

The effects of changes in exchange rates can either help or hurt the purchasing power and revenue of a firm, depending upon which of the two currencies involved is strengthened or diminished. This can be seen in the following examples.

Example 1: The Price of Imported Newsprint

A newspaper corporation in the United States agrees to purchase 50,000 metric tons of newsprint for its local newspapers from a Finnish newsprint company in the coming year at 400 per ton, at a total price of 20 million payable in euros. At the time of the contract the exchange rate is such that the newsprint will cost the company $21 million.

If the exchange rates change, however, the newspaper company will pay more or less than the $21 million. For example, if the exchange rate for the euro rises just 5 percent in favor of the European currency, the newspaper company will lose more than $1 million because it will have to exchange $22,050,000 for the euros.

Example 2: The Price of CDs

A British record company sells compact discs featuring its recording artists in worldwide. The firm sells approximately 10 million copies annually in India at an average annual price of 500 rupees producing a turnover of 5 billion rupees. Past experience has shown that lowering the price by 50 rupees will result in an increase of sales of 500,000 copies, producing a turnover of 4.725 billion rupees but a decline of 275 million rupees in revenue.

If the pound diminishes against the rupee by 10 percent and the prices for the imported CDs are lowered accordingly, the company will increase sales by 500,000 CDs. The increased sales will provide additional income for the company's artists, but the company itself may be helped, hurt, or relatively unaffected by the change depending upon its costs structures. If the net profit from the increased sales is more than 275 million rupees, the company will benefit from the increased sales. If the net profit is less than 275 million rupees, the company will be harmed by the change in exchange rates, even though sales have increased.

Example 3: Selling Post-Production Services

The value of services received is also affected by exchange rates. For example, a production house in London that films and provides post-production services for television advertisements can have its workload reduced by the effect of exchange rates on its prices.

If a Japanese advertising agency is considering the company for the production of an advertisement, the choice between the British firm and an equally proficient production company in Los Angeles may be based on the value received for the cost.

If the Japanese yen is weaker against the British pound than the U.S. dollar, the agency may choose to use the U.S. firm. If the agency views the two firms' abilities, skills, technology, and creativity as equal, the decision may be primarily based on the amount of yen that must be exchanged for pounds or dollars to obtain the same services.

media companies can be monitored regularly using both general and sophisticated methods.

Most of the influencing forces creating changes are regularly reported upon by the business press in publications such as *The Wall Street Journal, Financial Times, Investor's Business Daily, Barron's,* and *Business Week.* These stories result from monthly and quarterly statistical reports from government agencies and central banks and sometimes include forecasts for future developments. A variety of other business and economic publications and newsletters track developments in the general economy in individual nations. By attending to such stories a manager can get a reasonable understanding of where the economy is in a business cycle and what the short- and mid-term prospects are for the overall economy.

More sophisticated methods of tracking and forecasting are available by specific and regular tracking of the economy in the national and local markets in which firms operate. These can be conducted by corporate intelligence or research departments or by collecting and tracking available economic data at the company or unit level each quarter. Some firms, both large and small, keep economists on contract or in part-time or full-time employment to track and forecast economic developments and how these developments will affect the firm's operations.

With a good understanding of economic trends and forecasts, the management of a magazine corporation can decide whether it is an auspicious time to expand or contract operations, introduce new magazines or online services, increase employment, acquire or reduce debt, or make other decisions affecting financial operations. If the economy is expanding and expected to continue growing in the coming quarters or years, increased costs can be expected to be offset by increased revenue as sales increase correspondingly. If the economy is contracting, that expectation is unrealistic and the managers may even need to prepare contingency plans for reductions in expenditures.

PREPARING FOR CHANGES IN INFLATION

Inflation is rarely a sudden and unexpected development, absent extraordinary shocks to the economy such as war. In developed economies, inflation tends to develop more slowly so that monthly and quarterly reports provide sufficient time to respond.

As previously discussed, inflation has the effects of reducing asset values and inducing economic choices that slow the general economy.

When inflation is high, the manager of a newspaper company will ensure that company reserve funds for future capital expenditures are held in investments that will not be adversely affected by inflation. If the inflation rates are rising significantly in a short period of time, managers will work to collect accounts payable more rapidly or shorten times for payment so that the value of the accounts are not diminished by the inflation.

PREPARING FOR CHANGES IN INTEREST RATES

Interest rates tend to change slowly, rising or falling monthly or quarterly. By following the prime rate or the basic business loan rates from a firm's primary bank, a manager can determine the direction of changes. By monitoring the general economy through general and specialized methods, a manager can see the trend of change over time.

Preparation for changes in interest rates is important if the firm is expecting to borrow capital or has adjustable rate debts.

If a cable system operator, for example, is planning to borrow capital to upgrade its system into a multiple-use optical fiber network, managers will find it prudent to base financial plans on several potential interest rates if changes are anticipated. If these different projections are used in making the decision of whether to go ahead with the project, the managers will not encounter great surprises in their financial performance based on the interest rate the loan ultimately requires.

PREPARING FOR CHANGES IN EXCHANGE RATES

In order to minimize the financial effects of currency rate changes, managers of media firms operating internationally can use a variety of currency exposure management techniques. They begin with regular, often daily, monitoring of currencies in countries in which they have subsidiaries, divisions, or significant sales. When currencies become unstable they may engage in hedging practices to offset assets with equivalent liabilities in local currencies. Because both assets and liabilities in the local currency are affected equally, exchange issues do not become a financial factor in the health of the firm.

If managers fear that the value of the currency will decline, they can reduce cash that will be affected by the change in the worrisome currency through purchases of inventory or fixed assets. They can also reduce trade credit extended or terms of credit in nations with worrisome currencies so that the value of these current assets is not significantly affected.

Managers can also borrow in domestic currency to replace advances by the parent firm in a stronger currency or vary the currency in billing for international transfers of components, goods, or services. They can also engage in forward exchange rate activities (a form of buying and selling currency futures) or use swap arrangements in which it is agreed to exchange currency at a future date and specified rate. The latter strategies provide a form of insurance against significant changes in currency value.

Managers need to be aware of the influences of these economic factors on a company and its operations. By understanding their impact, following trends and forecasts, and preparing plans to respond to changes, managers of media firms prepare their firms for survival and the creation of greater stability in the financial performance of the firm over time.

SUGGESTED READINGS

Barro, Robert J. 1989. *Modern Business Cycle Theory*. Cambridge, Mass.: Harvard University Press.

Baye, Michael R. 1999. *Managerial Economics and Business Strategy*. New York: McGraw-Hill.

Corden, Warner Max. 1986. *Inflation, Exchange Rates, and the World Economy*. Chicago: University of Chicago Press.

Ellis, Joseph. 2005. *Ahead of the Curve: A Commonsense Guide to Forecasting Business and Market Cycles*. Boston: Harvard Business School Press.

Maurice, S. Charles, and Christopher R. Thomas. 2007. *Managerial Economics*. 9th ed. New York: McGraw-Hill.

Samuelson, William F., and Stephen G. Marks. 2008. *Managerial Economics*. 6th ed. New York: John Wiley & Sons.

Wessels, Walter J. 2000. *Economics*. Hauppauge, N.Y.: Barrons Educational Series.

CHAPTER 6

Audiences and Consumers

The concepts of consumers and audiences are not synonymous when dealing with media and communications industries. Despite the tendency to use the two interchangeably in common discussion, the differences between the two concepts are important and affect how their activities are measured and understood.

Consumers are individuals or firms who acquire and consume something, typically through a monetary exchange. Individuals purchasing subscriptions to satellite television systems or buying CD players are clearly consumers, as are online content providers purchasing the rights to content to place on their sites.

The term *audience*, however, focuses not merely on acquisition but upon actual use of the product or service by people. Members of an audience may or may not fall into the category of consumers depending upon whether they pay for the media or communications product. This later distinction is a fine point, however, because even if individuals don't make monetary payments for a product or service, they must exchange the very scarce resource of time when they use media or other communications products or services.

In the last two decades, as the number of television, cable, and satellite channels have risen dramatically across the developed world, the amount of time spent on television viewing has not risen proportionally because demand for more content has grown more slowly than the supply of programming. This is further constrained by the fact that the time available for television viewing is limited due to the human need for sleep, work, and other daily activities.

Table 6-1 shows the basic relationship requirements for use of media and communications products and services; individuals who use them are variously consumers, audiences, or both.

This chapter explores these audience and consumer relationships with media and issues that influence how companies deal with the individuals with whom they interact.

AUDIENCES

We need to understand the idea of the audience as an abstract concept denoting those persons who attend to a communications channel. It is not the population. It is not those who have access to a medium or channel. It is those who actually select a channel for use. The audience is the whole of those persons that is measured as a collective. Nevertheless, it is made up of individuals and the behavior of these individuals dictates the behavior of the audience.

These individuals are different persons who use communications to satisfy their different wants and needs for information, ideas, and diversion in different ways. They spend different amounts of time satisfying their different wants with different media and in doing so create multiple audiences, that is, multiple collections of individuals seeking to serve those needs simultaneously.

The audience for a particular media channel is never stable. It is a constantly changing collective. A single audience for any media channel rarely exists; instead most channels have many audiences.

A central reality of audiences in a multiple channel world is that they cannot be controlled but can merely be courted. In order to court audiences in this highly competitive environment, media managers in broadcasting, cable, and publishing—especially magazine publishers—tend to engage in audience segmentation. This means that they work to serve an audience with characteristics that differ from the general audience for their medium.

The forces promoting these segmentation efforts are made possible by advances in audience measurement that stem from the audience fragmentation created by multiple channels, from audience polarization to specific content of their choice, and from advertiser interests in reaching specialized audiences.

Media content providers tend to segment the audiences by their motives for using media, the dominant characteristics of these groups of persons, and their interests. In doing so they make efforts to appeal to different groups with different types of content and to offer a package of content that maximizes the audience that they have chosen to reach.

	Hardware	Software/Content	Additional Consumption Required
Newspapers		Consumer of copies Audience of copies	
Magazines		Consumer of copies Audience of copies	
Books		Consumer of copies Audience of copies	
Telephone	Consumer of telephone/line	Consumer of telephony services	
Radio	Consumer of radio receiver	Audience of programming	Electricity/batteries
Television	Consumer of television receiver	Audience of programming	Electricity
Cable television	Consumer of television receiver	Consumer of service subscription and decoder Audience of programming	Electricity
Videocassette/ DVD Player	Consumer of television receiver/screen Consumer of videocassette/ DVD player	Consumer of recordings Audience of recordings	Electricity
CD Player/ Cassette Player	Consumer of CD or cassette player	Consumer of recordings Audience of recordings	Electricity/batteries
Internet	Consumer of computer Consumer of modem Consumer of telephone line or mobile hardware	Consumer of telephony services Consumer of Internet access service Audience of Internet content	Electricity

At the broad level, print media and newspapers in particular tend to emphasize serving the information-seeking motives of audiences, whereas electronic media typically emphasize serving entertainment issues. This does not mean that entertainment or diversionary material are absent from print media or that informational material has no place in electronic media, only that the overall emphases differ in terms of motivations served.

Even within a media firm efforts exist to appeal to different audiences. Thus, a television channel may offer a variety of programming that caters to women staying at home during daytime, young people home from school in the afternoon, workers arriving home in the early evening, and a broad general audience in the evening itself. Similarly, a sailing magazine may have material of general interest to all sailors, recipes and cooking tips for those who prepare food on board, technical materials for those who make repairs, and games for children who may be aboard.

In order to segment and target audiences effectively, media managers make significant efforts to understand the wants and needs of audiences.

WANTS AND NEEDS OF AUDIENCES

As noted above, media and communications users have individual purposes, desires, and use patterns. Collectively, however, these individuals constitute the audiences with collective wants and needs that are served and sought by content providers.

These wants and needs include information on events and public activities occurring at the local, national, and international levels, discussions of ideas and opinions, entertainment or diversion, and information on how to meet other wants and needs. This latter category includes information in the form of advertising about the availability and pricing of goods they consume, information on employment offers, or listings of community activities.

Individuals and audiences want media that can be acquired or accessed with ease. This means that they do not want to engage in complicated processes to receive media and that the systems for delivery should be easy to operate. These needs are served, for example, by publishers who made it easy for people wanting to obtain subscriptions to magazines or newspapers to do so through simple postcards, phone calls, or web sites. Similarly, manufacturers of hardware and software designed to make recording television programs easier are serving the need for easy acquisition of the programs.

Media users also want the costs of acquisition to be low because, like all consumers, they have limited financial resources and use those resources for a variety of purposes. This is why free media such as free television typically have larger audiences than subscription media. And when payments are required, audiences want the payments to be low. This, of course, serves as a counteracting economic force to media and communications firms that want the payments to be as high as possible.

In addition to the desires for easy and inexpensive acquisition, audiences want to have high-quality media and communications products. This concept of high quality should not be confused with the concepts of high and popular culture. In this market sense, high quality refers to production qualities evidenced in writing and editing, acting or performance, direction, imagery, reproduction, and so on.

The degree to which media and communications products serve these various needs affects their success in generating audiences. A significant limitation on the ability of managers to meet these wants and needs is that there are conflicts among the wants and needs and conflicts in patterns of how they are fulfilled. Audiences, for example, want high-quality television programs but are not willing to pay for everything they watch. Also the amount of information and the pattern of information and entertainment content sought differ widely and media managers try to find a balance or methods of serving these different wants and needs.

AUDIENCE MEASURES

Media managers spend a great deal of effort and money in trying to understand audiences and their behavior so they can create strategies to serve optimally the conflicting wants and needs. The tools of audience research are used for these purposes, and they include business data analysis, market data analysis, survey and focus group methods, and monitoring methods.

Three major types of audience measurements are employed. First, demographic measurement methods are used to help identify the basic characteristics of an audience and to identify dominant audience elements. This measurement is concerned with describing *who* the audience is and includes data such as age, gender, income, language, and race/ethnic group.

The second type of measure is psychographic measurement, which is concerned with the internal attributes of an audience. It focuses on *what* audiences are and *how* they think. Indicators used in this type of analysis focus on attitudes and opinions, values, needs, personality, preferences, and interests.

A third type of measure develops profiles of audience groupings by lifestyle. It is concerned with how audiences live and what they do with their time. To make these determinations, researchers study time expenditures, activities, social contexts, purchasing behavior, product uses, and media use patterns.

Audience measures are used to help position media products, to differentiate them from other media products, and to differentiate audiences that

Challenges of Troublesome Audiences

Media companies have historically been relatively unconcerned about and at times even disdainful of individuals in their audiences. Publishers produced newspapers in formats and at times that was convenient for them. Television channels offered programs on a take-it-when-offered basis.

Audiences used to be treated and sold as commodities. In their sales pitches to advertisers, media executives presented audiences as a unified group, promising to advertisers that they were purchasing the same group of people any time their ads were carried. The reality is that audiences have always been individuals who change constantly, but media companies pretended otherwise in order to sell them. The façade put up by media companies is eroding rapidly and this is one reason why there is so much unease and shifting of advertising expenditures among media in advertising markets today.

The ascendancy of customer relationship management and personal marketing, and the personal identification of audience members in interactive media, has moved businesses to view their customers as individuals. Businesses recognize that approaching customers on an individual, rather than mass, basis increases return on their marketing and advertising investments.

Media companies are waking up to the nightmare that many advertisers find the idea of mass audiences less appealing. Unfortunately most media companies are finding they know everything and nothing about their audiences. They know their average characteristics, habits, and purchases, but they know little about their individual lifestyles and how they individually consume media and other products.

One of the first lessons media executives are learning is that human beings are troublesome. They tend to do what they want, when they want, and how they want. They resist being constrained and controlled. They are prone to changing their minds and interests. They want flexibility in their lives. They make it difficult to predict their preferences because their tastes and needs change over time. They are fickle consumers who have the audacity to behave as individuals rather than as an aggregated group.

Some consumers want music while they are walking to the office; some want news about stock prices at 10 A.M.; others want short video entertainment when they have a coffee break at 2:30 P.M.; some want to view a prime-time TV program at 5:30 P.M. when they are taking the commuter train home; still others want a recipe from a cooking magazine at 6 P.M. when they get home or a video of their choice at 8 P.M. These demands are highly problematic because few media companies have the competence or infrastructures to handle the new demand-driven world of media.

Media companies need to make understanding audiences and individuals that join their audiences a central point for management attention. They need to find ways to develop better relationships with them and then to find technologies and business models that allow them to be served as individuals if they are to prosper in the ever-changing media environment.

can then be made available to advertisers. The results are used to make market and product strategy choices that segment audiences by audience motives, type, usage, interest, and quality of use.

The audience measures and their usefulness are not universally lauded although they are widely used by media and advertisers. A number of problems have led to criticisms over inaccuracies in measurement and different means of measurement. Advertisers are wary of data reported by media and have sought to have the data audited by independent organizations to ensure accurate and standardized reporting of media use and audience characteristics. These are typically done by organizations created jointly or supported by advertising and media companies. The earliest auditing organizations were created for newspapers but organizations now provide similar auditing of audiences for magazines, free newspapers and advertising sheets/direct mail, radio, television, and Internet media.

Over the years, perceptions of what should actually be measured and debates over what is actually measured has changed. Depending on the method employed, audience research measures availability, reception, penetration, and reach, or actual use of a medium.

In measuring audiences in the newspaper and magazine industries, for example, one can measure output by the number of copies produced in a press run, by the number of copies delivered to homes and retailers, by paid circulation, household penetration, readers per copy, or circulation within the population.

Cable television audience research can measure households passed by cable or homes with televisions as a measure of availability. But it can also measure reception by types of subscriptions, the penetration by number of homes with cable, and the reach of cable television by the number of people in those homes. In addition, research can measure cable use by demographics, the amount of use, how it is used, under what conditions it is employed, and for what purposes.

In studying television and cable television use, researchers employ a variety of methods. Sometimes diaries are used and television audiences record when they watch and what they view. The diary method is problematic, however, because it requires literacy and viewers must remember to complete the diaries daily. This method may also skew results because research has shown that diaries are more likely to be completed by women than men.

Another method is to employ a use recorder that electronically tracks usage. A problem with this method is that it merely records when a television is on and to which channel it is tuned. It does not record actual viewing or who is viewing. To overcome these problems researchers created technologies in which individual viewers sign in regularly to show who is actually watching. The reliability of results obtained by such methods have been criticized, however, because many viewers contacted by researchers refuse to use them, because men are more likely to record their use than women, and because younger television users are more likely to record use than other persons.

Difficulties with the accuracy, representativeness, and use of broadcast media ratings aside, critics have also argued that firms rely too much on ratings in programming and advertising decisions and that important statistical significance issues in the data are often ignored.

Advertisers and online media firms are currently wrestling with determining how to measure audience use of the Internet. Some have used measures of the number of computer users, but this is highly problematic because using computer penetration to measure Internet use is like using literacy to measure magazine readership. Others have argued that online service subscription is an appropriate measure, but the availability of the Internet is not synonymous with its use. Some advertisers and media prefer the number of hits and unique viewers on a particular site, but these may be the result of multiple hits by a few users and do not necessarily mean that a hit was effective use. Others have argued that the time connected or the time spent viewing a site is important because a longer connection presumably means more use and exposure to messages. Others argue that the proper measure should be interactions such as click-through, downloads, or orders.

The debates of measures of audiences will continue as technologies change and the ability to measure different audience aspects changes. Media managers need to be aware that the type of measures they are given result from the methods employed and that the methods used must be taken into consideration when making decisions about audiences and content.

AUDIENCE FRAGMENTATION AND POLARIZATION

The basic problems of audience creation, segmentation, and measurement are compounded as the number of communication channels increases. As the number of choices rise and individuals' behaviors diverge, the mass audience fragments. *Audience fragmentation* is a term that describes this process and the result of de-massification of the audience. It represents the breakdown of a mass audience into smaller audiences.

Audience fragmentation is the inevitable and unstoppable consequence of increasing the channels available to audiences. It is true whether one is discussing publishing, broadcasting, Internet, or other forms of communications involving multiple content providers and individuals.

When one looks beyond averages at actual television and cable markets, one finds that some channels must struggle to survive with only 1 or 2 percent shares after about a dozen channels are available because they fall below the average share of the total television audience. This occurs because it is rare that audiences watch each of the channels equally and the fragmentation pattern results from individual choices.

This, of course, raises the question of whether individuals view channels or programs. When the number of channels is low, viewers tend to watch channels. As the number of channels increases, however, particular programs become attractive regardless of channel. Nevertheless, individuals tend to focus most viewing on a relatively few number of channels, even in a multichannel environment.

Some national and industry structural factors reduce the rapid decline of audiences in some markets. National language can be a significant protection and changes that provide content in that language tend to have higher than average ratings when other channels provide content in other languages. Similarly, when domestic news, domestic cultural content, and domestic entertainment content are available from only a few channels, these tend to get higher than average ratings.

These fragmentation issues and patterns create an environment in which managers' choices are constrained, and many pursue similar types of strategies that limit innovation and diversity in content and approach.

In addition to fragmentation, media use is also polarized. Fragmented audiences separate into extremes of use or nonuse. As a result, small but loyal audiences can exist for television channels, magazines, or radio stations that most of the potential audience avoids. This polarization is created by the reach of specialized media that are designed to serve audience niches. Polarization is apparent the more time an individual spends viewing, listening, or reading a channel, station, or magazine compared to others and to the higher the share of overall viewing, listening, or reading time given to a channel, station, or magazine by viewers, listeners, or readers as a whole.

TIME AND MEDIA USE

Time is a scarce resource that is becoming increasingly significant to the media environment and media and research. The temporal demands of modern society are placing increased pressure on individuals' leisure time and media use.

Time spent for media and communications is part of the overall time use patterns of individuals and audiences. Approximately one-third of the hours in a day is unavailable for media use in average lives because it is used for sleep. Another third is typically consumed by work, schooling, and other daily routines during which only limited media use can occur. The final third of the day is allocated to commuting, shopping, eating, and leisure.

Large portions of media use can thus be considered one of the myriads of possible leisure time activities such as sports, performances, and hobbies. It is the time available for these types of activities that media seek as well as that time when limited use can occur as other activities take place.

Individuals make personal time decisions but there are collective uses of time for overall activity and media use. Americans, for example, collectively spend about two-thirds of their media time use on electronic media and only about one-third on print media (see Figure 6-1). These use patterns reflect a difference in the ways and purposes for which audiences use different media.

Companies that are introducing new media or increasing the number of units of a medium must then try to induce audiences or consumers to alter their media time use patterns or to increase their overall media use time by taking time away from other activities.

CONSUMERS

As previously noted, consumers in a media and communications context are the individuals and companies who purchase media and the individuals and companies who purchase advertising.

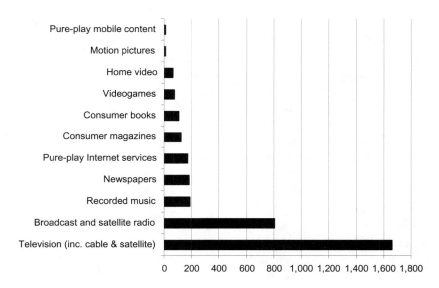

FIGURE 6-1   Average U.S. media use hours for selected media types, 2005 (Source: U.S. Census Bureau. Statistical Abstract of the United States, 2008. Table 1098.)

Consumer spending data reveal how much revenue is available from consumers, how consumers are dividing their spending among media, and how demand is shifting over time. Spending is typically measured by tracking actual monetary expenditures and expenditures as a percentage of all spending.

Actual monetary spending focuses on the amount of money paid by consumers, for example, for mass media or all communications products and services. Such expenditures are typically reported as the total amount of money spent, the total amount of money spent per each household or individual, or the total amount of money spent on each type of media or communications product or service.

The actual amount of money spent, however, does not give us an understanding of the relative importance of the media expenditures in comparison to other spending. This is typically done by comparing media expenditures to total spending.

When dealing with individuals or households, the best figures are based on disposable personal income (DPI), because it is based on the actual money with which consumers make choices (that is, money left after taxes). Media spending can thus be reported as a percent of DPI.

It is often useful to compare spending patterns over time to gain an understanding of overall changes and trends. Such comparisons, however, face the two major problems of currency value differences and market size difference.

The first problem with comparisons results because currency value changes over time due to inflation and other factors. Thus, if consumers spent $500 million on audio recordings in 1940, it was more valuable than if they spent $500 million on audio recordings today.

The second problem with comparisons occurs because market size changes with time. The population is constantly changing and altering the potential for sales. For example, the world had only 2.5 billion people in 1950 whereas today it has six billion inhabitants. Thus, if five hundred million people bought magazines in 1950, it was a greater portion of the population than if the same number bought magazines today.

The primary means for overcoming these difficulties are to use currency figures in constant currencies that adjust for changes in monetary value and to adjust market size by using figures based on expenditures per household or individual.

Another means of understanding collective consumer behavior related to the media and communications products and services is measurement of household penetration rates. This allows managers to follow the acquisition of new products and services and to observe media and communications use patterns when constructing business strategies and plans.

When one looks at such patterns, one immediately sees significant differences in the penetration of various media and communications products and services in households, with radio, television and telephones being the most acquired products and services (see Figure 6-2).

Various types of penetration rates are also used to measure how rapidly different technologies have been adopted. One can, for example, study how rapidly telephones reached a certain number of households or a percentage of the population and compare the time to how rapidly mobile phones reached the same number of households or percentage of the population. This type of comparison must be made carefully, however, to ensure that the comparisons are appropriate, as shown in the box "Problems with Media Data Use."

Media companies are increasingly creating consumer relationships with those who read, listen to, or view their content through a variety of direct mail, e-mail, and social media activities involving services such as Facebook, YouTube, and Twitter. Much of this trend is related to financial demands created by increasing audience segmentation and fragmentation. The dominant business model of the twentieth century—particularly for commercial broadcasting—cannot produce sufficient revenue to cover operating costs as the audiences shares decline due to segmentation and fragmentation. As a result, audiences are being increasingly asked to bear costs they had not previously borne, thus being transformed into consumers making monetary payments for cable television, satellite television, and premium services. Even

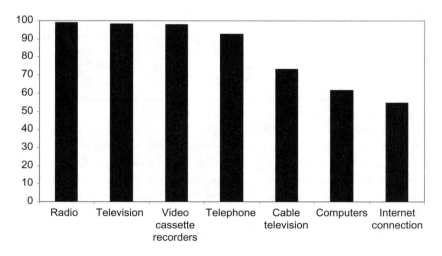

FIGURE 6-2   Penetration of selected media and communications in U.S. households (Source: U.S. Census Bureau. Statistical Abstract of the United States, 2008. Table 1099.)

Problems with Media Use Data: Did Consumers Really Jump to the Web Faster than Other Media?

In recent years it has been argued that the rapidity of expansion of the Internet is unusual and that consumers' acceptance shows it is an extremely desirable technology. A widely distributed group of statistics used to illustrate the point shows the number of years it took for the World Wide Web to reach fifty million users globally.

Telephone	74 years
Radio	38 years
Personal Computer	16 years
Television	13 years
World Wide Web	4 years

Setting aside issues of whether the numbers themselves are accurate, can one accept the figures as meaningful comparisons, as many observers have done? Unfortunately, the comparisons are highly problematic for a number of reasons.

The first reason is that the different media were introduced at times when the population differed greatly. Gaining fifty million users in the year 2000, when the global population was 6.1 billion, represents a different success rate than reaching fifty million users in 1900, when world population was estimated to be 1.65 billion. As a result the consumption comparison of World Wide Web penetration is fallacious. To improve the calculation, one would at least need to adjust comparative data for the population at the time of the introduction of the technology and the date at which it reached the fifty million users mark.

The cost of acquisition of the technologies is hardly comparable as well. Even by today's standard, the cost of a television is far higher than the cost of acquiring World Wide Web access if one already has a computer. This doesn't even begin to account for the issues of the value of currency and the differences in disposable income available to consumers at the different points when the technologies were introduced.

in print media, where advertisers had previously borne large portions of the expenses, additional costs are beginning to be shifted to readers because advertisers are no longer willing to pay as much for de-massified audiences. Many online, multimedia, and mobile telephone content services operate with direct payments from users, but users are currently resisting making payments for materials on most newspaper and magazine online operations.

How important consumers are to media firms can be seen in the fact that for every dollar that advertisers pay for media worldwide, consumers pay three. This relationship is even stronger in the United States where for every dollar advertisers provide to media, consumers provide seven. In such an environment considerable power is in the hands of consumers rather than suppliers.

Even then, however, the comparison would be highly problematic for several reasons.

First, the existence of the telephone requires electricity and a telephone network. The penetration of the telephone occurred almost concurrently with the rise of electrification in many parts of the United States before and at the turn of the twentieth century, and the penetration of both technologies was related to population mobility, urbanization, and the development of large businesses. Because the availability of electricity and telephone networks was limited, much of the U.S. population and that of the rest of the world—even in relatively developed nations—could not have had a telephone even if they wanted one at that time.

Radio was similarly affected by the fact that electrification was needed and the ability to receive radio broadcasts was required. Because electrification of locations such as North America and Europe were still underway when radio was introduced, and because many persons with electricity could even then not receive signals because transmitters were not located within their reception area, they could not have made use of a radio receiver.

Television and the World Wide Web were introduced at much later states in development. Both are dependent upon electrification and telephone systems that were already in place throughout the developed world and to a lesser extent elsewhere. And both were able to use the technologies and infrastructure developed by heavy investments in the creation and development of the Internet and the World Wide Web by the U.S. military and the European nuclear science community. Thus, the comparison to the earlier technologies that did not have pre-existing infrastructures upon which to build gives a false picture of consumption desires or abilities.

Those factors taken into consideration, it really is impossible to tell from available information whether the Internet attracted consumers more rapidly than other media. The example, however, illustrates that one must have a critical approach to consumption and audience data upon which one is basing business strategies and decisions in media firms. As with all statistics, one must consider how they were gathered, the purpose for which they were gathered, what they actually measure, and whether they are comparable to other data.

In 2005, American consumers spent an average of $787 annually per person on media consumption with the largest expenditures going for television and cable, video recordings, and books (see Figure 6-3).

DEMAND AND PRICES OF MEDIA PRODUCTS AND SERVICES

The basic economic principle of demand indicates that the willingness of individuals to consume is related to price. When prices are high consumption decreases and when prices are low consumption increases.

The Power of Consumers

In order to protect music sold through music downloads, the four major recording companies (Warner, Sony BMG, Universal, and EMI) all started placing software protection software on their downloadable files in 2005 and 2006. The digital rights management software blocked users from moving downloads from their computers to portable music players or even to new computers.

The software incensed many consumers because it forced consumers to purchase multiple copies or to bypass illicitly the software if they wanted to use music they had purchased on more than one platform. Many felt it was unfair that one did not "own" the download in the same way as a CD, book, or DVD and voiced their frustration in blogs, music forums, and to the record companies. Opposition grew so strong among consumers that consumer rights and competition authorities in both the United States and Europe began to investigate and question the practice.

In 2007, EMI and Universal Music Group dropped the DRM measures and Warner Music Group and Sony BMG Music Entertainment followed suit in 2008.

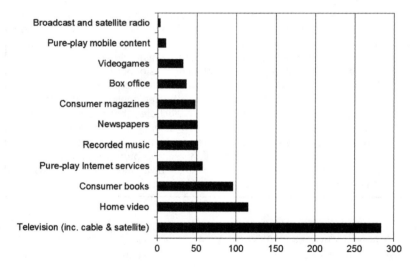

FIGURE 6-3   U.S. consumer spending on media per person, 2005 (Source: U.S. Census Bureau. Statistical Abstract of the United States, 2008. Table 1098.)

In addition to price alone, the willingness of individuals to consume is affected by a variety of factors including consumers' perceptions of the state of the general economy, the stability of their employment or income sources, or whether the product requires additional purchases.

Individuals who are concerned that the economy is becoming unstable or that they may lose income, for example, tend to postpone additional consumption in order to pay debts or save some money for use if income is reduced. Companies tend to behave in the same way as individuals when the economy is unstable or in decline.

Consumers also consider whether their purchases require additional consumption for use. A consumer purchasing a DVD player, for example, cannot use the equipment without also making additional expenditures to purchase or rent DVD recordings. Similarly, persons can purchase an advanced mobile telephone but cannot use it to access the Internet, use WAP services, or make telephone calls unless they also purchase a data service. As a result, one can make the general observation that the more additional items a consumer must purchase to use a medium, the lower the penetration of that medium.

If one considers the list of services by household penetration shown earlier in Figure 6-2, one immediately sees that the greatest consumption tends to come in basic media and communication products and services. Other possibilities that serve less basic needs or require additional expenditures for hardware, software, or services, tend to have significantly lower penetration because demand is lower.

CUSTOMER SATISFACTION

One factor affecting the willingness to continue consuming a media product or service, or to remain a customer of a particular company, is customer satisfaction that results from customers' perceptions and choices regarding issues of quality, price, and service.

From the business perspective, creating customer satisfaction is the driver of success for a company. If the product or service does not create customer satisfaction, the company will experience a constant turnover of customers, and the reputation of the company will decline. Thus satisfaction is key to finding and keeping customers. For media companies, this issue applies both to audiences and consumers.

Producing satisfaction thus becomes a critical component of quality management, and managers need to understand the expectations and requirements of their customers and how well their company and competitors are meeting them. They then can use that information to develop strategies and standards for their operations and programs to improve their performance.

A newspaper, for example, may develop methods to track and improve delivery problems. A cable system may work to reduce the number of service calls it must handle by improving the quality of its equipment and installations. An Internet portal may work to increase the ease with which customers can use the site if the current site creates dissatisfaction.

A wide variety of product/service attributes, customer service attributes, purchase attributes, and billing issues affect the satisfaction of audiences and customers of all media and communications systems. By carefully considering these attributes and what customers want, one can make regular determinations of customer satisfaction and track performance over time.

A variety of methods and tools for measuring satisfaction exist and are being increasingly applied to media and communications as competition and audience and consumer choice increases.

AUDIENCE SUBSTITUTION OF MEDIA AND COMMUNICATIONS

The basic issues of demand and satisfaction, as well as the uses that audiences and consumers make of media and communications, affect their willingness to substitute the use of one medium for another.

Although it is tempting to think that all the products and services are interchangeable, they are not. One needs to be aware of the difference between media and communications products and services and the inherent advantages and disadvantages in content and use. Further, the ability to substitute products and services are limited by the availability and penetration of the necessary communications technology in the market.

In determining the degree of substitution among media products and services one needs to ask fundamental questions about interactions that occur. First, does a price change in one product increase demand for the other? A change in price for cable television service, for example, will not have a significant effect on book sales. A change in price of CDs, however, may increase or decrease demand for digital downloads. Thus price is sometimes, but not always, the determinant of substitution.

Second, do the media products and services actually serve the same customers? If one considers television and cable television audiences, one can reasonably say that cable audiences can substitute terrestrial television for their viewing. This applies, of course, only if terrestrial channels are available, if the audience is willing to give up use of additional channels available on cable, or if they cannot find something desirable on cable. Terrestrial television viewers, however, typically find less ability to substitute cable because cable is not universally available and requires additional expenditures associated with its acquisition and use.

Third, audiences and consumers tend to use a mix of media at different times and these times limit substitution. For example, while some employees may listen to radio or recordings in the workplace, they typically don't have the choice of substituting television. Similarly, commuters driving to work tend not to read newspapers and magazines during that period, using audio media instead.

How audiences react to the increasing amount of media channels and the rising entertainment and information choices available is important. In television viewing, for example, the addition of more television, cable, and satellite channels, and the availability of videocassette recorders and players, has not produced a significant change in other media time use, except in places where very little television had previously been available. Both the time and money spent on print media, audio recordings, and radio listening have not been significantly reduced as video media availability and use has increased. A reason for this pattern seems to be that most of the newer media have tended to seek smaller niche audiences by focusing on specific interests.

STRENGTHENING AND STABILIZING AUDIENCE AND CONSUMER RELATIONSHIPS

Because of the importance of creating audiences that advertisers want to reach and the necessity of income from consumer sales, media and communications firms use a variety of methods to strengthen their relationships with audiences.

Subscriptions, for example, are used by cable television services, newspapers, magazines, and online firms to create a stable consumption relationship that reduces the transaction costs associated with separate sales. A number of media and communications firms have audience clubs, publications, and web sites that are designed to increase frequency of contact with customers and to build a closer, stronger relationship. Some media provide gifts, special offers, or special reports or books as premiums for good customers or those willing to enter prolonged relationships.

The methods of strengthening relationships are supported by audience and consumer studies, efforts to brand media products and services, efforts to develop and improve content and its relevance, and efforts to improve the quality. In most firms, individual departments are responsible for these audience and consumer activities with separate efforts being made to strengthen relationships conducted by sales and circulation departments, marketing and promotion departments, and editorial and programming departments. Some media and communications firms are beginning to establish audience relationship teams comprised of staff from the various departments to help improve and coordinate efforts to strengthen the relationships with audiences and consumers.

Ball-Rokeach, S., and M. Cantor, eds. 1986. *Media, Audience and Social Structure*. Newbury Park, Calif.: Sage Publications.

Barwise, Patrick, and Andrew Ehrenberg. 1988. *Television and Its Audience*. Newbury Park, Calif.: Sage Publications.

Becker, Lee, and Klaus Schoenbach. 1989. *Audience Responses to Media Diversification*. Mahwah, N.J.: Lawrence Erlbaum Associates.

Ettema, J., and D. Whitney, eds. 1994. *Audiencemaking: How the Media Create the Audience*. Thousand Oaks, Calif.: Sage Publications.

Napoli, Philip M. 2003. *Audience Economics: Media Institutions and the Audience Marketplace*. New York: Columbia University Press.

Neuman, W. 1991. *The Future of Mass Audience*. Cambridge: Cambridge University Press.

Webster, J. G., and L. Lichty. 2000. *Ratings Analysis: The Theory and Practice of Audience Research*. 2nd ed. Hillsdale, N.J.: Lawrence Erlbaum Associates.

Webster, J., and P. Phalen. 1997. *The Mass Audience: Rediscovering the Dominant Model*. Mahwah, N.J.: Lawrence Erlbaum Associations.

CHAPTER 7

Media, Advertisers, and Advertising

Advertisers are critical to the success of commercial media because they provide the primary revenue stream that keeps most of them viable. Broadcasters, trade magazine publishers, and newspaper publishers exhibit the highest levels of dependence on advertising income among media firms (see Figure 7-1). Advertisers, however, do not provide these financial resources in order to make media possible, they do so in order to pursue their own interests and purposes.

As a result, those working within and managing media enterprises need to understand the purposes and choices of advertisers and the dynamics of the relationships between media and advertisers if their media enterprises are to be more successful.

WHY ADVERTISING EXISTS

Advertising is designed to spur consumption of specific goods and services. Consumer advertising began to appear when excess goods and services developed after the Industrial Revolution. Before that time, most trade was in raw materials, and the number of sellers of the few finished goods and services available were relatively small and did not require significant advertising to gain the notice of potential customers.

Even as manufactured goods began to appear, advertising primarily promoted products to distributors and retailers. Because companies sold all the products and services they could, heavy advertising to consumers was not necessary. When the amount of goods increased and differences between

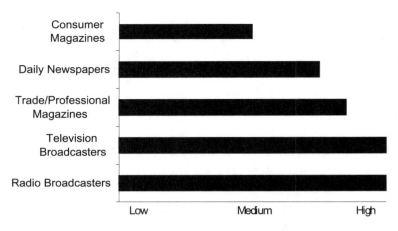

FIGURE 7-1   Relative dependence of selected media on advertising income

products appeared, advertising began being directed toward consumers to attract their attention and influence their choices. Today the wide range of products and services with different attributes that are available requires companies in both the consumer and business markets to advertise their goods and activities.

Because advertisers must cover the expenses of planning, producing, and placing advertising through the purchase of advertising space and time, advertising adds monetary expenses to the costs of a good or service. These costs are spread across all sales and, if consumption of the good or service increases sufficiently, the costs for the good will normally go down over time because the increased sales reduce unit costs.

Advertisers' wants and needs are served by media that are designed to attract broad general audiences with a variety of informational and entertainment types as well as focused media that present information or entertainment with a narrow focus or that focus content and activities toward a particular group of persons or a geographic location.

In selecting among the many potential advertising opportunities, advertisers seek to gain access to specific target audiences made up of persons most likely to use their product or service. Many media outlets try to create the largest possible audiences to attract advertisers. This approach was the basis of the business model adopted by commercial newspapers and broadcasters in the nineteenth and twentieth centuries, and this audience maximization strategy assumes that all members of the audience are equally valuable to advertisers. This is, of course, inaccurate because consumption of goods and services among consumers differs widely. Thus, for advertisers, members of the audience that consume, or are likely to consume, their products or services are more valuable than other audience members. Because of the difficulties in separating them from the mass audience many advertisers assume that more customers and potential customers exist among larger than smaller audiences if they are not able to differentiate the audience by programs or titles that produce niche audiences that contain their primary customer base.

During the second half of the twentieth century many niche print and broadcast media developed—especially in the magazine, radio, and cable television industries. These outlets, and the growing number of specialized Web sites, create smaller groups of individuals with common interests that make them attractive for specialized advertisers.

Although access to the target audience is a primary purpose of their activities, advertisers also seek a suitable message environment in which their advertising messages are not diluted by a clutter of advertising, are not ignored by the audience, and are not sullied by the media content. In addition, advertisers want a high-quality media product, a low price for the space or time purchased, and high-quality service and billing from the media firm with which they do business.

Advertising, however, cannot be considered in isolation as *the* method in which advertisers pursue satisfaction of their wants and needs. It is only one part of the marketing mix through which companies manage brand images and promote sales. It is only one method used and advertising is usually employed concurrently with a variety of advertiser marketing communications activities, including sales promotion, direct marketing, and public relations (see Table 7-1).

TABLE 7-1 · SELECTED MARKETING COMMUNICATIONS ACTIVITIES

Media Advertising	Direct Marketing	Sales Promotion	Public Relations
Newspapers	Catalogs	Point-of-sale displays	Publicity
Magazines	Flyers	Exhibitions	Product information
Free sheets	Direct mail	Sponsorships	Company information
Television/cable	Personal letters	Product placement	
Radio	Social media	Product Web sites	
Outdoor		Social media	
Cinema			
Online			

Although these other marketing communications activities are not the direct concern of media firms seeking advertising expenditures, their existence is important to how media sell advertising, to how advertisers divide expenditures among media and other marketing communications activities, and for projecting the resources that media can expect in the future. To be effective, media personnel need to understand specific advertisers' strategies that integrate and coordinate all of these activities and how the strategies affect their willingness to purchase advertising, their objectives and goals for the advertising, and the importance of specific media in pursuing those strategies.

DIFFERENCES AMONG ADVERTISERS AND THEIR STRATEGIES

Although many observers think of advertisers collectively, they are differentiated in terms of their types, their needs, and their advertising behavior.

How companies advertise varies depending upon the price and frequency of purchase for a given product. Fast-moving consumer goods typically have low purchase prices and purchases by consumers reoccur regularly. These include items such as packaged foods, toiletries, detergents, and beverages. The primary purposes of advertising these products are to attract new customers, develop and maintain loyalty among existing customers, and strengthen brands. Durable goods, such as kitchen appliances, television

---

The World's Biggest Advertiser

Procter & Gamble is the world's largest advertiser and operates in three global business segments: beauty care, household care, and health and well-being. It operates in 180 countries and had sales of $76 billion in 2007 for its branded products including Tide, Ivory, Duracell, Pampers, Folgers, Pringles, Clairol, Gillette, and Crest.

In 2007, P&G spent $7.9 billion on media and in-store advertising. The firm advertises heavily on television, but also makes significant investments in print and online media.

The company has been a leader in seeking high return on investment of advertising expenditures for many years and in ensuring that expenditures drive not only sales but build the asset value of its brands. In recent years, it has flexed its economic power and changed compensation methods for advertising agencies to include pay-per-performance elements based on increases in product sales rather than merely payments for advertising and media buying services.

---

sets, and automobiles, tend to be higher priced and are infrequently purchased. Advertisements for such products tend to emphasize brand characteristics, product attributes, and quality and value so that consumers will be more inclined to consider and buy the next time they make the purchase.

One can think of advertisers as being part of four major categories or types. First, national advertisers are typically producers of brand-name consumer products or large national retailers. These advertisers need to reach audiences throughout the nation in which they are active. Second, there are large and mid-sized regional and local advertisers that tend to be retail establishments such as department and grocery stores, auto dealers, and real estate firms that are intent on reaching regional and local audiences. Third, there are small local advertisers that are typically smaller retail stores and business that need to reach audiences within their local market area. Finally, there are nonbusiness advertisers such as churches, organizations, and individuals that typically want to communicate with local audiences.

Because of the different needs of these advertisers, and because different media provide different types of access to audiences, media firms get varying portions of their advertising revenue from the different types of advertisers. Television, cable systems, and consumer magazines are highly dependent upon national advertisers, whereas radio stations and newspapers are highly dependent upon local advertisers (see Table 7-2).

These differences in sources of advertising income affect the levels of competition experienced for advertising expenditures at the local and national levels.

In addition to these general patterns, different types of advertisers employ different strategies to get their messages across to audiences. As a result, advertising agencies do not sell ready-made advertising campaigns to clients and spend a great deal of time determining which media and mix of media are best for reaching the audiences that are intended to respond to clients' advertisements.

TABLE 7-2 · AVERAGE SOURCES OF ADVERTISING INCOME FOR
SELECTED U.S. MEDIA

	Local Television Station	Cable System	Radio Station	National Consumer Magazines	Newspapers
National	70%*	80%	25%*	95%	15%
Local	30%	20%	75%	5%	85%

*Including spot ads.

The underlying purposes of these strategies are important in understanding why advertisers select different media in which to place their messages. Although most advertisers ultimately want to increase their revenue by spurring sales, specific advertising campaigns may have different purposes. Some are designed to promote sales by inducing consumers to purchase a product, by telling them where to buy the product, or by telling them about special offers. Other campaigns are designed to provide information about the attributes and availability of products and additional uses for the products. Still other campaigns are designed to position products and services to establish or to change consumer perceptions about a product or to establish and maintain brand preferences.

Media, then, serve as a bridge between advertisers and audiences. The bridge is built by media content attracting audiences, by making it possible for advertisers to reach the audiences the media attract, and by providing mechanisms for targeting specific groups of people. Building and maintaining this bridge is not accomplished without problems and conflicts. Because commercial media are dependent upon income from advertisers, audiences must not see evidence that their interests are not harmed by that dependence or they will lose confidence in the bridge and it will lose its effectiveness.

Media must seek to build and maintain stable relationships with both audiences and advertisers. As noted in the last chapter, media engage in a variety of activities including subscriptions, audience clubs, and premiums. Similar methods are employed to strengthen advertising relationships. Advertisers are offered special prices if they will enter long-term contracts for quantities of space or time or regular purchases. Media companies offer a variety of customer service strategies involving proofs, pre-use information, preferential positioning, after-sales contacts, and follow-up information. In addition, a wide range of advertiser events, tie-ins and cross promotions, advertiser publications, and advertising research are offered as a means of strengthening relationships with advertisers.

Many media companies use key account managers to help solidify relationships with their most important advertising customers. Although this is done for a limited number of customers, they are typically the top ten to twenty companies that provide the bulk of the advertising income. Key account managers work to ensure consistency of service, to understand the customers' businesses and needs, to provide regular contacts and information, and to help develop strategies that mutually benefit both the media company and the advertisers and lead to long-term relationships. The *Los Angeles Times*, for example, uses key account managers for consumer sectors such as food and auto advertisers and *CFO Magazine* uses key account managers for its top advertising clients as well.

Sat 1, the giant German satellite programming provider, offers its advertisers and potential advertisers *Sat 1 Report*, a monthly newsletter containing ratings data, information on future programming, and other topics related to television, television advertising, and Sat 1. Similar types of publications are offered free of charge to advertisers by many large media firms.

Responsibility for these activities is often divided among the advertising, marketing, and research departments and only a few firms seek the benefits of creating unified advertising relationship activities.

EFFECTIVENESS OF DIFFERENT MEDIA

Media differ in their abilities to serve the wants and needs of advertisers because of differences in their characteristics, their relationships with audiences, and the way they are used by both audiences and advertisers.

Advertisers seeking to nurture a brand image for their products and services typically find that television, magazine, Internet, and outdoor advertising best suit that purpose. Advertisers, especially retailers, wanting immediate sales typically turn to newspapers, free distribution sheets, or direct mail. Advertisers that are intent on providing information about their products, services, and locations tend to turn to magazines, Internet, direct mail, and telephone directories. The reason for these choices is that each medium has different strengths and weaknesses from among which advertisers select media that best suit their purposes (see Table 7-3).

Because individual advertisers serve different wants and needs at different times, they tend to use a mix of media, rather than only one medium, as a means of reaching and influencing audiences.

These choices are also dependent upon whether advertisers want to reach broad or narrow geographical coverage and mass or differentiated audiences. As shown in Figure 7-2, advertisers wanting to reach mass audiences with narrow or broad geographic coverage have a variety of media choices available that permits them to implement a variety of strategies for choosing and mixing the media that best suit their needs. If differentiated audiences are sought, the number of choices is more constrained but the variety of choices and strategies available are greater when advertisers need to cover a broader geographic area.

Today, advertisers and advertising company executives give no media primacy in meeting their needs. For many years television held that position and it was a must buy—especially for national advertising campaigns. Now all media are considered more neutrally and are more clearly evaluated in terms of what they can deliver to the specific advertising campaign or a specific advertiser.

TABLE 7-3 · STRENGTHS AND WEAKNESSES OF SELECTED MEDIA FOR ADVERTISERS

	Strengths	*Weaknesses*
Television	Broad coverage Ability to repeat messages Highly visual Good for image development	Market targeting limitations Ignored messages Advertising clutter Limited information content possible High cost
Radio	Ability to target local markets Formats attract different audiences Audience uses in mobile situations Rapid ability to change message Low cost	Narrow audiences Audience instability Ease of station change Limited information content possible
Newspapers	Target market coverage Ability to change size and type of advertisements High frequency Cost advantages High information content possible	Advertising clutter Audiences read quickly Reproduction quality limited Short lifespan
Magazines	Target audience selectivity Excellent reproduction Long lifespan for advertisement High information content possible	Low overall market penetration Long lead time for ad changes
Online	Interactivity Immediacy Easy to change advertisements High information content possible Strong targeting ability	Low market penetration Low response rates

MECHANISMS OF ADVERTISING

Commercial media operate advertising departments designed to sell space or time in the product offered to those wanting to buy access to the medium's audience. These departments prepare a variety of sales promotion materials describing the product or service, describing its audience, and providing other information designed to produce sales.

Advertising departments engage in both direct and various forms of surrogate sales. Sales personnel call on potential advertisers in an effort to generate sales and then manage customers and orders that are produced. When relationships with major advertisers develop, these relationships are typically handled by experienced key account managers.

Mass Audience

local/regional newspapers, local/regional radio, local/regional magazines, local/regional Internet portals	national television, papers, and magazines, national radio (unformatted), national general Internet portals
local/regional formatted radio, local Internet portals, free sheets, direct mail	topical magazines, business and trade press, national formatted radio, specialized Internet portals, direct mail

Narrow geographic coverage (left) **Broad geographic coverage** (right)

Differentiated Audience

FIGURE 7-2　Matrix of advertising choices

Some companies also take part in sales networks that involve a number of units of the same medium. When these networks generate sales, a percentage of the income from those sales is paid to the network. Advertising sales networks in the newspaper industry, for example, make it possible for advertisers to purchase space in some or all newspapers in different geographic areas through one organization, thus reducing their transaction costs.

Within the advertising industry, advertisers contract with advertising agencies that provide a variety of research, planning, creative, and purchasing services. Sales personnel for media call upon those who place advertising in these agencies and on specialized advertisement placement firms in an effort to attract advertisements. Agencies that place advertisements in media receive part of their compensation in the form of commissions paid by the media firms.

Media also provide extensive information to specialized firms that publish information about the services, prices, and requirements of media firms.

ADVERTISING SPENDING ON MEDIA AND MEDIA PRODUCTS

The amount of money expended on advertising is enormous. Advertisers, for example, spent an estimated $163 billion on advertising in the United

States during 2006 and U.S. advertising alone accounted for 33.5 percent of worldwide spending (see Figure 7-3).

Different patterns of advertising expenditures exist among nations reflecting the availability of media, domestic media use patterns, and other market conditions. In the United States, the share of expenditures for television and cable and direct mail grew steadily in the last decades of the twentieth century. Television surpassed newspapers as the primary choice for advertisers and direct mail became a nearly equal rival (see Figure 7-4).

Internet advertising has grown rapidly in recent years, and by the year 2007 it accounted for about 8 percent of total advertising spending in the United States and 4 percent worldwide. Although this represents a significant amount of funds upon which to base Internet business models, it has not yet taken significant amounts from other advertising expenditures on specific media, with the exception of about one-third of the total volume of classified advertising in U.S. newspapers. In most cases advertisers have used other marketing funds or increased advertising expenditures in moving to the Web, but they may begin allocating funds that were previously used for other advertising in the future.

DEMAND AND PRICING OF ADVERTISING

The needs of manufacturers, service providers, and retailers drive the need for advertising and those needs fluctuate depending upon the extent of product supply and consumers purchases. Because of the dynamics of the market, supply and demand are rarely equal and this produces periods in which more or less advertising is necessary.

In addition advertisers have periods during which the majority of their commerce occurs that affect the extent to which they advertise. Although sales of groceries and other basic household products remain relatively stable throughout the year, retailers of other goods have periods when higher sales

FIGURE 7-3   Percent of global advertising spending by area, 2006

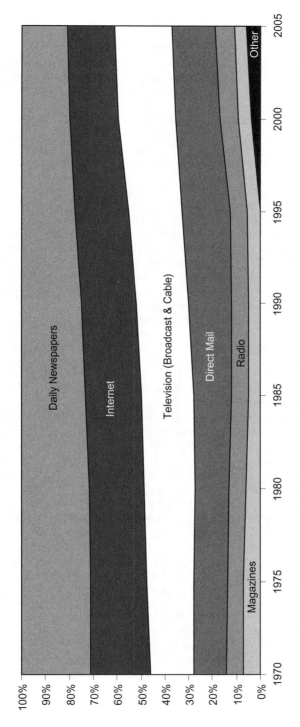

FIGURE 7-4 Shares of U.S. advertising expenditures by media, 1970–2005

Advertising on the Web

Online advertising is developing a different approach than that found in traditional media. This new approach developed because of advertisers' unease with the penetration rates of Internet services in the population and because of difficulties in measuring audience size and characteristics.

In traditional media, in which future audience sizes and characteristics can be predicted at the time of sale, a simple fee for agreed-upon amounts of time, space, or audience rating is the norm. As Internet advertising began to take hold, major Internet portal companies such as Yahoo!, AOL, MSN, and Google began offering similar types of arrangements to manufacturers, retailers, and e-retailers. Because interest in the Internet was strong and major portal and topic sites generated significant use, they were well positioned to induce many companies to sign advertising contracts at fairly high rates and, in some cases, to accept multiyear contracts. Sites with fewer users were not able to command such high fees and could only offer relatively low rates based on the number of page views. As a result they began to seek new ways of charging advertisers based on the interactive aspects of Web sites and many advertisers found these to be attractive offers.

Some sites began carrying clients' ads and taking transactions fees of 3 to 12 percent for e-commerce generated, while others began to offer flat-rate fees or fees based on the number of click-throughs. Over time these have had the effect of creating strong support for performance-based fees in online advertising. Today, about half of all revenue results from a pay-per-performance model and half from a CPM impressions model. Advertising prices based on performance are relatively high, whereas prices for CPM impressions are relatively low.

As much as 70 percent of online advertising inventory (advertising slots) is unsold at any time, so many sites turn to ad sales networks that broker advertising on hundreds of sites to fill the slots at a low price. Some of the largest sites, such as ESPN.com, however, have begun to refuse dealing with networks in order to gain more control over the types of advertising and to target advertising to their users more carefully. Other sites such as MSN, Yahoo!, You Tube, and Facebook are investing heavily in proprietary ad serving and targeting technology in order to be able to improve the value of advertising delivery.

Because of the increasing interest in the Internet as an advertising vehicle, overall online advertising expenditures in the United States grew to $21.2 billion in 2007 (see Figure 7-5), and has been growing at an average annual rate of about 30 percent for several years. Today, U.S. online advertising represents about two-thirds of all online expenditures worldwide.

About 40 percent of the revenue comes from payments to influence search engines and for keyword listings, about 20 percent for display advertisements, and about 15 percent for classified listings. General consumer product and services, financial services, computer and software products, telecom services, and media companies are now the largest online advertisers.

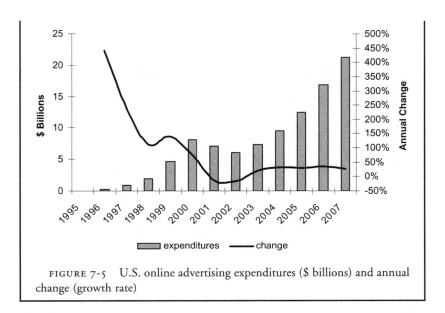

FIGURE 7-5   U.S. online advertising expenditures ($ billions) and annual change (growth rate)

take place. In some months, auto sales, home sales, clothing sales, and gift purchases are higher and retailers increase advertising during these times.

In addition, business cycles and economic developments affect advertising demand. When economies slow, advertisers receive less income and, consequently, tend to reduce their advertising expenditures. Because of the differences in types of advertisers and advertising carried among media, print media advertising tends to be reduced more as economies slow than broadcast media.

There is a relationship between the size of media audiences and advertising rates because advertisers of products and services intended for general use are willing to pay more to reach larger groups of people. Although other factors influence demand, the size of the audience is generally seen as the primary factor in the pricing of advertising space or time.

Because advertisers are seeking access to audiences and larger audiences tend to serve the needs of the largest advertisers, as well as many smaller firms, the price of advertising rises with audience size when the size or length of an ad, placement, and discounts are equalized.

Another relationship linked to price and audience size involves the cost per person. It is generally understood that this cost declines with increasing audience size, but the decline is not continuous.

The relationships between advertising prices and audience size can be seen in Figure 7-6, using a newspaper industry illustration. The figure illustrates that cost of advertising rises with circulation but that cost per

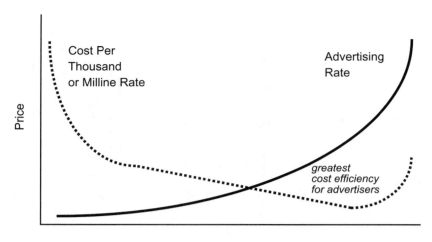

FIGURE 7-6   Relationships between advertising price and newspaper circulation (Source: Robert G. Picard, "A Note on the Relations Between Circulation Size and Newspaper Advertising Rates," *Journal of Media Economics*, 11(2):47–55, 1998.)

thousand persons as measured in milline rate (cost per line per million circulation) declines to a point and then rises. It reveals that advertisers' ability to achieve the greatest cost efficiency occurs in a relatively small area to the right of the point at which advertising rates and cost per thousand cross but before cost per thousand rises. Similar dynamics exist for other general-content mass media such as television and general consumer magazines.

For media with specialized audiences, advertisers are willing to pay a higher cost per thousand than available in mass media because the media are able to deliver audiences with specific characteristics that the advertising may be targeting. Thus, a manufacturer of snowboarding equipment will be willing to pay a higher cost per thousand to advertise in a snowboarding magazine than in a general magazine because the snowboarding magazine delivers an audience committed to the manufacturer's product and thus increases the effectiveness of the ad.

MEDIA SUBSTITUTION BY ADVERTISERS

Because of the different types of audiences delivered and the characteristics of messages that can be carried in various media, media tend to coexist rather than directly compete for advertiser expenditures.

Little real estate advertising is carried on radio and television, for example, because print media provides a better ability to convey information about specific homes and buildings available for sale or lease. Similarly, major fast food restaurants tend to use broadcast media rather than newspapers to convey their messages because the messages are primarily brand images, which are conveyed best through the audio and visual characteristics and repetition possibilities of television and radio.

In addition, the choice of which media to use tends not to change based on the prices offered. Price changes in television advertisers, for example, do not have a significant effect on demand for direct mail. And changes in the prices of Internet advertising do not have a significant effect on demand for radio advertising.

This is not to say that substitutability of media among advertisers does not exist, but the substitutability tends to be over the long term rather than the short term. Direct mail, for example, has become a growing choice for newspaper advertisers as household penetration of newspapers has declined. Cable television became a substitute for television advertising as cable penetration and audiences increased.

Advertiser substitution of media products, then, tends to involve media with similar types of production forms and functions rather than all media equally.

Within specific media markets there is often a must-buy phenomenon that reduces the choices available to advertisers and reduces the amount of money that can be spent in other advertising media. For example, the size of the audience or the qualities of the audience offered may require an advertiser to use a particular advertising medium or outlet as their primary choice.

For advertisers marketing to mass consumers, media or media units that reach the biggest audience become must-buys. For advertisers marketing to specialized or niches of consumers, media or media units that reach the greatest amount of those consumers become must-buys. In these cases, access to the target audience becomes the primary factor in demand rather than price.

The end result of this requisite purchase of advertising in a dominant medium is the reduction of funds available for advertising in other media or units of the same medium. As previously noted, no one media or media unit can perfectly serve an advertiser's needs and they must typically seek a media mix to serve their purposes effectively. When the advertising budget is constrained by the must-buy phenomenon, an advertiser is forced to diminish the amount of advertising expenditures used to achieve the mix, to reduce the number of media in the mix, or to reduce the outlets of each media in the mix from which advertising space or time is purchased.

MEDIA AS ADVERTISERS

Media themselves are increasingly becoming advertisers. In the past, media rarely purchased paid advertisements, relying primarily upon nonpaid promotional ads internal to their own media product, along with some point-of-purchase promotion and direct-mail marketing. This occurred because competition was typically limited in media markets and markets were saturated. As a result, making advertising expenditures produced few results.

In recent years, increases in the number of television and cable channels, radio stations, magazine titles, and online companies have produced heavier competition for audience time and monetary expenditures. Declining household penetrations for newspapers have also produced efforts to stabilize and increase readership. These factors have led to increases in purchased advertisements in other media and are making media not only purveyors but consumers of advertising services.

SUGGESTED READINGS

Avery, Jim, and Bruce Bendinger. 2000. *Advertising Campaign Planning.* 3rd ed. Chicago: Copy Workshop.

Davis, Joel J. 1997. *Advertising Research: Theory and Practice.* Upper Saddle River, N.J.: Prentice-Hall.

Jones, John Philip. 1999. *The Advertising Business: Operations, Creativity, Media Planning, Integrated Communications.* London: Sage Publications.

Parente, Donald. 2005. *Advertising Campaign Strategy: A Guide to Marketing Communication Plans.* Florence, Ky.: South-Western College Publishing.

Reekie, W. Duncan. 1981. *The Economics of Advertising.* London: Macmillan.

Schmalensee, Richard. 1981. *Economics of Advertising.* Amsterdam: North-Holland.

Schultz, Don E., and Beth E. Barnes. 1995. *Strategic Advertising Campaigns.* 4th ed. Lincolnwood, Ill.: NTC Business Books.

CHAPTER 8

Competition in Media Markets

Competition in media markets represents the rivalry of media firms to provide products and services. Many media managers believe their firms face high competition in their product markets but, in reality, the competition they face is relatively moderate or low, depending upon their product and location. By comparison to other industries, the degree of competition among media products is not very high because of limited choice. In many cases, competition is noticeably low.

Media firms face little product competition by comparison with producers of undifferentiated agricultural products such as milk or pork and lower competition than that faced by dishwashing detergent manufacturers, shoe retailers, and beer producers. This is illustrated by the fact that the number of pizzerias in the United States is sixty times higher than the number of newspapers, there are three times as many soft drink brands as cable channels, and there are five times as many ice cream shops as consumer magazines.

The perception of heavy competition in media industries has developed in the past few decades as social, technology, and policy changes have increased the number of media and direct competitors and altered the relatively secure and profitable media markets and structures of past decades. These have created new choices for audiences and advertisers and have raised the level of competition felt by media and communications firms significantly.

Thus, direct competition among media, such as newspaper versus newspaper or magazine versus magazine, is really not very high. However, overall media competition for audience time and advertisers' expenditures is high, especially when close substitutes are involved, as is competition for resources such as capital and technology, and competition to be the market leader.

Nevertheless, the levels of competition experienced by media companies are constrained because of differences in technologies, formats, and audience use patterns, as well as product differentiation and differences in geographic markets served by firms.

COMPETITION AND MARKET POWER

A market exists where companies provide the same or highly substitutable goods to the same group of consumers. In media terms this means that firms that produce and disseminate similar types of media products to users in the same location operate within the same market. This chapter, however, shows the limitations on the degree to which media firms compete in markets and that a number of factors limit substitutability of media goods and services.

The characteristics of media markets and the effectiveness with which they work are determined by a number of factors, including the number of media users, their temporal and monetary expenditures, the number of media firms, cost structures of the firms, barriers to entry, product differentiation, and a variety of other factors.

Historically, markets have been local and national but they are increasingly becoming international as well. However, all media do not participate in the potential markets or seek access to all potential audiences. In the United States, for example, 99 percent of cities are served by only one daily newspaper. The newspapers in these cities focus on their home market and do not attempt to compete in the other cities. Similarly, there are 210 television markets. Television stations broadcasting in one market do not compete in other markets, so their direct competition is limited to the other stations in the market in which they operate.

Also, the size of markets varies widely depending upon the size of the metropolitan area or city encompassed by the market. Most markets are small to mid-sized and the number of competitors serving them is constrained by the economies of the markets. Some markets are very large and media in them experience much stronger competition because those markets can support many more competitors. The top ten cities in the United States, for example, account for one-third of the nation's population (see Table 8-1), and the top twenty-five markets account for nearly half.

Within markets there are different levels of competition, and the degree to which any firm or small group of firms controls or influences activities such as pricing and production affects the effectiveness with which that

New York	7%
Los Angeles	6%
Chicago	3%
Washington/Baltimore	3%
San Francisco	3%
Philadelphia	2%
Boston	2%
Detroit	2%
Dallas/Ft. Worth	2%
Houston	2%

market operates. The more market power that any firm has the less effectively a market operates, thus making it possible to do harm to competitors and consumers.

As noted above, the degree of power is related to the level of competition present, but it is also affected by the level of dominance of leading firms. In a market with ten television stations, for example, if any one firm gains 40 percent of the viewers, it can effectively control much of the market's activities. This occurs because the leading firm becomes a must-buy for advertisers. If they want to reach the largest portion of the viewing audience, they are forced to purchase advertising at the price set by the leading television station, which, in turn, provides the station with financial resources to obtain and produce more desirable programming to continue as the leading station. At the same time, the must-buy expenditure reduces the amount of advertising budgets available for other purchases. Ultimately, this reduces the financial resources available to the station's competitors, diminishes their ability to obtain desirable programming, reduces their profitability, and can even result in bankruptcy.

Although it is not illegal to become successful or reap the harvest of that success, competition agencies and policy makers seek to ensure that market power is not used illicitly or cannot develop to the point that it damages markets. Antitrust regulations are used to limit a wide variety of activities that harm markets through the creation or damaging use of market power. This includes actions against mergers or acquisitions that create high market power, predatory pricing, and other anticompetitive behavior. Legislative bodies and regulatory agencies often place limits on the number of media units owned, crossownership, and percentages of audiences served by media firms as a means of constraining the development of unhealthy market power that limits competition.

PRODUCT AND AUDIENCE DIFFERENTIATION CONSTRAINS COMPETITION

Product differentiation is a strategy used by firms to make their products unique or have different properties than those of competitors. This process is designed to reduce the substitutability among products and limit the level of competition they encounter because the differentiated products are no longer equal choices.

In media, differentiation tends to focus on choices involving content, the time when content is made available, and production choices. Such differentiation gives firms a means of targeting specific audience groups based on demographics, place of media use, and sales methods. Even simple differences in design and presentation tone are widely used in print media to create publications that appeal to different audiences. This is seen in the differences between broadsheet and tabloid newspapers such as the *Times* of London and *The Daily Mirror* and *The New York Times* and *The New York Post*. It is also illustrated by the differences between women's magazines such as *Cosmopolitan* and *Woman's Day*.

Media can also choose to differentiate themselves by the characteristics of the audience they want to attract. One medium or media unit may choose to attract general audiences whereas another may decide to seek a well-defined and narrow audience. A magazine, for example, may seek an audience of male music lovers, who are between the ages of thirty-five and fifty-five, who earn high incomes, and who live in urban areas only in the northeastern portion of the country. In order to attract a differentiated audience, all personnel in the media company will have a clear understanding of that audience and the activities of the editorial, marketing, advertising, and circulation departments must all work to serve and reach that target audience.

The number of differentiation choices available to media managers depends on the variety of elements related to content, format, sales, and distribution that can be controlled. Thus, the degrees to which differentiation strategies can exist depend upon the characteristics of the media and markets. Some of the types of choices that can be made in creating strategies for different media are shown in Table 8-2.

A product differentiation strategy obviously influences the audience reached and an audience differentiation strategy influences the product offered, so both strategies must be coordinated and pursued simultaneously.

The Relevant Market

The relevant markets of media firms are increasingly becoming the focus of discussions of regulators and policy makers worldwide as they respond to increasing crossmedia activities, consolidation, and globalization. Central to the discussions is the definition of the relevant market for media and media products and services. The debate is not merely semantic; its results will be crucial in determining the form of legal and regulatory measures and actions taken by competition and trade authorities.

In economic terms markets are recognized as consisting of sellers that provide the same good or service, or closely substitutable goods or services, to the same group of consumers. When applied to analyses for public purposes, this general concept is refined to include a specific relevant market for a product or service and a geographic area in which exchange takes place. It thus recognizes that there are many markets and that participants may be active in only some, or many, markets individually or simultaneously. Advertising-supported media, for example, compete in two markets because of their dual product characteristics. When they compete, they may compete with others in both the audience market and advertising market, only in the audience markets, only in the advertising market, or only in part of the advertising market.

The coexistence of a wide variety of media and audience use patterns that involve multiple media tends to indicate that the degree of substitutability among media is imperfect. Competing media firms often seek niches within media types as a strategy to further limit substitutability. The availability of media units, product strategies, and a variety of other factors influence substitutability, and the determination of which media are included in the relevant product market in economic terms is unique to each situation.

In contemporary relevant market debates there are difficulties assessing the extent of crossmedia activities and how they affect the relevant market. A newspaper, for example, may be distributed only in a single city, but its web site and mobile services may be available nationally and internationally. Such issues come to prominence if the company owning that paper wants to have a television station in another city or at the national level, raising questions about whether the purchase would reduce competition.

In recent years, media-specific policy approaches to relevant markets have appeared in some nations. These approaches tend to use broader product and geographic market definitions that exclude or ignore economic determinations of the existence of markets and assert the presence of markets. In this approach, there is a tendency to view media as single rather than dual products and to use geopolitical definitions of markets. In this frame of reference, policy makers tend to define the relevant market in terms of the television market in a nation (including both national and local television as competitors) or the newspaper market in a province or state (including daily, nondaily, and free publications). These approaches exist in countries such as Germany and the United Kingdom.

	Product Differentiation	*Audience Differentiation*

Radio Stations	Programming offered:
	  Music (rock, jazz,
	  classical, urban, etc.)
	  News
	  Talk
	  Sports
	Broadcast time:
	  Length of day
	  Counterprogramming
	Language use
		Target listeners:
		  General
		  Demographic group
		Place of use:
		  Home
		  Office
		  Commuting
		Segmentation by
		  program
		Geographic location of
		  audience

Magazines	Product type:
	  Consumer
	  Trade/professional
	Content type:
	  General interest
	  Specialized interest
	Frequency
	Language use
	Production choices:
	  Size
	  Inks
	  Paper
		Target readers:
		  General
		  Demographic group
		  Interest group
		Geographic location of
		  audience:
		  Zoned editions
		  State/regional magazines
		  National magazines
		Sales method:
		  Subscription
		  Single copy
		  Both

Newspapers	Distribution time
	Editorial orientation:
	  Coverage
	  News focus
	  Presentation tone
	  Readability level
	  Graphic/photo use
	Production choices:
	  Size
	  Inks
	  Paper
		Target readers:
		  Mass
		  Specialized
		Place of use:
		  Home
		  Office
		  Commuting
		Geographic location
		  of audience:
		  Local
		  Zoned editions
		  Statewide
		  National
		Sales method:
		  Subscription
		  Single copy
		  Both

	Product Differentiation	*Audience Differentiation*
Television/Cable Networks or Channels	Programming offered: Variety Specialized Sports Movies Music Lifestyle Cultural Broadcast time: Length of day Counterprogramming Language use	Target listeners: General Demographic group Segmentation by program Geographic location of audience

The ability to differentiate content in multiple ways is being heightened by information and communications technologies. This is increasingly allowing media firms to personalize content to the interests and needs of specific customers or customer groups and for customers to request specific types of content. The primary media taking advantage of these abilities today are magazines and online content providers, but television service firms are expected to take advantage of the possibility when digital television penetration and broadband distribution capabilities increase.

THE ROLE OF GEOGRAPHIC MARKETS

Geographic markets are particularly important in understanding competition involving media because of the strong links of audiences and advertisers to particular locations. As noted in Chapter 7, advertisers need to reach specific audiences that are often defined by geographic locations adjacent to stores they operate or geographic areas in which their products or services are distributed to retailers.

Thus, different types of media and different units of the same medium tend to provide services intended for specific geographic markets. In the magazine industry, for example, a national publication devoted to travel and tourism will include content on domestic and worldwide possibilities and attract readers nationally and advertisers nationally and globally. Another travel magazine, however, will target a region or a state for its coverage, readers, and advertisers. Still another publisher may produce a local travel or tourism magazine for a city filled with local content and local advertising, and intended for persons who visit or live in that city.

Geographic markets are critical to the survival of multiple media units because they make it possible for multiple media units to exist without competing with each other. This is seen in the fact that there are about 12,000 radio stations in the United States. These stations, however, are spread throughout the country and the number that can be readily received within any one city is limited and exceeds two dozen in only a small number of metropolitan areas.

Geographic markets also limit the degree of substitutability of media products. *USA Today*, for example, is a national newspaper available in all fifty states and internationally. That paper does not provide the range or types of news coverage necessary to understand the events and developments in the community in which a reader lives, however, and it cannot provide useful access to the readers that most local advertisers want to reach.

The degree of competition experienced in any market can change if market conditions are altered. In general, competition increases whenever new competitors enter the market, when the number of competitors is high, when the market is well divided among the competitors, when the market involves undifferentiated products, and when the market is mature or growing slowly.

In media markets, competition tends to be increased if the content provided is similar, if audiences can easily choose among competitors' content, and if advertisers can gain access to similar audiences with different media products.

BENEFITS OF COMPETITIVE ADVANTAGES

Competitive advantages are factors that give one firm advantages over another in a competitive situation. These advantages exist only for a limited period of time, however, because competition is dynamic and constantly evolving. There are always new products and new market strategies put in place by competitors, and unless a firm is constantly working to capitalize upon and maintain advantages, these competitive advantages can be lost.

Advantages arise from constant efforts to improve the performance of firms and upgrade products and services. In order to achieve advantages, a firm needs an internal atmosphere and value system that support change and innovation.

Competitive advantages include the ability to produce the product or service less expensively than competitors. For example, book printers in nations such as the United States or Germany tend to have higher cost structures because of labor, social costs, and taxes than book printers in Singapore or Mexico.

As previously noted, product differentiation is a method of reducing competition but it also is a competitive advantage, especially for differentiated products commanding a high price in a segmented market. Bang & Olufsen audio systems, for example, have competitive advantages related to their design innovation and differentiation over other audio products.

Another advantage is a proprietary asset such as a specialized process, technique, or patent that is not available to other providers of the good or service. Quality is also a competitive advantage when consumers perceive one product or service as providing higher quality. Other advantages come through advanced features and innovations, more efficient production that reduces costs and the ability to develop new products more rapidly so that a company can respond to changes in demand faster than competitors. A television channel that can control its programming production methods so that it can commission and begin broadcasting a new program within six months, for example, has distinct advantages over a channel that requires twelve to twenty-four months to do so.

BRANDS AND BRANDING AID IN COMPETITION

The concepts of brand and branding are increasingly associated with media products and services, but their use is often merely the use of a contemporary industry buzzword rather than one of understanding of the competitive advantages of a brand and its further use. Branding and the development of brands are not merely marketing practices and process, but strategic activities that can add value to the product or service and require significant thought and resource allocation to achieve.

The concept of brands has moved into communications from the retail and service industries, where it has been used to induce customers to purchase a variety of vegetables available under the Green Giant brand, because of the brand's image of freshness, size, and high quality. Branding is also used to build preferences for services such as Federal Express delivery services through creating and supporting an image of speed and reliability.

Brands are names or designs that help distinguish products and convey attributes or images of the product that are designed to attract and maintain customers. Both users and nonusers of a product and service recognize effective brands. The importance of brands is shown in that strong brands for retail products and services maintain loyalty, are linked to repeat purchases, and give advantages to the firm as it grows. Having a strong brand is especially important to a firm as the number of competitors increases, so it is no accident that the concept was adopted in the media and communication industries as the number of competitors exploded at the end of the twentieth century.

Although new to many media firms, branding has been used for many years in the magazine industry, where it was first introduced in the internationalization of magazine titles. *Reader's Digest*, for example, established the title in many nations in local languages, taking steps to ensure that its editorial profile of stories on human triumphs, condensed readings, clean humor, and inspirational readings were maintained across the titles despite localization of the content.

In addition to the names of the product or service, media companies have made a variety of uses of sub-branding. American Broadcasting Company was one of the first to do so when it branded its Friday night programming using "TGIF Friday" to brand a family-friendly evening of programming that could be marketed as a package rather than individual programs. Later, National Broadcasting Company (NBC) attempted the same by introducing "Must See TV" for its Thursday night lineup and Discovery Channel branded "Shark Week" for an annual week of programming devoted to documentaries about sharks and a related web site.

Branding can also use a variety of techniques to separate some products from others visually. The *Financial Times* newspaper, for example, uses salmon-colored paper to help rapidly identify it on newsstands so that observers recognize the paper when they see other persons reading it. Visual branding is used to carry the image across multiple media products. NBC, for example, uses its well-recognized color peacock across its products, including the NBC Network, CNBC, and MSNBC, thus conveying the strengths of the brand image to all its products.

Brand images are best established, developed, and maintained when companies consistently strive to solidify the images in all production, distribution, marketing, and customer service activities and by communicating the image in all marketing activities, including logos, slogans, advertising, sales promotion, and direct marketing.

Brands can also be extended to include more than the original product under a brand name and image. This provides particular competitive advantages to firms launching new products or services because it encompasses the secondary product or service with the same brand identity of the established primary product or service.

ESPN, the leading cable sports channel, expanded its brand by starting a second cable channel ESPN2 to carry even more live events. It then expanded its brand through the establishment of regional sports networks such as ESPN West to provide more intense regional coverage and ensure that regional team games could be viewed even if they were not on its national channels. The firm further expanded its brands with the establishment of ESPN Classic Sports to rerun excellent games it had previously covered on its live networks. Ultimately, it moved out of cable to establish the *ESPN* sports magazine, ESPN sports radio network, and an ESPN on-line operation.

The French magazine *Marie Claire* expanded its products by transferring its editorial profile of fashion and living coverage for affluent working women to national editions published in countries ranging from the United Kingdom to Japan. It also began brand expansion into other magazines on related topics such as *Marie Claire Maison*, a home magazine designed for the same readers as its primary magazine.

Brand extension can be a successful way to more easily establish and develop audiences for new media products. However, managers of media firms must be careful with brand extension because it loses effectiveness when products and services embraced by the brand are less central to the core brand identity or if lower-quality products or services are encompassed that weaken the brand image of the original product or service.

In addition to their competitive effects, development of strong brands has significant financial effects on the companies because strong brand equity translates into asset value on company balance sheets.

COMPETITION AMONG AND BETWEEN MEDIA

The nature and structure of media markets and the kinds of products provided influence the degree of competition each firm faces. Because true monopolies are rare in media today, competition among media units ranges from low to moderate to fierce depending upon the market. The fiercest

---

"Law & Order" as a Brand

"Law & Order" is not only the longest-running crime series on U.S. television but one of its strongest brands that created a strong relationship between Wolf Films and NBC Universal. The New York–based crime series was created by Dick Wolf, premiered in fall 1990, and features both the investigation and prosecution of a crime.

The success of the show led to the 1999 spinoff "Law & Order: Special Victims Unit" that follows the investigation of sexually based crimes and crimes against children and then "Law & Order: Criminal Intent" that follows the major case squad using psychologically based approaches to solving crimes. The program premiered in fall 2001.

In 2007, French and Russian versions of "Law & Order: Criminal Intent" were established. The French edition "Enquêtes criminelles" is set in Paris and airs on TF1. The Russian version is set in Moscow.

The success of the series established earlier helped pave the way for the launch and success of subsequent series, and the success of the U.S. series generated interested in adopting the format and title in other countries.

---

competition tends to arise when there are many firms, low entry barriers, and less product differentiation, and these can have negative effects on content by reducing available resources (see Table 8-3).

As competition grows stronger, strategic choices available to companies diminish and competition typically moves from product differentiation and quality choices to competitive actions designed to lower costs and price and to compete with others for the largest and most desirable audience and consumer groups. Ultimately, the only way to prosper in this environment is to be the leader in low costs and to undertake portfolio strategies of operating multiple titles or channels and process strategies designed to streamline and create the most efficient operations possible.

Competition among and between media can be understood as intermedia and intramedia competition. Intermedia competion involves the competition that takes place among different types of media such as television and radio, whereas intramedia competition involves competition among units of the same medium, such as two radio stations. The two occur simultaneously as illustrated in Figure 8-1. Intramedia competition, such a competition among satellite television channels, takes place within the overall intermedia competition among all media types.

INTERMEDIA COMPETITION

In the content product market, intermedia competition primarily involves competition for the attention and time of audiences and sometimes for expenditures by consumers. The competition among media is not equal, however, because of wide differences in availability and demand factors. As

TABLE 8-3 · COMPETITIVE STRUCTURE AND COMPETITIVE CONDUCT IN MEDIA

Competition	Structure	Conduct
Moderate	Small number of media organizations with significant market power	Product innovation
		Strategy is based on product rather than price
	High barriers to entry and exit	
	Media operate in market niches	Efforts are made to attract different groups of consumers
Fierce	Many media organizations (some of them rivals for the same audience)	Process innovation
		Strategy based on price
	Low barriers to entry and exit	
	Absence of economically significant market niches	Following public preferences, competing for the same (mostly dominant) audience group with other media

FIGURE 8-1   Intermedia and intramedia competition

shown in Chapter 6, these factors produce wide differences in the penetration of media in average households, in the amount of time that is allotted for use of different media, and in the purposes for using different media. These factors limit the degree to which different media directly compete, and it is useful to think of the existing competition in broader terms of gaining a portion of the overall use of different types of audiences.

In the market for providing access to audiences for advertisers, competition is limited by audience acquisition and use issues and also by the characteristics of different media and their ability to deliver certain types of advertising messages. As a result of such factors, intermedia competition is constrained, and advertisers typically purchase advertising in more than one type of media. The primary competition among media almost always involves the size of the share of the advertiser's expenditures rather than an all-or-nothing choice among media.

A useful general rule for understanding audience and advertiser competition is that the more common characteristics there are among media the more intermedia competition will exist. Thus, audiovisual content delivered by terrestrial television channels will experience more competition with content delivered by satellite systems than a magazine will with content delivered by radio broadcasts. These differences, however, are being eroded as more and more physical products and services move some of their operations into electronic format for online distribution (see Figure 8-2). In doing so, they also alter the amount of competition that they traditionally faced.

INTRAMEDIA COMPETITION

The highest levels of competition for audiences and advertisers' expenditures take place among units of the same medium, particularly if they serve the same audiences in the same location. Two Internet portals serving the same metropolitan region, for example, will be engaged in heavier competition than two portals that operate in separate metropolitan markets because

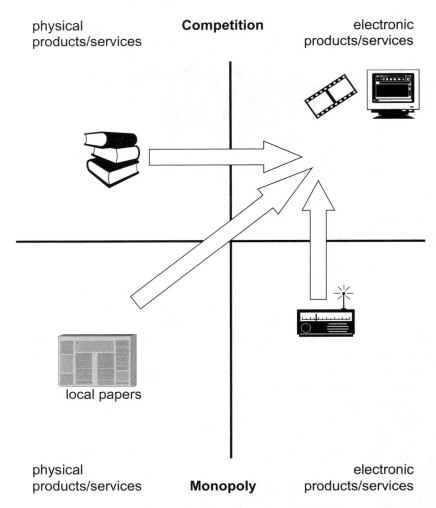

physical products/services   **Competition**   electronic products/services

local papers

physical products/services   **Monopoly**   electronic products/services

FIGURE 8-2   Limitations on competition are eroded by digitalization and the movement from physical form

of the choices of local users and advertisers. Similarly, a radio station operating in a market with twenty stations will face far greater intramedia competition than if only ten stations existed in that same market.

The nature of intramedia competition is determined within specific markets and the number of competitors, the population, the number of potential advertisers, and the degree of market power held by market leaders must be considered in each individual case. As noted above, twenty radio stations face greater competition than ten stations in one market, but another market with ten stations may have greater competition than that market with twenty stations because of differences in the market characteristics.

Managers and observers who want to comprehend the nature of media markets need to accurately assess the amount and degree of competition among units of the same medium and media as a whole. With that knowledge they can then develop appropriate strategies and make informed choices that limit the competition, use advantages available to them, and make them more effective in their competition against others.

SUGGESTED READINGS

Chan-Olmsted, Sylvia. 2006. *Competitive Strategy for Media Firms: Strategic and Brand Management in Changing Media Markets*. Mahwah, N.J.: Lawrence Erlbaum.

Compaine, Benjamin M., and Douglas Gomery. 2000. *Who Owns the Media: Competition and Concentration in the Mass Media Industry*, 3rd ed. Mahwah, N.J.: Lawrence Erlbaum.

Eastman, Susan Tyler, and Douglas A. Ferguson. 2008. *Media Programming: Strategies and Practices*. Belmont, Calif.: Wadsworth Publishing.

Koff, Richard M. 1987. *Strategic Planning for Magazine Executives*. Stamford, CT: Folio Magazine Publishing.

Küng, Lucy. 2008. *Strategic Management in the Media: Theory and Practice*. London: Sage Publications.

MacFarland, David T. 1997. *Future Radio Programming Strategies*. 2nd ed. Mahweh, N.J.: Lawrence Erlbaum Associates.

Norberg, Eric G. 1996. *Radio Programming Tactics and Strategy*. Woburn, Mass.: Focal Press.

Porter, M. E. 1985. *Competitive Advantage: Creating and Sustaining Superior Performance*. New York: Free Press.

Todreas, Timothy M. 1999. *Value Creation and Branding in Television's Digital Age*. New York: Quorum Books..

Tungate, M. 2004. *Media Monoliths—How Great Media Brands Thrive and Survive*. London: Kogan Page.

Wilkinson, Earl J. 1998. *Branding and the Newspaper Consumer*. Dallas: International Newspaper Marketing Association.

CHAPTER 9

Concepts in Media Financing and Financial Management

Financing involves meeting the monetary needs of a firm so that it may be established, operated, and developed. Issues of financing range from creating sufficient funds to establish a firm, to obtaining money to pay for operations, to gathering funds to invest in growth.

Certain types of financing tend to be available only at particular stages in company or product development. Those intent on creating and developing companies need to understand the constraints and relations that result from seeking capital at different stages.

The research stage represents the point at which ideas are pursued and elements that are necessary to make them into workable products and services are brought together to determine whether the product or service can be effectively produced and offered.

Media companies are rarely active in basic research; they typically leave such efforts to suppliers and other hardware firms and then later find ways to exploit new communications inventions. The primary types of research done in media firms involves market research to improve the effectiveness of marketing existing media products or to find markets for new products such as a new magazine, cable channel, or online service.

During the research stage, cash flow is negative because nothing is being sold and producing a source of revenue. As a result, this process is typically carried out by investors or in the research and development activities of companies and funded by those individuals and firms. Without the investment of that funding and support, the equipment, personnel, and supply costs necessary for the research could not be carried out.

After research is completed, efforts must be made to develop the concept into a workable product or service. The development stage includes assembling the personnel and equipment needed and then preparing the product or service to be offered to the public, and creating the managerial or company structure for its operation. This stage includes the preparation of an introductory issue of a new magazine, the construction and preparation of a new radio station, and the preparation of content and planning for marketing and operation of a new web site.

During the development stage, in which the negative cash flow continues because nothing is being sold, funding typically comes from the entrepreneur or company involved or from venture capital firms. Very little outside funding has traditionally been available for media firms at this stage. In recent years, however, a number of venture capitalists and public-private joint ventures have created *new media incubators* in the United States and Europe to help fund the creation of new products and services and to provide a variety of managerial and marketing services and expertise to start-up firms.

The third stage is the introduction period, in which the new product or service is first offered to the public. During this stage, the company has a highly negative cash flow because it must be fully operational and make large marketing expenditures. There is no guarantee that the market will accept the product or service and the revenue stream develops slowly as the market initially responds.

At this stage, funding comes from the entrepreneur or parent companies and any trade credit the firm may obtain from suppliers. Unless the product or service has unusual potential for high returns, only a limited amount of venture capital or risk funds will be available because such investors tend to pursue products and services with high yield potential.

If a product or service survives its introduction, cash flow begins to become positive as the product gains acceptance and improvements are made. During this establishment stage, stock markets and some traditional lenders such as banks begin to make capital available to help fund growth of the firm and further exploitation of markets.

When the product has achieved broad acceptance and has become highly profitable, the firm can employ bond markets and a wide range of conservative lenders to obtain financing.

UNDERSTANDING FINANCIAL FLOW

Critical to understanding financial needs of media firms is an understanding of how money flows within and around firms. Figure 9-1 illustrates the flow

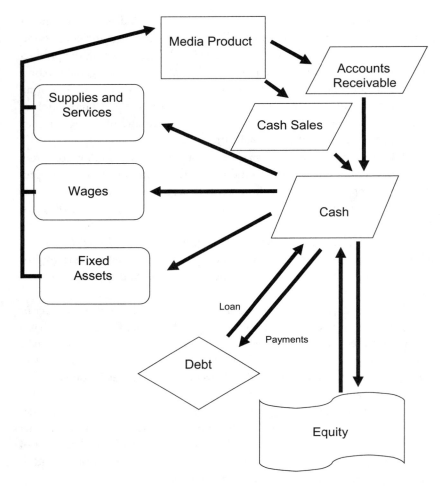

FIGURE 9-1   Financial flow in media with revenue from advertising and circulation

in a media firm and central to the flow is cash—money that is available to spend.

The money, of course, must have come from an original source and this may be the owner's contribution or debt. It is this cash that allows the firm to pay for facilities and equipment, labor, and supplies and services needed to produce the media product.

The media product is then sold to consumers and advertisers, producing cash through direct sales or accounts receivable. The money can be returned to the process to create the next issue of the media product.

Additional cash is used to make payment on debts and, if excess cash exists, returned to the equity of the owner.

The amount of money regularly returned to the production process depends upon the medium and management choices. Newspapers, magazines, and broadcasters must regularly return large portions of the cash obtained from sales to the production process because of the frequency of their operations. The amount returned, however, is more variable for book publishers and motion picture and multimedia producers, who tend to produce discrete separate products and must make specific decisions about what and when to produce.

PROBLEMS OF FINANCING A NEW FIRM OR PRODUCT

As noted above, the financing issue for new companies and products is very important because in the stages of research and development a company cannot count on income from consumers; and even though income begins to grow slowly in the introduction stage, it is generally insufficient to cover costs. This process is illustrated in Figure 9-2. Note that the company's cash flow is continuously negative during the initial stages; it begins to rise steadily if the introduction of the new product is successful and maturation occurs.

This is problematic for startup companies. It means that those intent on establishing firms must not only identify market needs that their companies will meet and have clear and reasonable business plans, but that they must

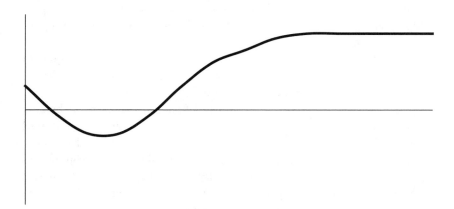

FIGURE 9-2   Cash flow during development and introduction of a new product or service

also have sufficient financial resources available to survive the period of negative cash flow.

The problem is compounded because the great majority of new businesses fail—sometimes because of poor financing, sometimes because of poor management, and sometimes because of market reasons. This risk makes such startup enterprises generally unattractive to investors.

As a result, most new businesses are financed out of the owner's savings, loans from relatives or in-laws, and occasionally with the support of small business loans that are backed by some governments and development authorities.

Media firms overall are not the most attractive ventures for startup and development financing because traditional media industries are not perceived as having the potential for growth. Most tend to be relatively unexciting to investors compared to high-tech, biotechnology, and other industries that are perceived as save investments for the future. The most attractive media-related firms today are those involved in online and other new media activities, despite problems in their current performance.

These perceptions are important because they mean that most media firms fall into traditional business analysis when it comes to financing and financial issues. Moreover, sources of venture capital and other forms of risk capital are not likely to see their potential for producing rapid growth through innovative products that can reward high-risk investment.

Media firms are also affected because most survive as small enterprises or can grow only to become mid-sized firms. Only a few develop into large firms.

The establishment pattern for media and communication firms, then, is to start as a traditional small firm built and operated with equity capital from their owners, with little credit or other financing available from suppliers and capital sources.

As the firms become more established and grow, they are able to obtain greater amounts of trade credit and secured loans that reduce their dependence upon revenue and their owners' financing.

These factors are important in terms of financial management because small firms tend to have more of their assets in cash, receivables, and fixed assets and less in fewer inventories than larger, more established firms do. Simultaneously they tend to have more of their liabilities in accounts payable and less net worth than more established and larger firms. This means those smaller firms have to pay greater attention to issues of working capital, to rapid collection of accounts, and to liquidity of assets.

Cash flow, however, is not only an issue for startup firms and small and mid-sized enterprises. Established and successful firms also face the negative cash flow problem when introducing new products. A record company, for example, will be spending money without offsetting income as it selects, records, masters, manufactures, distributes, and begins marketing a CD of a recording artist. When sales occur, revenue begins to offset the costs but initially not enough to pay for expenses. If the artist is successful, cash flow is no longer a problem and the company will benefit if it exceeds costs and reaches profitability.

The concern about negative cash flow during the introduction stage of new products is compounded by the introduction of upgraded products or multiple new products, because more than one product can have a negative cash flow simultaneously and create a significant drain on financial resources. If the company has insufficient cash resources it will run out of working capital before the new products have the opportunity to become successful, as illustrated in Figure 9-3.

The problem of insufficient working capital has been particularly difficult for emerging multimedia and software companies who must often introduce upgrades to their products or additional products before their initial products have become profitable. The same problem often presents difficulties for small independent book publishers and audio-visual producers.

In the late 1990s, however, because of the enthusiasm of venture capitalists and other investors for dot-com firms, many startup firms were able to obtain large infusions of capital by having their shares publicly traded or through other financial arrangements with investors. The sudden growth of financial resources in these firms led to a situation in which many managers with little experience managing cash believed their firms would never run out of cash, and this, in turn, led them to make mistakes that caused their firms to face financial crises and closure.

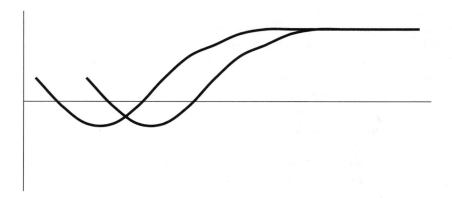

FIGURE 9-3   Cash flow during development and introduction of upgraded products and services

When a firm is established and cash flow has developed, it is still not unusual for revenue from sales to be insufficient to meet all the financial needs of the firm. For example, the firm may need to invest in expensive equipment or purchase buildings; or it may experience seasonal fluctuations in income that do not provide sufficient revenue during some parts of the year to cover operating expenses; or the firm may obtain an order that requires making a large initial expenditure that will only be recouped when the order is completed.

A DVD reproduction studio, for example, might receive a manufacturing order from a motion picture studio to produce 500,000 copies of a motion picture for sales and rental with payment being made upon delivery. This would require the reproduction studio to spend more than two million dollars on blank DVDs covers, employee time, and other costs prior to receiving its payment from the film company. Unless the firm already has sufficient cash to pay for those expenditures, it will need to find financing to cover the costs.

A magazine company may find that it obtains the bulk of its advertising revenue in two months during the spring and two months during the fall. If it has not reserved sufficient income from those months for the lean months, it may need to seek financing to pay expenses during some of the other eight months of the year.

CREDIT MANAGEMENT

Credit management in media firms involves controlling sales credit for customer purchases of advertising space and time, and service credit for purchases of subscriptions for media products by audiences.

Advertising sales account for the majority of income in most media firms. Purchases of advertising on credit create a need for significant attention to developments in those accounts. This need is particularly strong in commercial radio and television, newspapers, and most magazines. Cable systems and some magazines rely most heavily on sales of media products to consumers, and credit management in these firms tends to focus more on the customer accounts for services provided but for which payment has not yet been received. Because circulation sales are also important to newspapers, magazines, and cable companies, management of these customer accounts also receives attention in those industries.

Credit management involves deciding whether to issue sales or service credit, controlling the use of that credit, and collecting the accounts. Newspapers, magazines, and cable systems risk only a little money each time they

Obtaining Financing Through Secured Debt

When a company is new and not well established, or if an existing company's ability to pay off debts is uncertain, it is still sometimes possible to obtain financing for some activities by securing the debt with something of value that the lender can collect if the debt is not repaid.

Some common types of security are collateral, loans against inventory, and receivable assignment.

Collateral: Lenders secure debts with assets they believe have market value equal to or exceeding their loan. The lender receives a security agreement describing the collateral and it is filed with a public official giving notice of the lender's claim to the asset. Collateral includes assets that are fairly easily sold such as land and buildings, machinery and equipment, vehicles, and so on.

Inventory loans: If a firm is storing inventory that it has already purchased, that inventory has value and some inventory can be used as security on debt if it is deemed relatively imperishable and easily marketable. Depending upon the circumstances of the firm seeking a loan, there are a variety of arrangements in which the inventory can either be kept in the firm's storage facilities or moved to an independent facility.

Accounts receivable: Because these are liquid, current assets, the assignment of some accounts receivable are accepted for security on debt by lenders, typically for no more than about three-fourths of their value. Such financing is sometimes used to help firms fill unusually large orders for which they do not have sufficient internal resources or to increase cash on hand while awaiting payment from customers.

send issues or provide service to a customer who is billed after the service is provided. However, television stations, newspapers, magazines, and other media risk amounts totaling hundreds of thousands of dollars when they provide advertising services on credit to large advertisers or advertising agencies. As a result, these financial management functions are critical to the survival and profitability of media firms.

Many media companies operate unified credit departments to handle these functions. Some companies, however, choose to divide the credit functions among several departments. When a unified credit department exists, it may deal with both the advertising and media product sales credit. In other situations, typified by newspapers and magazines, the credit department will usually deal only with advertising sales credit. In these media, credit managers for the circulation departments typically handle subscription service credit.

In either case, those managers responsible for credit functions need to work closely with advertising and service sales departments to set policies and to ensure that credit activities help rather than hinder the overall marketing program of the company. Cooperation between the various departments is essential.

Some Important Types of Short-Term, Unsecured Debt

Media firms use a variety of arrangements to acquire capital for operations. Money used for this purpose is called *working capital.* If a firm does not have sufficient cash on hand in current assets and retained earnings and it is an established and credit-worthy firm, it may arrange several forms of short-term unsecured debt to acquire the working capital it needs for continuing operations.

Commercial loan: A commercial loan is designed to provide working capital to purchase supplies or finance production or distribution of products. It typically comes from a bank with whom the firm has a regular working relationship. It is a short-term loan, often ninety days, that is shown as a notes payable in the current liabilities section of the company's balance sheet.

Commercial paper: Large, well-established businesses, including some media conglomerates, have the ability to issue these unsecured promises to pay a debt and interest. Companies use these as a means of raising short-term cash at a rate lower than bank interest rates. Those who provide the cash in exchange for commercial paper benefit from greater flexibility in maturity dates than available in other investments. This allows them to invest excess cash for a short period of time.

Line of credit: This is a form of debt in which a bank and customer agree on an amount of credit that the firm may obtain to meet temporary cash needs or respond to seasonal variations in revenue. The agreement is usually made for a year and the customer usually pays for the creation of the line of credit, whether it is exercised or not.

Revolving credit: This type of credit between a bank and customer operates much like a credit card, with the customer borrowing and repaying up to a limit established by the bank and according to agreed-upon terms for interest and payment dates.

Trade credit: This is the most common type of debt for companies and is based on open accounts for goods and services from suppliers. This debt is a form of working capital extended to the firm by suppliers, because the firm can pay interest if it postpones payment of some or all of the account beyond the normal due date.

Regardless of the organization's structure and where responsibility for credit activities is located, credit management issues are similar. They involve credit evaluation and determination, credit risk management, and collection.

CREDIT EVALUATION

The decision to extend credit to a customer is made by evaluating the ability of the customer to pay for purchases made on credit and the willingness of the customer to pay as shown in past behavior involving credit purchases. Media managers use a variety of means by which to make such evaluations, including credit applications and credit investigations.

In some types of sales, no significant evaluations are made. This is particularly true in the case of service credit requests for cable service or subscriptions to newspapers or magazines. Little investigation is made because the credit for service between the time the order is placed and payment received is small and the cost of an investigation outweighs the potential loss.

Because the potential losses from unpaid advertising time or space is greater, credit managers spend a significant amount of time considering the credit worthiness of new advertisers by requiring them to provide information about themselves or seeking such information before extending credit.

In some cases, a credit manager may request a specific credit investigation beyond the information reported on the application. Because of the expense involved, this is usually done only with new customers who are expected to purchase significant amounts of advertising and who request extensive credit. Such investigations usually involve seeking reports from credit bureaus or credit databases. In some cases a major investigation may be warranted and involve significant analysis of the assets of firms as well.

When the credit manager obtains information about the firm, he or she can make a rational decision. Every firm has its own guidelines for determining whether to extend credit and how much to provide. Such determinations involve weighing the performance of the applicant in past credit arrangements and the financial strength and stability of the applicant. The credit manager uses information on the application form and from credit investigations to evaluate the credit worthiness of the applicant. There is no easy way to determine what credit to extend; credit managers typically base their policies for what is an appropriate amount of credit based on past experiences and industry guidelines.

Decisions to grant or refuse credit, of course, must be made in accordance with appropriate laws and regulations. Similarly, laws and common sense require that credit conditions and terms must be made clear in the credit applications, purchase orders, and billing statements. In most cases these include provisions for the assessment of late charges and collection.

CREDIT RISK MANAGEMENT

Risk management involves controlling and lowering the risk that the customers will not repay credit that has been extended. Although sales personnel have incentives to sell as much advertising and as many subscriptions as possible, credit managers must ensure that payment is received. Most managers help manage advertising sales credit by treating certain types of advertisers differently and placing special requirements upon some.

In the case of advertising, credit managers generally set credit limits for classes of advertisers, and companies are not allowed to make purchases above that limit. Limits are often set based on the amount of time the customer has been in business or a purchaser of advertising. Some credit managers establish limits based on the operating budgets of a firm or some other estimate of how much a firm should spend on advertising. When dealing with large, regular advertisers, managers usually set separate limits based on the companies' past performance in paying for advertising purchased on credit.

COLLECTION

Media firms make collection efforts internally and externally. Collections involve getting timely payments from customers who are slow in paying on their advertising sales credit or service credit accounts, and getting payments from customers who have not paid. The collection process begins whenever an account is billed and payment is not received by the due date.

Because media companies value customers, and a variety of factors may account for late payment, collections involve different and progressively coercive steps. Company employees make the initial steps but final collection efforts are often done outside the media firm. Sending an account outside the media company is generally considered the last resort for non-payment. Turning the account over to an attorney or collection agency is expensive because in many nations collection agencies keep as much as one-third or even half of what they collect as their fee.

A variety of national and state laws cover collection efforts, so persons engaging in collections internally and externally must be familiar with the range of permissible collection efforts and those activities that are forbidden.

If collection efforts fail, media companies may sue advertisers or persons responsible for accounts in courts of law. In reality, however, companies do so only when the amount of money owned warrants the additional costs of legal action.

BAD DEBT

When collection steps ultimately fail to generate payment, the company must deal with the account receivable that cannot be collected. In order to take it out of the accounting system, the uncollectable credit account is transferred to the bad debt account.

Media firms maintain bad debt accounts as a budgeted operating expense item. Obviously, it is in the interest of the firm to keep bad debt as low as possible because of its effects on operating expenses and the profitability of firms. Although bad debt losses are generally written off as tax-deductible business costs, the benefits of doing so are far outweighed by the costs. In order to help minimize bad debt, media credit managers track bad debt carefully and make regular comparisons to past performance as a means of evaluating collection effectiveness.

INTERNAL CREDIT MANAGEMENT REPORTS

In order for the manager to efficiently manage credit operations, he or she needs regular reports about the condition of accounts. Important management information is found in aging reports, delinquency reports, and bad debt reports. Many media companies have computer programs that automatically generate such information.

Aging reports provide a look at the status of all the accounts and provide data on credit outstanding, payments received, and payments due. Many companies use aging reports to produce delinquency reports, special reports that show which accounts are overdue or delinquent.

A standard calculation used to indicate the efficiency of a credit department and the rate at which accounts receivable are paid and collected is *days sales outstanding* (DSO). The figure factors in credit sales and receivables and is normally calculated monthly, quarterly, and annually. DSO figures are used for comparative evaluative purposes to show performance of the credit department over time and as indicators of usually contemporary developments in credit management. One widely used DSO calculation is the average trade credit receivables for the past three months times ninety, and then that amount is divided by the total credit sales for past three months. This figure provides an indicator of the quantity of the daily sales outstanding. Media firms are operating most efficiently when the DSO figure is low.

Bad debt reports indicate those accounts that cannot be collected and thus are losses to the company. Bad debt is generally reported as a percentage of credit or service sales, total sales, or service revenue for comparative purposes. Most media companies break down bad debt reports by source to gain a better understanding of where problems are developing.

CASH MANAGEMENT ISSUES

In addition to the capital and debt issues faced by companies, they also encounter issues involving cash that the firm receives from investors and operations. Capital and revenue received must be controlled to ensure its availability to pay for assets and future expense payments. Cash management involves the control of this cash in a firm's accounts in such a way that it produces the best possible results for the company.

This involves making choices about cash availability (liquidity) and interest income and choices about when to use the funds and for what purposes. Decisions are made regarding cash coming into a firm, cash leaving a firm, and cash held or invested.

Companies with significant daily income arriving by mail, for example, may choose to utilize banking arrangements whereby the bank collects the money several times during the day from the post office, collect the funds as rapidly as possible, and then posts the payments to the firm's accounts. This process is speeded up if the firm employs electronic payment systems by which customers make payments directly to the firm's bank accounts.

The virtue of this type of incoming cash management is that it reduces the time between the arrival of payments and when it is converted to cash that can be used by the firm. Accelerating the collection of payments can reduce the amount of cash that a firm must keep on hand to pay day-to-day expenses, allowing that cash to be used more effectively elsewhere.

Outgoing cash management is designed to delay payments that the firm must make in a way that permits it to use the cash but without harming its relationships with suppliers and others whom it must pay, or its rating with credit reporting agencies.

In order to achieve this goal, cash managers track payment due dates and time payments to arrive at the debtor just at the time it is due, a process easier to manage when a firm can use electronic fund transfers rather than checks. Managers also attempt to maximize the float time between when checks are written and will be cashed and to determine and maintain the lowest possible cash balances and compensating balances in bank accounts.

The combination of the tactics of rapid collection of incoming funds and slow payment of outgoing funds maximizes the cash that a firm can have on hand to finance operations and obtain income.

Cash management also becomes an issue for firms when they have excess cash from capital or current operations but want to save that cash for future operations. The need to preserve cash may be for either the short or long term. However, because the firm does not wish to have funds sitting ineffectually in checking accounts, finding appropriate methods to achieve a return from the cash while preserving necessary liquidity requires special attention.

Decisions on the management of cash are usually made by the manager of the firm or delegated to the accounting or treasurer's office. Depending upon the length of time that cash can be used for income production, a variety of arrangements are possible, ranging from the use of money market accounts or investments in certificates of deposit, bonds, commercial paper, or other investments.

The Problem of Large Infusions of Cash

Although it seems contradictory, suddenly obtaining a large amount of capital in the form of cash presents significant problems for firms because it requires that managers spend a great deal of time and effort maintaining and properly overseeing those funds.

This difficulty was encountered by a large number of dot-com and multimedia firms in recent years that made initial public offerings in the stock market and suddenly had hundreds of millions of dollars in cash in their accounts. If care is not taken in managing such funds, one risks following the pattern of rapid diminishment of the cash that was seen in many dot-com firms in the 1990s as they spent wildly and did not replace what they spent with revenues from sales of products and services (see Figure 9-4).

To avoid such problems firms with sudden wealth must behave more like banking institutions than media companies or they will misuse or mismanage capital that will be needed as much as four or five years after it is received. Managing such sudden wealth typically requires expertise not readily available in growing media and communication firms because the cash itself must be invested or lent as capital so that it is not wasted and accumulates appropriate returns before it is needed by the company.

In most cases it is appropriate for companies to hire a financial manager for these funds who has expertise in the management of cash capital, often a person from the banking or investment community. And the company board and management need to develop and implement specific policies to guide the use of the capital.

Even internally, companies benefit and make effective use of the capital by allocating it to growth and projects through processes similar to approaching investors or lending institutions. Decisions on what to fund and the amounts to provide internally should be made on the basis of sound internal business plans, research and development strategies, and other factors rather than less rigorous reviews or whims that lead to loss of cash capital or decisions that reduce the ability of the firm to make the most of its cash resources.

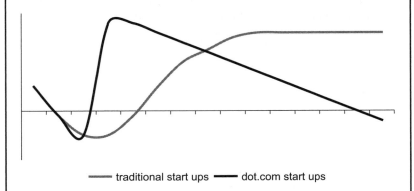

—— traditional start ups —— dot.com start ups

FIGURE 9-4   Cash flow in traditional startup firms and dot-com startup companies during the late 1990s

Financial issues play an important role in the development and operation of all media and communications firms and require that managers throughout the firms understand issues associated with capital, income, expenditures, and debt. Companies of all sizes require knowledgeable financial managers. That need is especially strong in startup firms, public firms, and firms coping with large cash flow.

The need for skillful financial management dictates that managers with special education and experience are in place to effectively serve the needs of firms. Other managers in the firm, however, also need to have a basic understanding of the issues and importance of these functions because their strategies and operations are dependent upon effective management of the financial resources available.

SUGGESTED READINGS

Broadcast Cable Financial Managers Association. 1994. *Understanding Broadcasting and Cable Finance: A Handbook for Non-Financial Managers.* Des Plaines, Ill.: Broadcast Cable Financial Managers Association.

Gitman, Lawrence. 2007. *Principles of Managerial Finance.* 12th ed. Boston: Addison-Wesley Publishing.

International Newspaper Financial Executives. 1993. *Newspaper Financial Management: An Introduction.* Reston, Va.: INFE.

Myddleton, David R. 1995. *The Essence of Financial Management.* Englewood Cliffs, N.J.: Prentice-Hall.

Van Horne, James C., and John W. Wachowitz. 2004. *Fundamentals of Financial Management.* 12th ed. Englewood Cliffs, N.J.: Prentice Hall.

Vogel, Harold L. 2007. *Entertainment Industry Economics: A Guide for Financial Analysis.* 7th ed. Cambridge: Cambridge University Press.

CHAPTER 10

Capital Markets and Media Firms

Capital markets are locations in which individuals and firms seek money needed to create enterprises, to start new initiatives, to purchase new equipment and facilities, and to finance operations. Capital in the form of debt and equity are exchanged in organized and structured markets as well as placed through private sources. All companies, including media firms, must have capital and access to capital to continue operations.

When individuals save money they can use that money to buy goods and services or they can invest that money or lend it to others for a fee. Money that is saved can be placed in banks, investment funds, and other capital accumulation institutions, or lent directly to those needing capital.

The wealth of individuals or groups of individuals can be combined to create a firm and to obtain ownership or partial ownership of a firm. The existence of large amounts of capital through stock markets has helped create large companies that would have been impossible for individuals or a small group of individuals to create with their own capital alone and has made it possible for small firms to gain capital to introduce new products and services.

Those who obtain capital through ownership shares or borrowed capital use the funds to purchase raw materials, required materials and services, and labor necessary to produce their own products and services, and to market, distribute, and sell them to purchasers. The income from the transaction is then used to repay the capital and its costs of production, distribution, and administration of the firm.

Those with capital to lend want the highest possible return for the lending of the capital and, depending upon their strategies, they typically want that return in the short term or medium term. They also pursue different strategies with regard to degrees of risk and may seek to maximize return and security across loans or investments in multiple firms.

The desire for high return is tempered because the forces of supply and demand influence demand and supply of capital. If the price of capital rises, the number of borrowers and the amount of capital demand will decline. If the price declines significantly, those who have capital may use it in other ways that produce better returns and the supply may also decline. The price of capital affects the demand for capital, but monetary and fiscal policies of central banks and governments and the condition of the general economy also influence the price.

In addition to return concerns, those who make capital available for use by others wish to preserve that capital and to have the value of capital increase because of the return from the rent or ownership obtained through its use. Different persons and institutions with capital have different strategies in how they approach their wants and needs, the degrees of risk they will take, and the amounts of capital that they will place in risk situations.

The strategies and degrees of risk can be seen in a financial pyramid of investment options (see Figure 10-1). This pyramid also loosely represents

FIGURE 10-1   The financial pyramid of capital risk and capital placement

the amount of financial resources available in capital markets for different purposes. More capital is placed and available in lower-risk investments because most persons are not willing to risk losing any or very much of their money.

The base is built upon funds placed in safe, relatively liquid investments with a reasonable rate of return. This often takes the form of investments in treasury bills, bonds, or notes issued by national governments or state and municipal bonds. The second level represents investments intended for growth of capital or income and typically includes stocks and bonds in established, financially stable and growing firms that tend to be market leaders in their industries.

At the third and fourth levels the risks of no return or loss of investment increase significantly. Speculative investments are made usually in stock, bonds, or debt with a possibility for high return if the companies in which such investments are made prove to be successful. These speculative investments are often made in firms in emerging fields and often involve firms that are just changing from private to public companies. The highest risk investments, at the top of the pyramid, often take the form of venture capital in which return is uncertain but can produce very large rewards if a company or its products are successful.

All of these strategies are used in providing different types of capital to both new and mature media firms.

VENTURE CAPITAL HELPS FUND NEW COMPANIES AND EXPANSION

Venture capital is a form of high-risk capital that is made available to provide seed money, finance startup ventures, fund growth or expansion, or to help reverse the fortunes of an existing firm in poor condition by providing financial resources necessary to restructure and reinvest to improve its situation. Individuals and firms who provide venture capital typically invest only a small portion of their resources in venture capital and make it available only for short periods of time. These funds are typically provided to entrepreneurs who have a solid business concept and a product or service that may have a chance for success in the market.

The concept behind venture capital has existed for several centuries in which consortiums of individuals funded potentially profitable enterprises. During the latter half of the twentieth century, however, this process developed more effectively as part of an emerging private equity market. Acceptance of the concept of venture capital and the development of methods for spreading risk induced pension funds, insurance companies, holding companies, banks, and other organizations and individuals to place some of their funds with venture capital companies that invest and manage such funds or to become involved in direct investments in companies themselves.

Even the high-risk world of venture capital operates on principles of risk and reward and different venture capitalists have different strategies about the types of firms and industries in which they will invest, whether they will fund product development, company startups, or enter when companies first make shares available on stock markets.

Venture capitalists often seek a portion of the firm's profit, shares in the firm, or royalties from the innovative product or service for which financing is provided. In many cases they become partners in the management of the companies and seek positions on the board of directors so they can provide advice and other assistance and monitor the performance of the company.

Most media and communications firms in developed nations do not seek venture capital because they tend to be mature and in mature industries in which the risks are well understood. In recent years, however, online service and content companies and new media operations spun off from established firms have used venture capital to fund their development, startup, and introduction to the market. Similarly a good deal of venture capital has been placed with new online and mobile content firms whose ideas for new businesses have attracted interest.

In the United States during 2006, venture capitalists invested $25.5 billion, with $1.6 billion (6.3 percent of the total) placed in 299 media deals and an additional $4 billion (15.7 percent) in 645 Internet deals.

SELF-GENERATED AND BORROWED CAPITAL SUPPORTS MOST EXISTING MEDIA

After their establishment, most small and mid-sized enterprises operated along the lines outlined in Chapter 9 generated profits that can be placed in reserves for later capital expenditures such as new equipment or facilities, or for expansion through purchasing other firms.

This self-generation of capital is the primary means by which most firms develop and grow. Through creating wealth they make themselves more stable and valuable. When the capital needs are large, such as that for purchasing land and constructing new buildings, such firms typically seek to borrow capital from traditional lending institutions.

Most media firms operate independently of venture capital and capital available from stock markets, following the pattern found in most small and mid-sized firms. As a result, managers must make it a goal for the firm itself to be financially strong, developing its own wealth so that it can either directly use that wealth as capital or as the basis upon which capital can be borrowed.

This issue of generating money and making oneself strong so one may borrow capital applies to both commercial and not-for-profit media, both of which have future capital needs if they are to develop, respond to changes in technologies, and improve the quality of their content and services.

BANKS AND THRIFT INSTITUTIONS
AS CAPITAL PROVIDERS

A traditional source of capital has been banks and thrift institutions that invest customers' money by lending it to firms needing money for capital expenditures, to expand their activities to gain short-term financing for operations.

These lenders have tended to be more conservative than other capital sources in terms of the amount of risk they will accept. As a result banks and other thrift institutions tend to make loans only to established, stable media firms or under conditions requiring significant security.

Banks and thrift firms create profits on loans by lending it to users at a higher rate than they pay their depositors whose capital is pooled and used by the bank. The availability and price of capital from banks are thus affected by fluctuations in the amount of funds deposited, interest rates paid customers, and the state of the general economy.

The bank debt that a firm incurs through borrowing capital is typically divided by the length of time before full repayment is due. This is important because the two have different effects on the annual performance of a firm reflected in its accounting statements.

Long-term debt describes debt that is not expected to be paid within a company's fiscal year. Such indebtedness is often used to finance the growth and development of the firm and to acquire capital goods, machinery, equipment, and facilities needed for production. Because it is a multiyear debt, only the portion due in a particular year must be repaid and will affect financial performance during that year.

A radio station, for example, might use a long-term loan to purchase a new building in which to locate studios and offices. An advertising agency might use long-term debt to acquire capital to purchase a Web design firm, or a motion picture studio might use a loan to purchase equipment to update its editing studios.

Short-term debt from banks and thrift institutions tends to take the forms of financing designed to meet operation requirements of media firms. These typically involve various forms of loans that provide working capital such as commercial credit, lines of credit, and revolving credit as discussed in Chapter 9.

Stock markets are a means of capital accumulation that bring together persons and institutions with money to invest and companies that want to sell shares of their ownership in exchange for that capital. Companies *go public*, that is, list their companies on stock markets to obtain capital for growth and development, including the acquisition of other companies. In other cases, firms have gone public as a means of allowing its original private owners or heirs to obtain cash for other purposes and investments.

Major media companies worldwide are increasingly turning to stock markets to meet their growing needs for capital as investments in expensive technologies and global expansion dramatically expand their need for capital. In creating or transforming themselves into public companies, firms make an initial public offering (IPO) of the shares on the market of their choice. It is the first time that shares are given a market value that is based on projections of future growth and performance.

When a firm is transformed into a stock company listed for trade on public markets, it must comply with laws and regulations that govern such companies in the country of its origin. In addition, it must comply with procedures outlined in its articles of incorporation, bylaws, and other relevant managerial documents. The firm must also comply with relevant laws and regulations in countries in whose stock exchange its shares are traded. Thus a firm in Italy is governed by Italian corporate law and, if its shares are traded in the United States, by U.S. securities laws.

Unlisted stocks can also be traded in what is called an *over-the-counter market*. This type of trading is also governed by various national laws and

---

The Largest Media IPOs

Cable and television companies produced the largest initial public offerings in terms of capital raised among media companies and three media IPOs are among the top twenty largest IPOs of all time in all industries.

When cable operator Charter Communications went public in 1999, its shares produced $3.23 billion in capital making it the largest media IPO and the eleventh largest IPO ever.

Second and third place in largest media IPOs are held by Infinity Broadcasting and Fox Entertainment Group. In 1998, CBS spun off the broadcast station company Infinity Broadcasting in an offering valued at $2.87 billion, the fifteenth largest IPO of all time. It beat out the spinoff of Fox Entertainment Group from News Corp. that same year, which produced $2.81 billion, making it the seventeenth largest IPO.

The largest IPO ever was that for the credit card operator Visa, whose shares produced $17.86 billion when it went public in 2008.

---

regulations, but the requirements that must be met by companies are typically less rigorous than those for listed companies.

Shares in media companies are categorized as *cyclical* in stock market language because they are not recession resistant and are typically affected by the business environment. The performance of media stocks depend on multiple factors, including advertising volume, subscriptions and other sales, prices of essential resources such as paper or content, promotional spending patterns, labor relations, capital spending patterns, the availability of cash flow to fund new activities, cost-cutting moves, and consolidation in the industry. Obviously, these factors are influenced by larger economic and environmental concerns, so media share prices respond to economic climates and to expectations about the future.

In the late 1990s, investors worldwide expressed more confidence in the future of Internet and multimedia firms than in traditional media firms, so those share prices surged ahead of traditional firms. In 2000, following the realization that the new media firms were not being able to deliver positive returns even in the mid term, their share prices fell but many remained overvalued compared to traditional media firms. A few successful firms such as Google escaped that fate and are highly valued today; many others such as Yahoo!, AOL, and WebMD are more reasonably valued in terms of their returns. Among traditional firms, companies with significant production of television programming and motion pictures have tended to have higher prices in recent years than those firms that primarily operate broadcasting stations or channels and print media.

Although new media shares have attracted large investments, they are viewed as having low financial performance but the potential for significant growth and future profitability. Because of the uncertainty of the firms, their capital has primarily resulted from the risk funds of institutional investors. Traditional media have been more attractive to institutional investors desiring capital preservation, income, and predictable growth.

STOCK MARKET OPERATIONS

Domestic laws govern the operations of stock exchanges and regulations and the regulations established by those who operate the exchanges. Generally, persons who want to buy shares place an order with a broker who sends the order to the stock exchange, where traders find a seller (a shareholder in the listed company who wants to sell) who has made the shares available.

Before electronic communications, the process involved direct contact between traders, but the use of sophisticated computers now makes most of the process automated, with computers keeping track of prices, individual trades, and a variety of other information that makes trading and record keeping much more rapid than in the past.

Investors primarily fall into two categories: individuals and institutions. A third category, inside investors, can be either individuals or institutions. Individual investors are single persons who, depending upon their interests and wealth, purchase one or many shares in one or more companies. Institutional investors are the primary source of capital in stock markets and include pension plans, investment firms, insurance companies, banks, and other institutions that invest some or all of their available funds in stock markets on behalf of their clients and themselves.

Inside investors are individuals employed within a firm who own shares in that firm. The term insider is typically applied to those who manage or direct the company while owning shares, such as members of boards of directors, corporate officials, and company executives. Institutional investors are considered insiders if one of their executives is on the board of or an officer in a company in which it owns shares.

Different types of equity shares are offered on stock markets, providing different rights to managing and sharing in the financial performance of firms. The most important are common stock, classified stock, and preferred stock. In some cases convertible shares exist that permit holders of one type of share to convert them to another.

Common stock is the primary type of share available. It proportionally splits the equity in the firm and the rights to make decisions regarding the firm such as voting for directors and officers, making changes in the company charter, and approving new stock issues. Each share has an equal voice in the decisions.

Classified stock splits the equity in the firm proportionally, but limits or removes voting rights in one or more categories of stock. This is often done to limit the control of shareholders of publicly traded shares. The founders of the firm or their heirs typically hold the most powerful shares and these shares are not publicly traded. Among media firms, these are typically found more often in newspaper-based companies where strong social, cultural, and political orientations remain, and the original owners want to protect that orientation—and sometimes their own pocketbooks—from the powerful influence of outside capital.

Preferred stock is shares that pay dividends at a specified rate and carry preference over common stock when dividends are paid or the firm is liquidated. Preferred shares rarely carry voting rights. Convertible stock is typically shares of classified or preferred stock that can or must be converted at a specific price or time to common stock.

Shares of firms are constantly traded, and the price of any firm's shares is dependent upon the willingness of investors to purchase at a given price based on their view of the economy, the performance of the firm, and its future prospects. The price of shares is important to companies because they typically retain portions of the shares themselves and changes in price affect their wealth and the perception of their firms by investors.

Stock markets exist worldwide to facilitate the exchange of shares in public companies. Each operates with its own sets of rules and procedures and is guided by the laws and regulations of the countries in which it operates.

Today, the one stock market featuring the largest number of media companies is the New York Stock Exchange. In most cases, shares in the largest media companies are traded in the largest stock exchange in their nation of origin and they are sometimes traded in markets in other countries. The large number of U.S. media firms traded on NYSE has helped make it the location of the largest number of media stocks in one market.

Because of the complexities of securities laws in each nation, and because stock markets have traditionally provided sufficient capital for major domestic firms, these markets traditionally exchanged only shares of domestic companies. The growth of multinational firms needing capital worldwide, and telecommunications developments during the final decades of the twentieth century that permit rapid global communications and data exchange, however, have led some firms to list themselves on multiple markets.

The most important exchanges in the world are located in Frankfurt, London, New York, Paris, and Tokyo. Significant markets in other parts of

---

Effects of Share Price Changes

The prices of shares in companies rise or fall depending upon the price investors are willing to pay for shares. That willingness is affected by perceptions of a variety of factors including company profitability, dividends paid, company strategies, industry potential, and the general economy. Changes in the price of shares can both help and harm company strategies.

In February 2008, Google Inc. announced that its results for the final quarter of 2007 had failed to meet forecasts because of increased capital spending and higher costs for gaining new customers. Earnings per share were $4.43 rather than $4.47 expected by analysts. Immediately following announcements of the results, shares in the company fell to $510, a 9.5 percent decline.

In June 2008, antitrust authorities approved Cablevision Systems Corp.'s $650 million purchase of Newsday on Long Island, N.Y., from Tribune Company. The company, based on Long Island, is one of the largest cable system operators in the United States and owns cable channels and sports teams. Investors disapproved of the deal and shares dropped 37 cents to $23.23 on news of the approval.

---

the world include Buenos Aires, Hong Kong, Rio de Janeiro, Seoul, Singapore, and Sydney.

MAJOR MEDIA COMPANIES TRADED ON STOCK MARKETS

Shares in nearly every major media company in the developed world are now traded on one or more stock markets because few large firms have sufficient access to capital to keep them from becoming public. Among the hundreds of media firms in which investors can choose are companies such as Walt Disney Co., EMAP, Fairfax Ltd., Gannett Co., Legardère, News Corp., New York Times Co., Pearson, Quebecor, Thomsen Reuters, Televisa, Time Warner, Torstar, Viacom, and Washington Post.

Although broadcasting and motion picture companies entered the stock market around the middle of the twentieth century, newspaper companies were reticent to do so and most did not begin entering the market until the 1960s (see Table 10-1).

Public companies need not remain public in perpetuity and may be later sold, privatized, or delisted. Privatization reverses public ownership and puts the firm in the hands of private investors. Delisting is the removal of a firm from a stock market. These are illustrated by the sale of Knight Ridder Inc. that was sold to McClatchy Company in 2006, by the privatization of Tribune Co. in 2007 to an investor group headed by Sam Zell, and by the delisting of Journal Register Co. in 2008 after its share prices and market capitalization fell below minimum requirements.

As media companies worldwide have increasingly turned to stock markets for capital, they have gained resources that have allowed them to improve their content and its presentation, to upgrade facilities and equipment, to begin new initiatives, and to establish media products. They have gained funds that have helped them grow, acquire other companies, and create relatively large media companies and conglomerates. The interest in media firms can be seen in the value of investments, also market capitalization, in major firms. This value, of course, fluctuates as the prices of shares rise and fall.

Simultaneously new pressures for increased company performance have been placed on managers because of the obligations to shareholders whose interest is primarily the highest possible regular returns and this has caused managers to work for increased cash flows, return on sales, and higher net profit margins. These market pressures have led to short-term thinking in some media companies in which the management has determined that the best possible short-term performance measures are the primary objectives for the firm. This type of bottom-line orientation can result in management not paying sufficient attention to the reinvestment needs of the firm and its needs to grow and develop.

TABLE 10-1 · GOING PUBLIC: WHEN NEWSPAPER COMPANY
SHARES BEGAN TRADING

Before 1960	
	Dow Jones & Co.
1938	Times Mirror Co.
1960s	
1967	Gannett Co.
1969	Knight Newspapers Inc. (merged with Ridder Publications in 1974 to form Knight-Ridder Inc.)
	Ridder Publications Inc. (merged with Knight Newspapers in 1974 to form Knight-Ridder Inc.)
	Lee Enterprises Inc.
	New York Times Co.
1970s	
1970	Media General Inc.
1971	Washington Post Co.
1972	Harte-Hanks (privatized 1984)
1980s	
1981	A. H. Belo Corp.
1983	Tribune Co.
1986	Pulitzer Publishing Co.
1988	McClatchy Newspapers Inc.
	E. W. Scripps Co.
1989	Central Newspapers Inc.
1990s	
1993	Harte-Hanks Communications
1994	Hollinger International (American Publishing Co.)
1996	Providence Journal Co.
1995	Journal Register Co.
2000s	
2003	Journal Communications
2006	GateHouse Media

Market Capitalization of Media and Communications Firms

Market capitalization is a term used to determine the comparative value of firms traded on a stock market. The value is created by multiplying the market price and the number of its issued and outstanding common shares.

The largest media and communications companies have market capitalization and revenues in the tens of billion dollars range and eleven have value exceeding $20 billion (see Table 10-2).

TABLE 10–2 · MEDIA FIRMS WITH MARKET CAPITALIZATION
EXCEEDING $20 BILLION, 2008

	Company	Market Capitalization ($ Billions)
1	Walt Disney	59.1
2	News Corp.	58.9
3	Comcast	57.7
4	Time Warner	50.1
5	Vivendi	45.7
6	DirecTV	28.5
7	Reed Elsevier	26.6
8	Viacom	25.4
9	Liberty Media	23.4
10	Time Warner Cable	22.5
11	Thomson Reuters	21.5

Some media critics also argue that the major problem with stock ownership is that it causes many owners and managers to move away from a public-service orientation toward a commercial orientation equivalent to that of any big business and that this affects the type of content and nature of service provided by public firms.

Shares in media companies can be categorized, to use a traditional Wall Street term, as *cyclical*. Cyclical stocks are defined as stocks that are not recession resistant, and typically are strongly affected by the business environment.

The performance of media stocks depend on multiple factors, including advertising volume, subscriptions and other sales, prices of essential resources such as paper or content, promotional spending patterns, labor relations, capital spending patterns, the ability of cash flow to fund new activities, cost-cutting moves (which can result in operating leverage), and consolidation in the industry. Obviously, these factors are influenced positively and negatively at various points by larger economic and environmental concerns. Media share prices respond to recessionary economic climates and to expectations for the future.

In recent years, investors worldwide have expressed more confidence in the future of Internet and multimedia firms than in traditional media firms, so those share prices have surged ahead. Companies with significant production of television programming and motion pictures have tended to have higher prices than those who are operating primarily broadcasting stations or channels and print media. Many investors have lost confidence in the future of the newspaper industry because of troublesome audience and advertising trends, resulting in declining share prices and creating a capital crisis in that industry (see the box "The Capital Crisis of Newspaper Companies").

THE GLOBALIZATION OF MEDIA CAPITAL

A phenomenon of the last quarter of the twentieth century was the growing internationalization of capital as a whole. In practice this has meant that the location in which capital is produced need not be the location in which it is invested. As a result, capital accumulated in the United States can be invested in Brazil, capital gathered in Netherlands can be available in Japan, and capital collected in Singapore can be borrowed in Korea.

The reasons for this capital flow are that those institutions and individuals with capital look for opportunities to achieve the best returns or growth opportunities. Because of differences in national economies, those returns may occur in different nations at different times.

The desires of capital sources to find better returns have been supported by developments in communications and financial systems. As the mechanisms and processes for better information and capital flow matured, media firms began to feel the effects of the international capital market.

A prime example of these effects on U.S. media is the motion picture industry, which was primarily a domestically financed industry until the 1980s. As international capital became easily available, producers began to see it as a means of bringing new money into the industry. A large number of film productions began to be financed by capital from France, Japan, and the United Kingdom. The industry then became a target of direct international investment and by the 1990s, the majority of U.S. motion picture studios were purchased by firms from Japan, Australia, and France.

The Capital Crisis of Newspaper Companies

Diminishing newspaper readership, discontented advertisers, lack of growth in overall newspaper advertising expenditures, and lack of vision among newspaper company executives of how their firms will survive and prosper in the future have combined to create a capital crisis in the U.S. newspaper industry. The situation is evident in disputes between investors and companies, declining dividends and share prices, and debt problems.

After a prolonged dispute with dissident shareholders, the board of Knight-Ridder Co., the second largest newspaper company in the United States, decided to end operations and sold the firm to McClatchy Newspapers in 2006. The following year the board of Dow Jones & Co. sold that company, including *The Wall Street Journal*, to News Corporation, after enduring several years of limited reinvestment and imperfect working capital. In 2008, the Sulzberger family attempted to alleviate disputes with its shareholders over financial performance by giving rebel shareholders seats on the board and a proxy battle for control of the board of Media General broke out.

Poor prospects for the industry and declining dividends produced declining prices for newspaper company shares and they dropped dramatically during the first decade of the millennium. McClatchy Newspapers prices, for example, fell from $35 in mid-2000 to $4 by mid-2008. During the same period shares in Gannett fell from $60 to $17 and shares in New York Times Co. fell from $40 to $13. The financial conditions of the companies and the effects of the recession continued to drive prices down in 2009. McClatchy's shares fell below 50 cents before rising to $5 in 2010; Gannett dropped below $2 before rebounding into the high teens; and New York Times Co. shares declined below $5 before increasing into the low teens.

The decline in share prices was so sharp that it made it difficult for some firms to remain listed on major stock markets. In 2008, the Journal Register Co. was delisted from the New York Stock Exchange because its share price remained below $1, reducing its market capitalization to about $12 million, less than one-fifth the capitalization required to be traded on the big board. The Sun-Times Media Group stock also continued trading below $1 and its market capitalization dropped to $61 million, drawing a delisting warning from the New York Stock Exchange.

During 2008, debt ratings agencies lowered the ratings on company debt for McClatchy Co., New York Times Co., GateHouse Media and many other publicly traded and privately traded firms.

Part of the debt problems resulted because some newspaper firms raised capital in the 1990s and early twenty-first century to make acquisitions of other newspaper companies and additional media businesses with debt based on the value of their existing assets, their market capitalization, and the strength of advertising growth rates. When the growth rates for advertising declined, financial problems rapidly appeared. Because the financial arrangements for the debt were based on expectations of growth in advertising, companies suddenly had to scramble to find ways to pay their obligations and they began to do so by cost cutting. The debt payment problem was compounded in many cases because interest rates on the debt increased when the value of company shares declined, requiring even deeper budget cuts.

European capital also flowed to the United States when companies such as Hachette Filipachi, Groupe Legardère, and Bertelsmann Co. made massive purchases of American magazine and book publishing firms that catapulted those firms into the leading magazine and book publishers in the world.

Large amounts of capital flowed to foreign media firms from the United States as well. By listing their shares on the New York Stock Exchange, firms such as Australia's News Corporation, Britain's Pearson Corp., Japan's Sony Corp., and Spain's Telefonica have gained access to billions of dollars in U.S. capital.

The globalization of capital is increasingly separating ownership of large media firms from the nations in which they were established and forcing managers to take a more international outlook and approach to their strategies and operations.

SUGGESTED READINGS

Bradley, Edward S., and Richard J. Teweles. 1998. *The Stock Market.* 7th ed. New York: John Wiley and Sons.

Cranberg, Gilbert, Randall Bezanson, and John Soloski. 2001. *Taking Stock: Journalism and the Publicly Traded Newspaper Company.* Ames: Iowa State University Press.

Dufey, Gunther, and Ian Giddy. 1994. *The International Money Market.* 2nd ed. Englewood Cliffs, N.Y.: Prentice-Hall.

Golis, Christopher C. 1999. *Enterprise and Venture Capital.* 3rd ed. London: Allyn and Unwin.

Harvard Business School Press. 2003. *Finance for Managers.* Cambridge, Mass.: Harvard Business School Press.

Robertson, Robert J., and Mark Van Osnabrugge. 2000. *Angel Investing: Matching Startup Funds with Startup Companies—A Guide for Entrepreneurs, Individual Investors, and Venture Capitalists.* San Francisco: Jossey-Bass.

Sincere, Michael. 2003. *Understanding Stocks.* Columbus, Ohio: McGraw-Hill.

CHAPTER 11

The Development of Large
Media Companies

Large media companies result from the creation of an administrative organization that is used to pursue growth-oriented business strategies. Until the last half of the twentieth century, media firms tended to be small and mid-sized enterprises. Even the companies operated by publishing giants such as Hearst, Northcliffe, and Pulitzer were relatively small enterprises in terms of revenue, employment, and facilities when compared to other industries.

The development of large media firms resulted from changes in technologies that produced additional types of media, from strategies of growth and expansion, and from the availability of capital, particularly through equity markets, to finance expansion and further development of media firms. In the United States, commercial radio networks begun in the first half of the twentieth century expanded into television and rapidly grew into large media firms by the 1970s. In the 1970s and 1980s, a number of newspaper companies began expanding and many became large firms by emphasizing newspaper, magazine, and book publishing holdings before deciding to expand into other media. Similar movements can be seen among publishers in other major companies as cable and satellite developed and government policies permitted commercial television where they had not previously been authorized and other media opportunities.

Although important media firms have existed since the commercialization of newspapers in the nineteenth century, the rapid and seemingly unending expansion of communication conglomerates at the end of the twentieth century has fueled rhetoric that, taken uncritically, might lead some to believe that such conglomerates are self-sustaining, continually expanding, nearly immortal organizations.

This view, however, ignores widely differing degrees of success in media firms that result from differences in their strategies, organization, and operation. Some have used centralized management, whereas others use decentralized management; some require standardization among their media products, but others permit individuality. Some firms operate as single entities, others operate with divisions and subsidiaries; some are operated with a strategic vision, others are not. Some firms seek higher degrees of integration than others; some seek more product and geographic diversification than others. These types of factors create differences in behavior and the ability of communication firms to grow or survive, so one cannot view all media empires as similar and behaving in the same manner.

Media companies have grown in size for a variety of reasons. First, some have become large firms as part of the aspirations of strong leaders who have reinvested profits and often gathered new capital—in many cases by becoming publicly traded companies—to undertake strategies of growth and expansion. These leaders have sought out opportunities for expansion and exploited the weaknesses of other firms through acquisition or creating mergers. In recent decades, this has been seen in the case of the Australian company News Corporation, led by Rupert Murdoch, and the U.S. firm Gannett Co., which was transformed from a small, relatively unknown local newspaper company into one of the largest media conglomerates by Allen Neuharth. Similarly, Viacom developed into one of the world's largest media and entertainment firms under the leadership of Sumner Redstone.

The growth of media firms is possible because of the ability of company leaders to translate their visions into actions. Large firms are not created only to serve the aspirations of leaders, however; sometimes growth is precipitated by the firm's regular need for resources that it does not currently have available. In such cases it may purchase important suppliers such as programming production companies, paper companies, or distribution service firms.

Efforts to stabilize the finances of a firm also have played a role in the development of media firms. They increase in size and scope to help reduce the effects of changes in specific market segments or market locations or to make themselves less dependent upon changes in prices by suppliers and distributors.

Because of the desire to stabilize resource supply, some newspaper firms have purchased newsprint mills. From the desire to stabilize distribution arrangements, some magazine companies have purchased magazine distribution companies. Expansion to reduce dependence on a single type of music or a few recording stars, as well as to achieve economies in production and distribution, has led audio companies to purchase additional record labels.

Companies have also grown to reduce economic risks, seeking geographical diversity to reduce the effects of economic cycles or downturns in a particular region. Others have grown to diversify their operations by pursuing multimedia strategies designed to reduce their dependence upon a particular type of media.

Companies also expand their operations and diversify to acquire a greater share of the market and its profits, to enter industries and industry branches that offset slower-growing existing operations, and to move into emerging industries related to their operations that may have profitable futures.

Size is no guarantee of success, however. It is both an advantage and disadvantage. It can both empower as well as constrain a manager's actions. Size can provide strength and economies of scale, but it can also make enterprises difficult to manage and cause inertia or slow response when change is needed. Size can create greater dependence on outside capital or vulnerability to rapid economic changes. As a result, it is important to understand the reasons for growth and the rationales and strategies necessary to guide that growth so the company can be successfully managed to gain the advantages of size while minimizing disadvantages.

GROWTH PRESSURES AND STRATEGIES

Questions of how a firm grows and the strategies it can employ for growth interest managers, who are focused on developing their firms by increasing their size. Natural growth occurs when resources are used more efficiently and productivity is increased, or when firms offer new products and services that are successful in the marketplace.

Growth can also occur by using financial resources to expand one's market or by acquiring other firms. Because firms experience unequal growth, some firms grow larger than others and may have the ability to purchase some of the smaller firms. In other cases mergers are sought between existing firms to create an even larger enterprise.

Growth is sometimes sought as a means of reducing risk by diversifying a firm. Growth through diversification may be pursued in geographic terms as a firm expands the markets in which it operates to reduce the effects of economic fluctuations in any one market. The diversification may add subsidiaries that are not in the original business of the firm to reduce its dependence on one product or service.

Growth can also occur if a firm engages in vertical integration to control resources needed for their operations or to control or participate in the distribution or marketing of the end product or service.

Growth can also occur as the result of special opportunities, such as those that force the sale or divestiture of other companies.

The Problematic America Online–Time Warner Merger

Many social critics used the takeover of Time Warner by America Online in the year 2000 to illustrate the power of large companies. It was certainly a massive deal and created the world's largest media company. To observers with a business perspective, however, the merger was more illustrative of weaknesses driving firms together than an exercise of economic strength and raw corporate power.

The merger created a firm with $350 billion in market value and revenues in excess of $30 billion annually. AOL shareholders received 55 percent of the new firm, whereas Time Warner shareholders received 45 percent. The deal was certainly large enough to raise eyebrows everywhere, but when considered using questions from a business standpoint it becomes understandable in a different way.

How could AOL take over a firm that had sales revenue five times larger than its own? Why was it possible for AOL to acquire a firm with a net income more than double its own? How does a firm with 12,000 employees take over a firm with 67,000 employees?

The answer lay in the fact that both firms had significant impediments to their ability to compete individually in the emerging content-driven broadband distribution environment. It also lies, equally significantly, in the fact that AOL had capital. Its market capitalization was nearly twice that of Time Warner, thanks to the stock market's infatuation with Internet shares.

Although AOL was a preeminent U.S. Internet service provider and content organizer, it was vulnerable because it could not easily gain access to cable systems for broadband distribution services and because it was dependent upon Internet subscriptions. The company was established in 1985 and became the first Internet firm to make a profit in 1998, just two years before it became the dominant player in the merger with Time Warner.

The company had a strong understanding of Internet operations and markets, operating the AOL family of services that includes CompuServe, DigitalCity, and MovieFone. However, its own financial performance was weak by comparison to the price of its shares. At the time of the acquisition AOL shares were priced at fifty-five times its earnings. AOL executives realized that the firm had vulnerabilities that could be ameliorated by acquiring or merging with a firm with hard assets and a large cash flow.

Time Warner was one of the largest media conglomerates and enjoyed the benefits of well-known media brands such as Warner Bros., *Time*, *Sports Illustrated*, and CNN. Its strength as a content creator was also supported by its position as the second largest cable operator in the United States. But Time Warner also had weaknesses. Although the firm was well known, it was perceived—as many traditional media firms have been—as being slow to respond to changes in communications technologies and unable to fully exploit opportunities in new media.

The firm had been carrying a huge debt load accumulated by upgrading its cable systems, financing the merger of Warner Communications and Time Inc., and paying for acquisitions made during the 1990s. It was also limited in its ability to move its content across different platforms because the Internet was becoming an important part of that ability and Time Warner did not have strength in Internet operations or knowledge.

Joining the two firms thus combined their strengths and eliminated some of their significant weaknesses. It presented increased opportunities for on-line distribution and e-commerce in music, video, and other Time Warner content and additional opportunities for cross marketing and brand enhancement.

But to make the deal, which involved a swap of shares, AOL had to discount the value of its shares by one-fourth, a clear indication that its management recognized that its shares were not worth their price in the stock market. With that discount the deal was palatable to Time Warner shareholders and still perceived as beneficial for AOL shareholders. The value of the deal for Time Warner shareholders is seen in the fact that the day before the deal was announced, Time Warner shares were trading for $65 dollars. Under the terms of the merger, shareholders received the equivalent of $110, about 70 percent more value than they had in the stock market.

News of the merger in January 2000 boosted AOL shares from $68 the day prior to the announcement to $74 on the day of the announcement. Time Warner shares shot up from $65 to $92. The following week, however, AOL shares dropped to $60 and Time Warner shares to $79. At the beginning of February, AOL shares had dropped to $55 and Time Warmer to $77.

Part of the decline was due to a decline in share prices across the U.S. stock markets, but the initial buoyant reaction to the merger was also restrained when the deal was considered from a financial standpoint. In order to produce a real rate of return of 10 percent annually for investors, the combined company will have to grow at 15 percent per year for fifteen years and maintain a price-earnings ratio multiple of about thirty. To gain a 15 percent return, the growth rate would have to be in the range of 22 percent a year. Although these were not impossible goals for the company, they placed a great deal of pressure on the management to increase cash flow, keep costs low, and ensure high operating profits.

In the years since the merger, things have not gone well for the combined company. Problems and resentments in having less experienced Internet managers oversee well-established print, broadcast, cable, and entertainment operations soon appeared and the inability of the new media operations to produce significant income led to internal disputes. That discontent spread to investors when in 2002 the company posted a loss of $99 billion—the largest loss ever reported by any company. Not surprisingly such developments affected the value of the company. Time Warner was the largest media company in terms of capitalization before the merger and AOL Time Warner was the largest after the merger. By 2008, however, it had dropped to fourth place and its value in terms of market capitalization had declined to 15 percent of what it was at the time of the merger.

Since that time, control of company management has returned to executives from the traditional media side and AOL has been dropped from the company name altogether. Today it is simply called Time Warner.

The effects of the merger continue to be felt throughout the media industries because it has made other firms wary of large acquisitions and mergers and induced many to seek benefits through strategic alliances, joint ventures, and networked operating structures instead.

Other factors promoting growth are:

Growing demand for a product or service
New technology that increases productivity and market size
Substitute products or services that can be offered by the firm
Available resources such as financial or managerial ability to create growth

Factors impeding growth include:

Poor management
Lack of capital
Company traditions
Lack of capacity
Declining demand for the product or service
Heavy competition from other producers of the product or service
Policy and legal control on growth

The rate of growth experienced by companies presents special problems for firms. Slow growth rates require that managers exercise great care in financial management and plan any debt increases or other company changes carefully.

Because slow growth is also indicative of mature markets or consumer disinterest in the product, media managers whose companies are experiencing slow growth need to consider carefully the reasons for the rate of growth and develop strategies to ensure they have sufficient resources or alternative products for the company to survive in the future. Newspaper publishers in North America and Europe, for example, are experiencing relatively lower revenue growth when compared to other media and no growth or negative growth in terms of the number of customers served. As a result, newspaper companies are implementing a variety of strategies to expand markets and products and spread costs across multiple products.

At the other end of the continuum is rapid growth. Although it presents a good deal of opportunities and is more desirable than negative or no growth, rapid growth presents critical issues that must be addressed or else firms can encounter disastrous managerial and financial conditions. The largest problems with rapid growth result from the inability of existing organizational structures or managers' abilities to effectively respond to and control the growth. This leads to inadequate financial planning and control, heavy financial leveraging, poor use of personnel, loss of focus, and growth taking the place of strategic planning. These problems have been experienced in recent years by a variety of online media and dot-com firms, cable and satellite television firms, and other companies who have benefited from rapid growth resulting from advances in information and communications technologies.

Growth—or the lack of it—thus creates issues that require careful attention by managers if the company is to benefit or survive the growth environment in which it exists.

GROWTH THROUGH DIVERSIFICATION

Diversification is a strategy used by firms to smooth sales and profit fluctuations, to stimulate growth faster than if they concentrated on a single product or service, and to ensure that performance is not dependent on the economic cycles of one location or industry.

Decisions on whether and the degree to which a company will diversify vary, but large media and communication firms typically diversify into a range of media and communication products and services. Company choices and investments change the pattern and amount of diversification. The Tribune Co., for example, was much more clearly a newspaper company in 1980 than it was in 2005 (see Figure 11-1), because of significant investments in broadcast and entertainment activities.

Patterns of diversification differ significantly among media firms (see Figure 11-2). Some newspaper companies are comfortable only diversifying into other print media or extending their publications online. Other companies choose to offer a wide range of media and communications products ranging from newspapers to magazines, from television to recordings, and from radio to online operations.

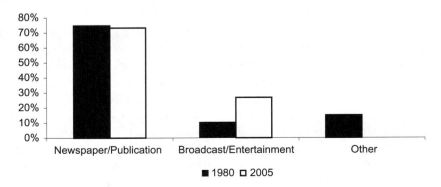

FIGURE 11-1   Example of diversification reflected in revenue sources of Tribune Co., 1980 and 2005

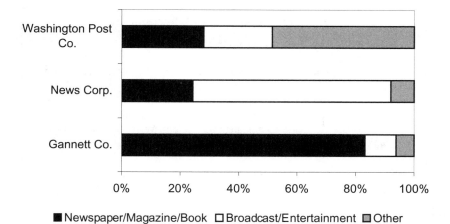

FIGURE 11-2   Examples of different diversification patterns shown in revenue sources of three large media firms, 2007

Diversification creates challenges for companies if it is not based on the existing knowledge of managers. If top personnel do not understand the dynamics and inner workings of an industry, its culture, the production and distribution activities required, or consumer behavior in that industry they can run into significant difficulties.

GROWTH THROUGH MERGERS AND ACQUISITIONS

Mergers and acquisitions combine companies by joining the companies together or through the purchase of one company by another. Despite the popular conception that such activities are designed merely to increase the size of firms, these fusions are only useful if they are part of a strategy to increase competitiveness of one or more of the firms involved.

They are a strategic method to improve companies, to rationalize operations, and to gain access to resources needed to compete in larger markets with a greater number of competitors. In media industries, for example, many mergers and acquisitions have occurred as firms have responded to weaknesses resulting from globalization, entry of competitors, and changing technologies.

Acquisitions or mergers, for example, are a means to enter new geographic markets. A publisher in Italy might purchase a publishing firm in the United States so that it may benefit from the larger U.S. market as part of a strategy of increasing its cash flow and distributing American materials in Europe and European materials in America.

Acquisition for Strength in Games

In 2007, Vivendi acquired a controlling stake in the game publisher Activision, which when combined with Vivendi Games would make the firm a major rival of Electronic Arts, the leading independent game publisher in the world.

Activision's strengths in console games such as Tony Hawk skateboarding games and Guitar Hero were seen as a strategic complement to Vivendi Games' strength in online games such as World of Warcraft. The combined firm was seen as having economic and market power that would make it a close competitor to Electronic Arts and allow the new firm to seek to transform its games across both console and online platforms.

In other cases mergers or acquisitions can aid entry into a media product market in which a firm has not previously operated. In this type of activity, a newspaper publisher may merge with a magazine publisher to enter the magazine market without the risk of having to start new titles. Firms also join so that they can acquire and use innovative products. A dot-com company, for example, might merge with a software company so it can gain the right to use a unique proprietary software that improves its customers' abilities to personalize the information they receive.

The desire to shorten the time required for delivery or to find a mechanism to better serve customers may promote mergers or acquisitions. An American recording company, for example, may purchase a recording distributor in France to increase the efficiency with which European retailers may order its recordings and to reduce delivery time because the orders will be filled in Europe and not the United States.

Successful mergers and acquisitions need to serve clear business strategy goals, not mere growth, or they actually can harm a company. This is why some divisions or subsidiaries of the joined firms are sold shortly after mergers or acquisitions and why there seems to be constant trading of media firms and divisions. As companies try to rationalize all the elements acquired during a merger or acquisition it is natural to shed those that do not serve corporate strategies and core business activities.

The primary value of mergers and acquisitions to companies, then, comes not merely from increasing its assets but from organizing the assets in a way that increases shareholder value. This occurs when the combined pieces are put together so that they are more valuable when joined together than they were when they were independent.

John Malone, who guided the growth of TCI and made it the largest cable operator in the United States before selling it to AT&T in 1999 and

Making the Pieces Fit: Harcourt General, Reed Elsevier, and Thomson Corp.

Ensuring that an acquisition serves the needs of an acquiring company was starkly illustrated when Harcourt General, the textbook and journal publishing company, was put up for sale by its owners.

Although both Reed Elsevier, the British and Dutch publishing conglomerate, and the Canadian publishing firm Thomson Corp. were interested in Harcourt, neither company wanted to purchase all of its operations because they could not be integrated into the strategies of either one. In the end, the two companies made an unusual $5.7 billion joint bid and purchase in which Reed Elsevier purchased Harcourt and then passed on about half of that company to Thomson in 2001.

The arrangement occurred because strategic decisions within each company had placed them on divergent paths and each could not use large portions of Harcourt in those directions. As a result of the decision to divide the company, Reed Elsevier was able to focus its acquisition on Harcourt's elementary and primary school publishing and its medical and science holdings, including about 500 scholarly journals. Thompson was able to obtain Harcourt's higher education and corporate publishing activities that fit well with its publishing strategies.

Making acquisitions fit into a company and getting the desired results is not simple and in 2007, Reed Elsevier decided that the school publishing activities it had acquired in the Harcourt deal did not fit its strategic and performance requirements so it sold those activities to Houghton Mifflin Riverdeep Group.

now heads Liberty Media, has been both lauded and reviled for his willingness and prowess in trading assets as a means of increasing shareholder value. One of the era's best deal makers, Malone is highly adept at finding firms or portions of firms that fill needs within his own organizations or create opportunities that are attractive to investors and increase the overall value of the firm.

Because consolidations designed to increase value are dependent upon the effects of the fusion of firms, whenever such mergers and acquisitions occur managers need to increase the efficiency and effectiveness of the joined firms to produce the desired results. This necessity is often the impetus for restructuring through blending operations, modifying organization structures, and selling or ending some operations. These activities, of course, affect personnel. Sometimes they force job changes, layoffs, buyouts, retirements, and relocations.

If restructuring is not handled sensitively or occurs too often, it leads to insecurity, resentment, career development concerns, reduced productivity, resignations of talented employees, and other problems that affect the long-term interests of firms.

Similarly, financial performance of the merged or acquiring firm can be harmed if technology, organization structures, company cultures, compensation and benefits, accounting and management information systems (MIS), marketing activities, production equipment, and sales and distribution methods are not rapidly and effectively fused.

These force managers to rapidly confront how the pieces of the company get put together for maximum efficiency by taking advantage of economies of scale, scope, and integration and complementary products or services. Mergers and acquisitions require that a shared vision must be built and a clear strategy for the integration of the firms be present and effectively communicated.

Large mergers and acquisitions often create public opinion that these deals are limiting competition. The number of mergers and acquisitions and the size of the deals rightfully raise concern over the possibility of anticompetitive practices. If mergers and acquisitions create unhealthy levels of market power or barriers for new firms to enter, there certainly is reason for public concern and the merger may attract the attention of competition authorities.

GROWTH THROUGH JOINT ACTIVITIES

Another form of company growth is seen in activities in which companies cooperate with each other through joint ownership in other companies, by creating joint ventures, or by establishing formal business networks.

Managers of large companies engage in these cooperative activities for a variety of reasons—government policies, weaknesses in firms, or uncertainty on the part of boards and managers. These activities are sometimes used when government antitrust or policy regulations block greater ownership. Most often, however, strategies of joint activities are employed when managers of firms want to respond to high-risk opportunities but cannot bear the risk alone or when firms have financial resource limitations and cannot afford to completely acquire a firm as a subsidiary. They are also sought when the knowledge base about new technologies or applications—or the skills and abilities of personnel—in a firm are limited but management wants to participate in and learn from a new media market because of its potential.

The partial ownership and other relationships that characterize joint ventures show that the participating firms are more *interdependent* than unconstrained powerful companies that are independent of outside influences. Although the relationships clearly show joint interest, these joint ventures in and of themselves are not evidence of the lack of competition between firms in other activities. Gaining advantages in that competition, as well as

Making Mergers and Acquisitions Work

If consolidating firms that are merged or acquired is not made a priority, internal conflicts and coordination difficulties will emerge among companies operating under one owner. As a result, acquisitions and mergers sometimes do not produce anticipated synergies, cost savings, or other advantages and may reduce the financial performance of the new larger firm. Other problems can result from issues related to company strategies, company organization and management, personnel, company cultures, and customer reactions.

Growth through merger or acquisition thus needs to be guided by process and strategy if it is to be successful. The overall strategy of the acquisition or merger involves choices such as whether the companies will operate independently or be integrated into one new firm and whether the acquiring firm will be active or passive in the operation of the acquired one. If integration and active management are the strategy, it means that senior management must work to increase the capacity and productivity of the entire organization, not just its individual parts. This requires a vision that will guide decisions and needs to be communicated to and accepted by personnel throughout the organization.

For a successful blending of firms, attention must be paid to the entire organization, not just the acquired firm. Managerial teams need to explore the effects on the technical and organizational system of the new and larger firm, as well as on the existing political and cultural systems of the existing firms. They need to explore differences and similarities in:

Management information systems

Accounting systems

Marketing programs

Management styles

Organization structures

Work forces

Production equipment and processes

Customer bases and needs

Competitors

Types of products

Distribution methods

A variety of overall questions need to be asked and answered such as: How do the firms differ in terms of structure and product lines? Can sales and marketing efforts be joined effectively for joint sales and cross promotion? Can joint purchasing and standardization of needed resources save money? Can some parts of accounting be centralized? What is unique, good, and bad in each division or unit?

Specific questions about operations also need to asked: Are there differences in the costs of production and distribution for the products? Are employees treated differently in terms of compensation and benefits? Can and should those differences be standardized?

Ultimately mergers and acquisitions are effective only if an integration plan is devised and implemented in a timely fashion that addresses the methods for management to put the pieces together, to take advantage of economies of scale, scope, and integration, and to make products and services complementary. The strategies and pace of change need to be set and communicated to everyone in the organization to reduce uncertainty and fear.

To be successful, a new culture must be created that is not merely a blending of the existing cultures. It must have clear values, strategies, and expectations that promote improvement and innovation. Not only employees but also customers must understand how the changes will affect their relationships with the firms and what benefits they will accrue.

changing corporate strategies, is what leads to alliances through joint activities changing so often.

THE PURSUIT OF SYNERGIES

The idea of creating synergies through the combination of cross-media activities has been widely touted during acquisition and merger activities in recent years. Company executives, analysts, and industry observers have argued that combining firms that produce different types of content and operate different distribution capabilities can create synergies that will improve the performance of the combined firm.

After a decade of efforts to find synergies among media operations, the goal of reducing costs or increasing profit through synergies remains generally elusive. Efforts to create synergies in the content by *retooling* content for additional uses, by trying to create successful cross-media concept products in film, books, and games, and by using staff from one media operation to provide services to another have not generally produced the desired financial results. These efforts, however, have produced some advantages in terms of brand development and strengthening. Those factors are, of course, difficult to measure in terms of impact on company financial performance.

The most visible financial improvements resulting from mergers seeking synergies have occurred in noncontent areas of media operations. Some cost savings have been achieved through the combination of subscription marketing, billing, and distribution when magazine holdings have been joined. Cross-media synergies producing financial results through economies have also been possible when the warehousing and distribution operations for books, audio recordings, and DVDs have been joined.

Joint Interest, Joint Ventures, and Competition

Many observers of the growing networks of activities among media firms, including partial ownerships and related joint ventures of subsidiaries, point to these webs of activity as evidence that competition is diminishing and that there is a convergence of interests among big companies that is leading to co-option and collusion. These critics often argue that joint activities are a means by which big media firms have become powerful companies that dominate communications in a cooperative manner. Such concern can be illustrated by examining the relationships that exist between two large Australian media firms.

Rupert Murdoch's News Corporation and Kerry Packer's Australian Consolidated Press Holdings Ltd. (ACP) dominate much of the Australian media scene. Both own significant publishing, broadcasting, and news media operations.

When one takes a look at those operations, one finds significant relationships that link the firms. For example, the firms are joint owners of *TV Week*, Australia's leading television guide, and they also own equal shares of Foxtel, a subscription-broadcasting firm that distributes signals through cable and satellite delivery. Murdoch's News Corporation and Packer's ACP own half of Foxtel and the other half is owned by Telstra, the public telephone company that is in the process of privatization. Observers who use these types of relationships as indications of the diminishment of competition and the rise of cooperation among companies might easily come to the conclusion that News Corporation and ACP have aligned their operations in a friendly sharing of the Australian market.

However, one cannot immediately accept all such examples of joint activities as evidence of co-option and collusion between firms. Anyone who is familiar with the Australian media scene knows about the extraordinary vigor with which the separate holdings of News Corporation and ACP compete and the explicit rancour between Murdoch and Packer and executives of their respective firms. There is anything but a cozy relationship with friendly market divisions between the firms; each firm actively pursues its own advantage and works to block the other from gaining any competitive advantage.

More recently, media executives have attempted to achieve synergies by joining traditional media firms with online firms. However, most of the initiatives launched do not really create synergies. Instead, these efforts usually represent a defensive mechanism against competitors, risk reduction in case of rapid acceptance of Internet-based media and distribution, and the creation of new sales and distribution mechanisms. The extent to which these efforts are successful for different types of media and communications products and services remains to be seen.

As companies grow, it becomes difficult for corporate managers to focus attention on the wide variety of operations within their firms, so they often create divisions within the corporation that are headed by managers responsible for those operations. Sometimes they have subsidiary firms, semiautonomous companies in which they have significant or controlling ownership, within the scope of their responsibilities.

Large firms can be either private or publicly owned. Although some large privately held firms exist, public ownership is more common among large media and communications firms because of their needs for capital.

The typical corporate organization for large firms is based on a board of directors made up of the major owners of the firms and, often, other persons selected for their expertise or perspectives. Boards make major strategic decisions and typically determine company goals and objectives. Firms are typically headed by a chief executive officer (CEO), who is concerned with overall strategy and corporate development, and a chief operating officer (COO) who typically holds the president's title and is responsible for managing the implementation of strategies and overseeing the operations of the firm. Below these persons are managers of divisions or subsidiaries, who typically hold corporate vice presidential titles and presidential titles for their divisions or subsidiaries.

Different types of vertical and horizontal hierarchies are employed because every firm is unique and has varying managerial requirements. In large media corporations, however, it is typical to place responsibility for print and broadcast operations in different divisions because of the significant differences in their characteristics and the media-specific knowledge required. Large companies also differ in terms of their degree of centralization of decision making.

COMPANY CULTURES

Every company operates within its own culture that is created by its values, traditions, methods of operations, relations among management and employees, and other factors. This company culture is a particularly important factor in the ability of firms to grow, to change, and to integrate with other firms through mergers and acquisitions.

Synergies in growing companies may not be created because people may be used to operating in other company cultures and do not have experience working together and are not used to thinking about ways they can help other portions of the firm. The result can be differences in goals, in what is perceived as important, in how issues and problems are understood, and in varying levels of cooperation among the divisions or subsidiaries.

Within the same firm, even a small one, different cultures may exist in different departments and this may result in problems in coordination and joint activity. The differences result from the types of persons and working environments in which they are located.

If one examines media firms, for example, one often finds some personnel working in an entrepreneurial culture while others work in an administrative culture, some work in a creative culture whereas others exist in a maintenance culture, some persons work within a sales culture while others work in a production culture, and some persons work in a process culture whereas others work in an outcome culture. Finding ways to work together and understand each other's perspectives is critical for achieving cooperation and success within the firm.

In order for companies, especially large companies, to operate successfully, managers need to understand the culture of their companies and departments. This is problematic because cultures are rarely explicit, that is, they are rarely written down and explained in company descriptions, handbooks, or employee orientations.

MANAGERIAL CONFLICTS

In large firms a certain amount of conflict among managers of the corporate parent, among corporate managers and divisional and subsidiary managers, and among the managers of divisions and subsidiaries is normal because of their different needs and responsibilities. That conflict can rise to unhealthy levels, however, and create significant problems. Strong personality conflicts, competition among managers, and differing visions among managers can reduce cooperation and the performance of the firm overall.

The problem that conflicting leadership styles can create was starkly illustrated in the 1990s in the relationship between Michael Eisner, CEO of the Walt Disney Co., and Michael Ovitz, who was brought into the firm to become its president. Eisner, who is reported to have an autocratic style, clashed with Ovitz's own strong personality. He left the firm within a year taking with him a severance package that cost the company more than $100 million. In the late 1990s more than half a dozen senior executives left the firm to take top executive positions in other firms, including its chief strategist, two chief financial officers, senior executive vice president, and the head of its studio operations. Disney was obviously a good training ground for upper management, but many managers apparently were unhappy with managerial relations and did not see desirable upward opportunities within the company.

In order to avoid conflicts, leaders with strong personalities and visions often seek top managers whose personalities complement rather clash with their own. Al Neuharth built the Gannett Co. into one of America's largest

Internal Conflict in Large Companies: The Dispute Over Bertelsmann's Deal with Napster

Differences in perspectives about strategies and potential business opportunities can create conflicts within large companies. Managers of various divisions and subsidiaries have different perspectives and goals, and there is a rivalry among these different portions of the company for internal resources. Differences in the importance and influence of divisions and managers, as well as the personalities of managers, can also create conflict in the management team. If the conflict cannot be resolved through accommodation or compromise, it can become divisive and harm the continued pursuit of corporate goals.

In 2000 leading music industry firms filed copyright infringement suits against Napster, the online music file-sharing company. Before the case was concluded, however, Bertelsmann, Europe's largest media company, withdrew from the suit and announced it had reached an agreement for an alliance with Napster that would create a pay service to compensate the copyright owners of music. The arrangement was approved by company CEO Thomas Middelhoff, who determined that Bertelsmann's e-commerce division would work with Napster to create a paid membership service.

The decision, however, was opposed by the executives of Bertelsmann's music operations who had brought the original suit against Napster. Their opposition reportedly included preferences for other online strategies, the wish to remain united with other major record companies against file swapping, and the desire not to be seen as rewarding Napster's previous copyright infringement. When Middelhoff approved the Bertelsmann-Napster deal despite their opposition, Bertelsmann Music Group CEO Strauss Zelnick and President Michael Dornemann resigned.

media firms, and in his autobiography he characterized himself as an S.O.B. The position of his second in command was filled by John Curley, who was not overly aggressive, who did not seek the limelight, and who was excellent at implementing Neuharth's visions. Curley became the CEO after Neuharth retired.

Managerial differences can also emerge after mergers and acquisitions if the leaders of both companies remain in the firm. Although Gerald Levin of Time Warner and Ted Turner of Turner Broadcasting made a workable arrangement that provided Turner the status and relative autonomy he desired when those firms merged, Turner's ownership share and influence within the firm was reduced when Time Warner and AOL merged.

HOW LARGE IS LARGE?

Large media enterprises face a variety of financial, economic, and organizational pressures that are unique to firms of their size, as well as those

Middlehoff's decision to align Bertelsmann with Napster was part of a larger corporate strategy to become the world's leading music company and a leading online distributor of content, something it was already doing with books through its position as the world's largest book publisher. In making the deal with Napster, Bertelsmann made a significant alliance with the file-sharing firm, loaning it about $50 million and obtaining an option to purchase a large share of the company when settlements were reached with the other major record companies involved in the suits.

When a partial agreement on the lawsuits was reached, Napster was relaunched as a pay service that proved unpopular because many record companies—still angry over its past practices—would not license their music for sale on the site. The company fell into bankruptcy and attempted to pass its assets to Bertelsmann, but the bankruptcy court refused and liquidated its remaining assets to pay debt. Bertelsmann, however, was still involved in copyright lawsuits because of its ties with the company and it agreed in 2007 to pay $130 million to end lawsuits over copyright infringement by Napster.

The Napster dispute, along with other strategic disagreements with the board of directors of Bertelsmann, ultimately led to Middelhoff's replacement as CEO.

The strategic position of Bertelsmann Music Group remained a point of contention within the company despite the ending of the Napster dispute. Bertelsmann entered a joint venture with Sony Music Entertainment to form Sony BMG Music Entertainment in 2004, but the arrangement lasted only four years. In 2008, Sony bought out Bertelsmann's interest in the combined firm and renamed it Sony Music Entertainment.

pressures that are shared with smaller firms. However, the concept of size is relative and determined by comparison to other firms.

Although large media companies such as Time Warner, Vivendi, Bertelsmann, and News Corporation are larger than most firms involved in media, they are not among the top companies by any measure of company size. If one considers big media firms in terms of revenue, the numbers are clearly impressive (see Figure 11-3). Companies with billions of dollars in revenue can hardly be thought of as anything but *big*.

Based on 2007 revenue, however, ExxonMobil is ten times as large as Walt Disney Co., Wal-Mart is eight times larger than Time Warner, and General Motors is seven times larger than News Corporation (see Figure 11-4). Although media companies are of significant size, when compared in business terms they are not as large, rich, and independent as some might assume.

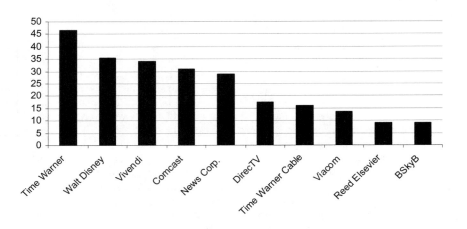

FIGURE 11-3   Revenues of largest media firms, 2007 ($ billions)

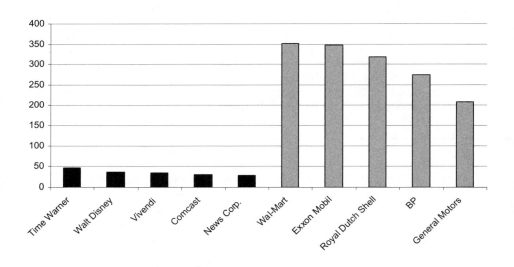

FIGURE 11-4   Revenues of media and largest firms in all industries, 2007 ($ billions)

SUGGESTED READINGS

Barnouw, Erik, ed. 1997. *Conglomerates and the Media*. New York: The New Press.

Baysinger, B. D., R. E. Meiners, and C. P. Zeithaml. 1981. *Barriers to Corporate Growth*. Lexington, Mass: Lexington Books.

Gaughan, Patrick A. 1999. *Mergers, Acquistions, and Corporate Restructuring.* New York: John Wiley & Sons.

Needham, Douglas. 1978. *The Economics of Industrial Structure Conduct and Performance.* New York: St. Martin's.

Penrose, E. T. 1959. *The Theory of the Growth of the Firm.* Oxford: Basil Blackwell.

CHAPTER 12

Trade and Globalization in Media Products and Services

Mid- and large-sized media companies are increasingly expanding their activities internationally as they attempt to benefit from additional opportunities and markets for their content and services. Even some small enterprises are finding innovative ways to operate globally. Their activities involve trade in their products and, sometimes, globalization of the firm by establishing itself in locations outside the country of its origin.

Trade is a term used to describe the movement of goods and services among countries and involves a number of activities ranging from shipping products to consumers outside the country of origin to establishing relationships with domestic distributors and retailers, who make them available in other countries.

Globalization is a term used to describe the increasing internationalization of business activities by companies worldwide that involve more than mere trade in goods and services to include establishment of subsidiaries and joint ventures worldwide, as well as activities such as the acquisitions of supplies and the manufacture of components or finished goods beyond the borders of the nation of a firm's origin.

A number of factors promote trade and globalization in media and communication product and services. The first is demand. Although media exist globally and some domestic production takes place in every location, large-scale content production capabilities—particularly in film and television—are not equally distributed and tend to be concentrated in a few countries. As a result, when desired products and services are unavailable domestically or when desirable products are elsewhere, firms in these nations look externally for content products they can use.

The uneven distribution of capabilities, amount of production, and range of content production has occurred because domestic needs and financial support for production in large content-producing countries such as the United States has made it possible for content-creation clusters to develop. These involve financiers, producers, studios and equipment, directors, actors, and other necessary personnel and support services. These resources have been used to create products and services to serve the domestic market and simultaneously seek additional uses in foreign markets.

Technical as well as policy changes worldwide have promoted trade and globalization in recent decades. Digitalization, global telecommunications, and transportation systems have combined to create mechanisms for easier distribution of media products outside their nation of origin. These changes have accompanied the liberalization of media and communications policies that has privatized much telecommunications infrastructure and created private commercial broadcast, cable, and satellite systems, increased the number of stations, channels, and networks, and generally heightened demand for information and entertainment products and services.

For some firms, globalization has occurred when ownership limits, antitrust regulations, or other governmental actions have blocked growth in a company's nation of origin. Some firms globalize when saturated domestic markets offer few additional opportunities or when revenue and profit levels plateau or decline in domestic markets and they seek horizontal and vertical integration opportunities elsewhere to increase revenue, reduce costs, or create economies.

Whatever the motivation for individual companies, trade and global expansion are becoming increasingly important activities for all sorts of media companies. In some cases they limit their activities to selected countries or regions. In other cases they engage in commerce worldwide depending upon their resources and strategies, and the demand for their media and communications products or services.

TRADE IN MEDIA PRODUCTS AND SERVICES

Trade in media products and services has occurred since the first person paid a publisher or contact in another country to send copies of books, newspapers, or other printed matter for personal or commercial use. The development of this trade often followed colonial lines. Colonists in Brazil and Indonesia wanted books published in their native Portuese or Dutch. Colonists in North America and India sent to England for copies of books and pamphlets. The needs of financial and business communities in Europe and North America led to the creation of financial news agencies—such as Agence Havas in France, Wolff's in Germany, and Reuters in the United

Kingdom—that began offering their information to clients outside their nations of origin more than 150 years ago. Today, there is vibrant worldwide trade in all types of media and communications, ranging from news and information to recordings to books to advertising.

EXPORTABILITY OF MEDIA PRODUCTS

Media industries have fundamental differences that affect exportability when compared to general goods and services, however. The properties of products and services such as automobiles, vacuum cleaners, and water filters make them easily traded among nations, assuming there are roads upon which to drive, electricity, and water systems. Media products, however, are different. The most important differences involve time sensitivity, language, and local or domestic content requirements.

Media products vary in terms of their time sensitivity depending upon their roles as information or entertainment providers. News and contemporary information must be disseminated rapidly to maintain its immediacy and currency to audiences. Information with less time sensitivity, such as feature materials and in-depth analysis, as well as entertainment materials, can be disseminated at a more leisurely pace without losing its attractiveness to audiences.

Time sensitivity is important because it affects the amount of lead time that is available before production, where the production takes place, the distances to which the product can be distributed (and thus market size), and the general exportability of products.

Newspapers have the highest time sensitivity because they are typically published daily. Magazines and periodicals have medium time sensitivity because they tend to have monthly frequencies, but a segment of the magazine industry has higher time sensitivity because of its weekly publication schedule. Books, motion pictures, videos, and audio recordings typically have the lowest time sensitivity.

Thus it is easier to export products with lower time sensitivity because the distribution time required in international trade does not make the product less valuable.

Language is also a significant factor affecting trade in communication products and services. Although many persons worldwide are bi- or multilingual, many others speak only their native language and most persons prefer content in their mother tongue. The result is that the majority of readers prefer printed news, information, educational publications, leisure, and cultural materials printed in their own languages, although this preference tends to be less strong in content of a scientific, professional, and technical nature. Audio recordings have been the most successful media products exported in their original languages, and motion picture and television programming producers have overcome linguistic problems by dubbing, subtitling, and other methods such as voice-over narration or secondary audio channels.

Media products, however, are not homogenous products that are relatively interchangeable once basic style and quality requirements are met. Because audiences use media for local news and information, and advertising associated with a particular city or region, information and advertising media such as newspapers are not easily substituted with products from abroad. Most magazines exist within a domestic framework, providing information that reflects a domestic culture and preferences. Domestic as well as foreign advertising is also served by this mechanism. The book industry also experiences strong domestic content pressure because literature, social commentary, current events, and history are domestic interests.

Acceptance of international audio recording artists is high, but domestic recording industries exist worldwide, providing music that reflects domestic culture and issues. The motion picture and television programming industries also produce highly exportable content and services, particularly from countries such as the United States, Canada, United Kingdom, Germany, France, Australia, Japan, Hong Kong (China), Egypt, Mexico, Spain, and Brazil. Despite this trade, domestic production exists in most nations, although financial and talent issues often limit the amount of domestic content available.

These issues of domestic content needs, language, and time sensitivity combine to affect the exportability of media products. The relative exportability is shown in Figure 12-2.

When a firm chooses to engage in trade, the number of factors affecting success rises rapidly and requires specific managerial attention. The company will now be affected by economic, social, and political developments in more than one nation. Therefore, its ability to conduct trade will require different types of financial structures and partners, additional planning and logistics, new marketing efforts, and a variety of changes in company strategy and organization.

For many companies, internationalization brings numerous benefits. However, risks are also present and companies need to be mindful of those risks when making decisions about how to engage in trade.

BARRIERS TO TRADE IN MEDIA PRODUCTS AND SERVICES

Trade barriers is a term typically used to describe the results of public policies that limit or halt the importation of products into one nation from another nation or the ability of foreign individuals or firms to do business

Trade in Records, Tapes, and Compact Discs

The recording industry is highly internationalized with recorded music regularly moving across national boarders. Trade takes place both as licenses of music to manufacture recordings in other nations and as direct exports of physical recordings.

The United States has played an active role in the global recording industry for the past seventy-five years. American artists have enjoyed significant success worldwide and have heavily influenced the rock, pop, jazz, and country genres. American artists such as Madonna, Britney Spears, Bruce Springsteen, Backstreet Boys, Mariah Carey, Nirvana, Carlos Santana, No Doubt, Michael Jackson, and Norah Jones have had great success outside the United States in the past three decades and made important contributions to the success of the U.S. industry.

If an artist or group has the potential for global success, the recording firms grant licenses to companies in other major countries to release and market the recordings there, but they also engage in direct exports of recordings to other nations. Because of a strong global market for recordings by American artists, physical records, tapes, and compact discs have a positive trade balance. Recordings are one of the products in which the U.S. has long maintained a positive balance.

In 2007, for example, exports of recordings to other countries totaled $4.95 billion and imports totaled $1.33 billion. This produced a positive trade balance of $3.62 billion (see Figure 12-1).

Because these are trade figures, the amounts represent only the value generated by physical recordings moving into or out of the United States. The data does not include the value generated by the domestic sales or the trade in licensing rights.

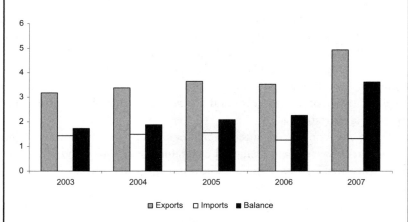

FIGURE 12-1   Total imports, total exports, and trade balance for records, tapes, and compact discs ($ billions)

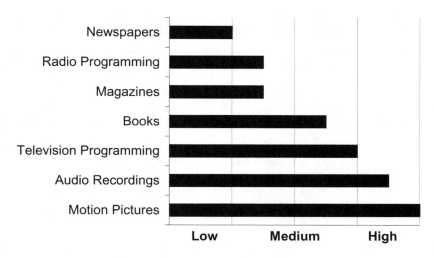

FIGURE 12-2   Relative exportability of different media products and services

or invest in a country. These are forms of barriers to entry. Most trade barriers emerge from good intentions of domestic policy makers, but some are erected as the result of poor intentions. Some barriers do harm to the global economic market by artificially harming competition in it. Others do harm to the competition for ideas by limiting the availability of ideas imported into a nation.

For the most part, trade barriers to transnational communication result from domestic efforts to respond to economic, cultural, and health and well-being issues. The primary economic rationales for barriers result from the desire to promote domestic economic activity, to protect or develop domestic employment, or to halt unfair competition such as product *dumping*, that is, selling below cost to gain greater market share.

Cultural rationales for trade barriers in communication products and services are intended to protect and promote domestic culture. This tends to be a concern of small nations or nations whose communication is overwhelmed by neighbors. There is also a cultural rationale intended to protect and promote subcultures, typically defined in ethnic or linguistic terms.

Health and well-being rationales for trade barriers in communication are typically designed to protect the public against harmful products and communications. The health rationale is typically used to place controls on advertising for products such as alcohol and tobacco. The desire to protect against harm to social well-being is seen in regulations intended to control depictions of violence, sex, or discriminatory and derogatory messages.

Strategies for Volatile Export Markets

The globalization of media company operations has created many opportunities for expanding the market base of companies. But the development has also created the new problem of handling volatile export markets. The decision to engage in foreign trade presents many additional challenges: new marketing and transportation needs, linguistic issues, banking and foreign exchange issues, dependency on trading partners, and the effects of changing foreign economies.

Each and all of these factors simultaneously tend to make foreign sales of media products and services more volatile than domestic trade. They also require that company boards and senior managers make specific decisions regarding export risks and that export operations be managed differently from domestic operations.

Although export markets are volatile, export operations yield great rewards in both the short term and long term.

Although risk is a natural part of any commercial activity, the level of risk acceptable to each media company differs. Companies engaged in exports must assess the risk individually and determine what level of risk they are willing to accept. If this is not done, companies are placed at the mercy of factors beyond their control and managers must respond rapidly with little or no planning to unanticipated changes in export markets.

The strategic issue of whether to accept the additional risks of exports and the amount of risk that is acceptable should be addressed by the company board that has the responsibility of setting company strategy. It then becomes the task of senior managers to monitor and control the risk within the levels set by the board.

Firms need accurate business intelligence on the export markets in which they have operations or are considering operating. Companies must also acquire and constantly update information about major firms with which they are doing business. These processes involve constant monitoring of economic, political, and social changes in the export markets for evidence of changes that may affect the trade.

A second strategy for benefiting from export markets involves limiting the dependency of a firm on exports or exports to particular nations or regions.

Policies affecting trade can be internally or externally oriented. Internally oriented policies prescribe action by internal firms or citizens in regard to communication. Externally oriented policies prescribe or address trade by external firms and non-nationals.

The internal approach is seen in domestic content policies that require domestic producers or distributors to include stipulated portions of the communications from nationals of a country. Canada, for example, requires that 60 percent of all programming and 50 percent of primetime programming must be of Canadian origin. Similarly, the European Union has established a 50 percent domestic content requirement for television broadcasts

Whenever a firm grows dependent upon another firm or a particular sector of its business, it increases the risk that it will be affected by adverse developments in the firm or sector. To protect against the risks of these changes, managers must try to diversify their trading partners and markets. This means doing business with more firms, providing products and services in different subsectors of the business that may be affected differently by changes in export markets, and diversifying both the nations and regions in which they do business so that the overall risk is minimized.

Because of such changes, boards of companies that engage in export trade need to manage that risk by establishing the level of risk of the overall activities of their firm. This risk level can be stated in terms of revenue or production capacity. A board may determine that no more than 15 or 25 percent of its revenues or profits will be the result of exports or the results of exports from particular countries. Or it may decide that it will devote only 10 or 20 percent of its capacity to export products.

Export markets also force companies to have clear strategies regarding facilities and equipment. The safest alternative is to use only excess capacity to serve export markets. The riskiest option is to invest in additional facilities and equipment to gain the capacity to serve them.

There is no right or wrong choice, but boards and managers should have a clear understanding of the implications of each strategy. The no-risk strategy limits the ability to gain additional benefits from export markets. The expansion-of-capacity strategy increases the dependence of the firm on exports and puts the firm at greater risk.

When companies begin to export products and services, they should develop contingency plans that answer questions such as, "What do we do if the market suddenly collapses? How will we need to restructure our operations to respond to increases and decreases in exports?"

These changes affect budgets, production scheduling, employment contracts, paper orders, and so on. Because export markets are often more volatile than domestic markets, these changes can occur so rapidly that little time is available to plan a response. By preparing contingency plans, a firm can respond more rapidly to the changes and reduce the potentially harmful effects on the company.

within its member states. Italy requires that one hundred days per year of each theater's operations must be reserved for Italian films.

In some cases, domestic production policies require that some or all of a product be produced within the country if it is to be distributed internally. These include provisions requiring that a domestic edition of an international magazine contain a certain percentage of domestically produced content or that advertising campaigns must be made within the nation.

The external orientation regulates activities of nondomestic firms. These include bans or limitations on foreign ownership, tariffs applied to foreign products, bans on importation, or requirements that foreign materials be translated, dubbed, or subtitled before importation. Mexico requires all imported programming to be dubbed in a neutral Mexican accent, generally taken to mean the accent spoken in the area of Mexico City, and that dubbing cannot use accents from other Latin American nations or idioms from other parts of the region.

A related conflict over regional dialect and language occurred recently when the Catalan region of Spain tried to use a law promoting Catalan Spanish to require the most popular films of any origin shown in the region be dubbed in Catalan, not in Castilian Spanish. Fines and closures would be levied on cinemas that did not comply. U.S. producers were especially concerned because of the additional costs of dubbing into Catalan and joined film distributors in challenging the requirement, which was subsequently struck down by Spanish courts.

REGIONAL AND GLOBAL TRADE AGREEMENTS

In order to standardize treatment and improve the speed of trade, nations worldwide have entered into agreements to make sales and movement of products and services across their borders easier. Some of these agreements are bilateral, that is, involving two nations. Other agreements are multilateral, that is, involving multiple nations. These agreements are designed to simplify customs regulations and taxes and to create an environment for easier flow of goods and services among nations.

Despite such agreements significant problems in trade in communications and information remain. These result from the fact that much activity in the communications field is typically classified as services and most international trade agreements have tended to cover goods but not services. In other cases, communication products and services have been specifically excluded in order to gain agreements on other products.

The primary multilateral agreements in recent years are those covered by what is known as General Agreements on Tariffs and Trade (GATT). In recent years, the United States and some other developed nations have attempted to get trade in information and entertainment products and services included in GATT. They have encountered strong resistance from other nations, primarily in the developed world, who insist on protectionist policies that assist development of their domestic information and communications industries. Other nations have resisted because they do not want nations with large communications industries to culturally dominate their media systems.

As a result, there are large multinational debates over media and communication products and services among members in the World Trade Organization (WTO) and in GATT negotiations that affect trade internationally.

In recent years these debates have focused on issues such as telecommunication services, databases, motion picture and television products, and advertising campaigns.

The Free Trade Agreement (1989) between the United States and Canada included information within its scope, but permitted the exclusion of motion pictures, audio recordings, and books through a cultural industry exemption clause. This allowed Canada and its provinces to provide advantages to Canadian producers and simultaneously implement policies to disadvantage U.S. products. When the North American Free Trade Agreement (NAFTA) came into play in 1994, covering trade among Mexico, the United States, and Canada, the exclusionary approach was extended and left films, TV programs, home video, books, and sound recordings out of the treaty. This permitted Canada to retain Canadian laws regarding copyright and foreign content and the ability to tax products differently.

This treatment of communications has made it possible for Canadian cable companies to retransmit U.S. broadcasts without payment to the U.S. stations or producers of the material, and for the United States to maintain its foreign ownership limits in broadcasting stations. A number of trade barrier conflicts have emerged among the two neighbors in recent years. One occurred when Canada tried to protect its magazine producers by prohibiting split-run magazines, in which U.S. firms produced a separate Canadian edition through dual use of the content of their U.S. editions and adding only a few pages of Canadian content and advertising. Canadian publishers particularly feared the effect on their advertising base and lobbied parliamentarians and ministers to create the protectionist barrier. The WTO ruled against the Canadian policy, but the Canadians have since attempted to preserve the protectionist effect by removing the tax deductibility of advertisements placed in Canadian versions of foreign-owned magazines.

METHODS OF GLOBALIZATION

Media firms use a variety of techniques to engage in globalization, including direct exports, licensing and rights sales, joint ventures, and direct foreign investment. Most of these were initially established in the early and mid-twentieth century by the magazine and motion picture industries but have now spread to the book, audio, and television programming industries.

DIRECT EXPORT

Direct export involves sending a product that is produced in one country to another country. In this form of export the producer acts as its own exporter or contracts with an exporter for the task. A book publisher in

Canada, for example, may market and sell its books in the United States through bookshops, direct mail, e-commerce, and other venues. Books are sent to stores and individuals when orders are received for the book.

PRODUCT LICENSING AND RIGHTS PURCHASES

Another form of internationalization that often occurs in the magazine, book, and audio industries involves firms in one country selling licenses to companies in another country to produce copies of the material or to translate it and then produce a domestic-language edition.

Many magazine publishers use this mechanism to acquire or sell rights to desirable titles and publishing concepts that they have created. Similar mechanisms exist in book publishing. In the audio recording industry, the rights to reproduce copies of CDs and cassettes are often sold by the original recording company to subsidiary or sister companies in other nations and to others interested in purchasing rights to sell the recording outside the original market.

Advances in electronic commerce and new rapid distribution systems are creating new problems related to rights purchases. These developments increase the need for firms to acquire rights territorially and to be protected against imports from outside the territory that diminish the value of the rights. This is particularly true when the same product is sold at different prices in different parts of the world to account for differences in income and demand.

FORMAT LICENSING

This form of licensing involves selling the rights to use an established television program format in another country. Many licensed formats involve game shows because of their worldwide popularity. Audiences, however, want the shows to involve domestic citizens and to involve domestic culture and personalities.

As a result, rather than selling the rights to broadcast an existing production of an American show, for example, the rights to use the format or concept are sold. As a result, domestic versions of programs such as "Wheel of Fortune" or "Do You Want to Be a Millionaire?" are produced worldwide under license from the original producers.

JOINT VENTURES

Another mechanism of media internationalization is joint ventures. These are often seen in the magazine publishing and television programming industry. In magazines, for example, the originating company and the domestic publisher enter a partnership to produce a magazine title and sometimes additional titles as well. Similarly, television and cable producers agree to jointly produce a series or motion picture with each gaining the first exclusive rights to the material in their nations or regions.

DIRECT FOREIGN INVESTMENT

This type of globalization occurs when a firm internationalizes by purchasing an existing company in another nation or by establishing a subsidiary firm in that country. This type of investment creates wealth for the firm by increasing its company's assets and, when successful, additional dividends for its shareholders. The ultimate result is that it strengthens firms, provides them with more resources, and increases their size.

Media firms engage in direct foreign investment for several reasons, usually beginning when they have exploited the mature, saturated markets in their nation of origin and better returns can be found by expanding abroad. Foreign markets provide opportunities for company growth without diversification into other businesses and create the ability for companies to continue developing the national market in which they originated. Unusually strong ownership regulation or heavier taxation in the domestic market than in foreign markets can also promote direct foreign investment.

PATTERNS OF MEDIA GLOBALIZATION

Whether and how individual media firms globalize is dependent upon their needs, strategies, and the types of products and services involved.

Many cultural critics have argued that U.S. media firms are heavily globalized and dominate communications worldwide. In truth, however, non-U.S. firms now dominate global communications. The erroneous impression is created because these critics do not separate ownership from products and content.

If one closely considers the activities of American-owned firms, one discovers that only a few have strong global operations today. U.S. media companies have made little direct foreign investment and have relied upon direct export, joint ventures, and licensing to move products worldwide. The size of the U.S. market, with its internal opportunities and linguistic limitations, and lack of foreign experience have kept most American media firms from making significant efforts to globalize their operations.

Today, only a few American-owned media firms are really globalized. The three with the largest activities worldwide are Time Warner, the Walt Disney Co., and Viacom. The primary and common activities that make these three important global players are television programming, motion picture production, and film and television program libraries that are marketed worldwide.

Large Global Players in Selected Media Fields

Audio Recordings
  Time Warner (USA)
  Sony (Japan)
  Vivendi Universal (France)
  EMI (UK)

Motion Pictures
  Time Warner (USA)
  News Corp. (Australia)
  Sony (Japan)
  Viacom (USA)
  Vivendi Universal (France)
  Walt Disney Co. (USA)

Consumer Magazines
  Time Warner (USA)
  Bertelsmann (Germany)
  Hachette Filipacchi (France)

Books
  Pearson (UK)
  Bertelsmann (Germany)
  Reed Elsevier (UK and Netherlands)
  Thomson Reuters (Canada and UK)
  Wolters Kluwer (Netherlands)

Television/Cable/Satellite Programming
  Time Warner (USA)
  News Corp. (Australia)
  Viacom (USA)
  Vivendi Universal (France)
  Walt Disney Co. (USA)

Cable and Satellite Systems
  Time Warner Cable (USA)
  AT&T (USA)
  Comcast (USA)
  Cablevision (USA)
  Direct TV (USA)
  News Corp. (Australia)

Online Services
  Time Warner (USA)
  Yahoo! (USA)
  Google (USA)
  Microsoft (USA)

Companies from other nations, however, have made significant direct foreign investments, particularly in the past quarter century. Many of those investments have been the acquisition of American content firms. The world's largest book publisher today is Bertelsmann A.G., the German multinational media conglomerate that owns such U.S. publishers as Random House, Knopf, Ballantine, Doubleday, and Bantam Dell. The biggest magazine company today is the French firm Hachette Filipachi (a subsidiary of Legardère), which owns more than two hundred titles, including *Elle, Car & Driver,* and *Woman's Day.*

Non-American firms also dominate the global music industry. Sony Music Entertainment, Universal Music Group, and EMI Group account for two-thirds of the revenue of the recording industry worldwide and release recordings by top musical artists from the United States and throughout the world. Warner Music Group, a U.S. firm that is part of Time Warner, competes with the other three major firms globally, but has a share of less than 15 percent of the global market.

The motion picture and television production industries are increasingly foreign owned. Universal Studios and Universal Pictures are jointedly owned by NBC and the French firm Vivendi Universal. Tri-Star and Columbia Pictures are owned by the Japanese electronics and entertainment giant Sony Corp., and Twentieth Century Fox is owned by the Australian conglomerate News Corporation.

Ownership of content libraries is increasingly important because of the global growth of television, video recording, and video on demand markets. The large foreign owners of studios have recognized this fact, and today, about half of the U.S. feature films in these collections are owned by non-U.S. firms.

Although the dominant ownership of media and content firms is increasingly non-American, U.S. produced media and content products and services are overwhelmingly represented in the products offered by those firms and dominate the global trade in motion pictures, television programming, and audio recordings.

Globalizing media firms and the sale of media products and services opens new markets and creates opportunities for media products and services, particularly entertainment products. The requirements of operating in the global environment, however, means that companies must adjust to the demands of multiple markets by structuring their companies in ways to accommodate those demands and the organizational necessities of larger operation.

Globalization is a multidirectional activity and alters capital availability, ownership, product demand, and business strategy patterns. Companies operating in the global environment encounter more competition than at the domestic level. Because communications, technology, and transportation improvements are reducing the importance of distance and the nation-state, global opportunities are increasing for a variety of types of media firms and products and services.

SUGGESTED READINGS

Albarran, Alan B., and Sylvia M. Chan-Olmsted. 1998. *Global Media Economics: Commercialization, Concentration, and Integration of World Media Markets.* Ames: Iowa State University Press.

Demers, David. 1999. *Global Media: Menace or Messiah.* Cresskill, N.J.: Hampton Press.

Freedman, Nigel, ed. 1991. *Strategic Management in Major Multinational Companies.* New York: Pergamon Press.

Gershon, Richard A. 1997. *The Transnational Media Corporation.* Mahwah, N.J.: Lawrence Erlbaum.

Prahalad, C. K., and Yves L. Doz. 1999. *The Multinational Mission: Balancing Local Demand and Global Vision.* New York: Simon and Schuster.

de la Sierra, M. Cauley, and Margaret Cauley. 1995. *Managing Global Alliances: Key Steps for Successful Collaboration.* Boston: Addison-Wesley Publishing Co.

Smith, Anthony. 1991. *The Age of Behemoths: The Globalization of Mass Media Firms.* New York: Priority Press.

Steinbock, Dan. 1995. *Triumph & Erosion in the American Media & Entertainment Industries.* Westport, Conn.: Quorum Books.

CHAPTER 13

Indicators of Financial and Economic Health of Media Firms

In order to evaluate the operations of their firms and to compare performance over time or among firms, managers employ a variety of economic and financial indicators to measure the health of their media firms. These include indicators of economic and financial health and indicators of internal company health.

INDICATORS OF ECONOMIC HEALTH

The economic health of media companies is exemplified by the state of its markets and consumers' desire for the products and services produced by those companies. Changes in these indicators of the health of companies and their industries can be observed to determine elements of their future and the potential need to alter company strategies to respond to those changes.

MARKET SHARE CHANGE OR MAINTENANCE

By considering a company's share of the market for a particular good or service, one gains an understanding of its position in the market and whether that position is being maintained, improved, or degraded. Changes in market share indicate that competitiveness has been maintained, improved, or lost by firms or that the market structure is being affected by entry or exit or better competitiveness on the part of other firms.

An online portal whose web site receives 15 percent of the hits for portals that organize and provide access to content will work to maintain and expand that market share as an evidence of its strength. If its market share declines to 13 or 14 percent it is losing portions of the market to other competitors who are seen by portal users as better meeting their needs or providing better service or quality.

Market share is measured in terms of circulation for print media, in sales for consumer products such as audio cassettes, CDs, CD-ROMs, videos, DVDs, and so on, and by ratings and share for most electronic media. As noted in Chapter 6, most of data regarding such items is provided by or audited by independent organizations that serve all media competitors and advertisers. These data provide means for monitoring developments regarding market shares.

In the past, a media firm was evaluated as healthy if its market share was growing. Today, with the proliferation of media, health tends to be evidenced in maintaining market share or growth within a small niche in which the firm operates.

CHANGES IN DEMAND

Changes in demand for a product or service can rapidly affect the state of any industry, so it is important for managers to monitor changes in demand.

In many economic studies, price is typically illustrated as the dominant force on demand. Although there is truth to this view, media and other products are affected by a variety of demand factors for individuals, including income, time for use of the product or service, requirements for additional purchases (such as software, CDs, DVDs, and so on), and skills required to operate products.

In additional, large-scale demand changes can be caused by the age of the users. In such cases, if the primary users of the product or service are older, they continue its use, but their numbers are reduced by mortality. In other cases, if the primary users are young people and birth rates decline, demand will be accordingly reduced in the future. Other cases of large-scale change include changes in linguistic needs of audiences caused by immigration, economic downturns, and the developments of new and more interesting products and services.

INDICATORS OF FINANCIAL HEALTH

It is important for managers to review regularly the financial health of their firms because financial data provides the key indicators of whether a firm is becoming or remaining a viable business entity. Basic indicators that need to be regularly reviewed involve sales and cash flow, profitability, the status of working capital, and the condition of the balance sheet.

Indicators provide both short-term and long-term indicators of financial health. Operating data, for example, tells what has occurred financially in the company during a given period and this can be compared to previous periods. But such operating data does not tell about the strength of the firm and its continued viability, so additional information from company balance sheets is necessary to gain a better understanding of its financial status and changes in that status.

SALES REVENUE GROWTH OR DECLINE

This measure is one of several financial growth measures that consider changes in financial performance. Firms whose sales revenues are growing are seen to have better relative health than those whose sales revenues are stable or declining. Sales revenues are indicators of the success that the company's products and services are having in the marketplace and the economic condition of the marketplace itself.

To gauge performance, revenue and change in revenue of a firm are tracked and compared to a similar period in the past. One could compare sales revenue changes from month to month, but this would present a distorted picture for two reasons: advertising revenue, in particular, is highly seasonal and use of certain products and services declines during holiday seasons. The months before Christmas, for example, are when most retailers achieve most of their sales. Consequently, department stores and other shops tend to spend most of their advertising budgets during that period. Similarly, telephone use tends to go down during summer months. As a result, media and communications executives compare revenues or change in revenue to the same period in previous years.

Because revenues are affected by inflation, current revenue amounts can only be understood if adjusted to account for the effect of inflation. A radio station that achieves revenue growth of 3 percent during a period of 2 percent inflation has actually achieved a true growth rate of 1 percent. If the inflation rate were 3.5 percent, the station would have a negative growth rate of one-half percent.

Healthy companies evidence regular growth of sales revenues. These can be interrupted by economic downturns, short-term product failures, and other factors. However, a company that is not able to achieve revenue growth over time tends to stagnate, have insufficient resources for product development and reinvestment, and ultimately declines.

In periods in which revenue growth is not shown, managers need to determine the reasons for the lack of growth and respond to the condition with budget reductions, product improvement strategies, additional marketing, and other efforts to improve performance in the marketplace depending upon the causes of the condition.

Basic Information You Need to Understand Media Industries and Firms

To comprehend the conditions and pressures on media businesses and media industries, one needs to have certain basic economic and financial information. At the industry level, data can be obtained from national statistics offices and industry associations. At the company level, information can be obtained from company registry information and annual reports.

Information is needed for the last year to obtain a contemporary view. However, to obtain a basic view of trends information is needed for the past five to ten years.

Industry-Level Data

How many companies operate in the field?

What is the total turnover (revenue) produced in the industry?
    What amount comes from advertising?
    What amount comes from viewers, listeners, and readers?
    What amount comes from other sources?

How has turnover changed?

What is the media industry's share of total advertising?

How has that share of advertising changed?

What is the industry's share of total consumer expenditures for media?

How has that share of expenditures changed?

How many people are employed in the industry?

How has employment in the industry changed?

CHANGE IN RESULTS

Results are indicators of profit and thus of the effectiveness with which firms use resources. These standard measures of performance are accounting-based figures that provide a view of what the company gained or lost due to its operations and other activities during a period of time. These are reported in operating statements.

DEBT GROWTH OR DECLINE

All firms carry debt in one form or another, ranging from invoices that have been received but not yet paid to money borrowed to purchase new facilities and equipment or to acquire other firms.

Managers must make a variety of strategies and choices regarding whether to incur debt and the amount of debt they are willing to carry. Carrying some debt at any given time may be desirable for a variety of reasons. Managers, however, must manage and monitor the debt incurred and this is typically done by tracking both short-term and long-term debts.

What is the value of imports and exports of products in the industry?

Who are the main customers of firms in the industry?

What social or economic changes are altering their purchasing and use choices?

Company-Level Data

What are the firm's turnover (revenue) and its sources?

What is the company's share of the audience market?

What is the firm's share of the advertising market?

What is the company's operating margin?

What is the company's net income before depreciation?

What is the firm's net income before extraordinary items?

What is the firm's equity ratio?

What is the firm's relative indebtedness?

What is the company's quick ratio?

What is the turnover per employee?

What is the value added per employee?

How much capital investment has been made?

What are the assets of the firm?

What is its share price?

What are the dividends it has paid to investors?

How have these indicators changed?

A healthy firm ensures that the debt load it carries is well within its abilities to repay and that it can manage the debt even if there are down-turns in revenues. Weak firms are often found to have used all the credit available to them and scramble to pay debtors merely interest on the debts.

CHANGE IN ASSET VALUE

Assets are tangible objects of material value that belong to a company. In healthy companies, the value of assets outweighs the value of liabilities and the value of assets grows over time. Company balance sheets indicate the kinds and values of assets that a firm possesses and they compare (or balance) them with liabilities to show the financial strength of a firm. In a healthy firm, assets exceed liabilities and in weak firms, assets are equal to or less than the liabilities.

If assets are not regularly increasing in value, managers need to consider the reasons and determine whether and what action is warranted. Asset values decline for a number of reasons and these need to be understood so that one can interpret the changes in asset value reflected on a balance sheet.

First, fixed assets, such as equipment, lose value over time because their use creates wear and reduces the length of time they can be used. This loss is accounted for through depreciation of assets in company financial records. Reductions in the value of assets because of their use can only be reversed through the purchase of new assets that provide additional value. For example, a transmitter and related equipment loses some of its value over time because of the wear and tear of regular use. If a television station purchases equipment to upgrade or improve the transmission system, the capital expenditure adds value to the system in the financial statements.

Second, the value of assets declines because of inflation. If the assets were purchased and valued when currency was worth more, inflation produces a decline in that value.

Third, the value of assets will normally decline if a firm divests by selling existing properties and does not, or is unable to, use the proceeds to purchase replacement assets or hold as cash.

A healthy company overcomes the natural decline in assets that takes place because of depreciation, changes in the general economy, and divestment. This is done through regular reinvestment in the form of capital expenditures, acquisitions, and appreciation of assets. Because cash for the reinvestment is typically produced by profits, managers need to produce regular profits for reinvestment and to build cash reserves for large reinvestments.

The issue of assets in modern media and communications firms is particularly complicated because much of the value is in brands, in copyrights, and in the personnel that they employ. Although methods have been created to place a financial value to intangibles such as brand names and copyrighted material, the value of knowledgeable and creative employees as a collective cannot be measured.

REINVESTMENT

Reinvestment is the return of profits to a firm to further develop the company and its activities.

If profits are continually taken from a firm without reinvesting an adequate portion in the company, it is denied resources needed to help it improve its operations, grow, and remain competitive.

The largest portions of reinvestment come in the form of capital expenditures. These involve reinvestment to improve or acquire capital assets such as buildings and equipment or other firms. Although a certain amount of capital expenditures occur each year, the amount required by any firm varies from year to year depending upon the age and conditions of the company's most important machinery and buildings, the necessity of immediate investments in newly available technologies, and the annual financial performance of the company.

Fixed assets, such as equipment, lose value over time because their use creates wear and reduces the length of time they can be used. This loss is accounted for through depreciation of assets in company financial records. Reductions in the value of assets because of their use can only be reversed through reinvestment that purchases new assets that provide additional value.

For example, a transmitter and related equipment lose some of their value over time because of the wear and tear of regular use. If a television station purchases equipment to upgrade or improve the transmission system, the capital expenditure adds value to the system in the financial statements.

The value of a firm's assets will decline if a firm divests by selling some existing properties and does not, or is unable to, use the proceeds to purchase replacement assets or hold as cash.

A healthy company overcomes the natural decline in assets that takes place because of depreciation, changes in the general economy, and divestment through regular reinvestment through capital expenditures, acquisitions, and appreciation of assets. Because cash for the reinvestment is most often obtained by using portions of the previous years' operating profits, the funds available for reinvestment vary from year to year. Similarly, the condition of existing assets and strategies that managers adopt that may put a lower priority on reinvestment in any given year affect the pace of capital investments.

Figure 13-1 illustrates fluctuations in capital investments by Tribune Co., one of the largest broadcasting, publishing, and new media firms in the United States.

FIGURE 13-1   Capital expenditures of the Tribune Co., 1980–2007 ($ millions)

Changes in expenditures can also be viewed at the industry level and these fluctuations in capital investment are illustrated by the U.S. cable television industry, which made significant investments around the millennium and after the 2001–2003 recession to upgrade capacity and capabilities of cable systems (see Figure 13-2).

INDICATORS OF COMPANY INTERNAL HEALTH

Indicators of company internal health focus on factors that managers can control through strategic and operation choices. Important indicators include productivity, capacity utilization, employee turnover, personnel skills and knowledge, and innovation and product development.

PRODUCTIVITY

Productivity involves the effectiveness with which firms use resources in their operations. Measures of productivity are made by the amount of output created by use of input such as labor and capital. A higher measure of productivity indicates that a company is using resources more effectively in creating products or services.

In media companies with well-established operations, the primary measure of productivity involves productivity of labor. This productivity can be measured in several ways. The simplest is calculating productivity as turnover per employee. Using this method, total turnover is divided by the

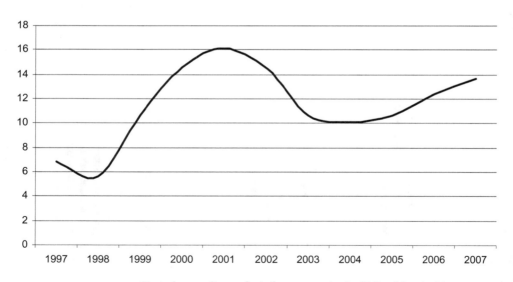

FIGURE 13-2   Capital expenditures for infrastructure in the U.S. cable television industry ($ billions) (Source: National Cable Television Association)

number of full-time equivalent employees. This method provides a measure of the amount of revenue (turnover) produced by the labor of the average employee. An increase in productivity is shown when the amount rises, a decrease when the amount declines.

When viewed in comparative terms, productivity data provides useful understanding of development in an industry. Recent data on productivity of cable and subscription program companies, for example, reveals that although productivity declined in the mid 1990s, it has risen about 70 percent since that then (see Figure 13-3).

Although this type of analysis is useful for industry analysis, it lacks the precision of measuring productivity using value added per employee. The value-added measure is obtained by subtracting the costs of production from total revenue and then dividing by the number of employees. Managers can use this better measurement because this internal information is available within companies.

This type of data is useful in strategic planning. It can be employed to review performance of a single firm or department over time, or to compare the performance of one firm with other firms to determine which is more effective. A manager of a magazine company with multiple titles, for example, could regularly compare productivity among the titles to determine which are most effective. Using this information, efforts could be made to improve the productivity of poorer-performing titles or to determine whether they should be candidates for divestiture.

A magazine firm with seven titles might produce productivity results as illustrated in Figure 13-4. A manager reviewing the chart can immediately

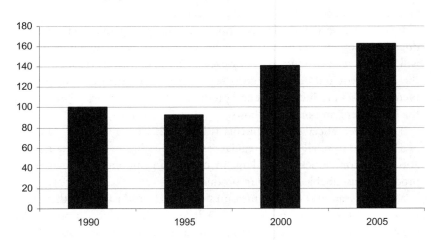

FIGURE 13-3   Index of productivity of cable and subscription programming companies, measured as output per hour (Source: U.S. Bureau of Labor Statistics)

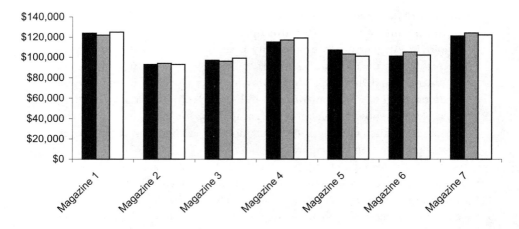

■ Value added per employee in 2006   ▨ Value added per employee in 2007   ☐ Value added per employee in 2008

FIGURE 13-4   Sample productivity display for a magazine company's titles (in value added per employee)

see that Magazines 1, 4, and 7 achieve the highest productivity, that Magazine 4 has achieved increases in productivity during the past three years, and that productivity has declined in Magazine 5.

Productivity analyses can be combined with profitability analysis to gain a very powerful tool for engineering productivity and profitability. Productivity measurements can also be applied to individual employees, but requires careful use in communications industries because mere output is not an appropriate measure of content production.

Investments in laborsaving equipment or equipment that increases production are often used by firms to increase productivity. These investments will only increase productivity, however, if the labor savings are higher than the investment and operating costs for the new equipment or if the equipment increases product output and produces additional income that exceeds the investment and operating costs.

The desired effect of investments is illustrated in Figure 13-5. Managers of a firm that normally makes regular capital expenditures to maintain operations may sometimes make a large investment in equipment or facilities to produce a sustainable increase in productivity.

Managers can also employ measures of capital productivity if they want to compare the returns on investment in multiple products produced by their firm. This technique is useful for managers of media and communications companies. A cable television firm, for example, might compare the

Measuring Productivity of Personnel

Productivity of personnel measures the output created by the use of employees. The measurement is meaningful for comparisons over time and between and among firms and industries.

The easiest measurement is revenue resulting from labor in the firm:

$$\frac{\text{total operating revenue}}{\text{full-time equivalent employees}}$$

A better measurement of productivity is the value added to goods or services through the labor of employees. It is more precise because it adjusts for that portion of the revenue related to the value of the materials used in preparing the good or service:

$$\text{value added per employee} = \frac{[\text{total operating revenue} - \text{cost of materials}]}{\text{full-time equivalent employees}}$$

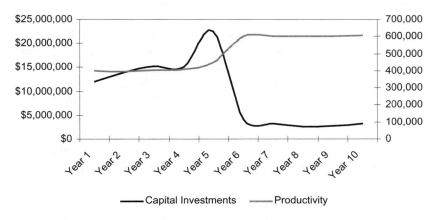

Capital Investments   Productivity

FIGURE 13-5   Desired effect of capital expenditures on productivity

returns on investment of various networks that it owns and operates. A radio station holding company might compare the effectiveness of the use of its capital in different stations, and an online media firm could use the measure to compare the effectiveness of its investments in different portals or other online services.

To make these kinds of capital productivity measurements, managers calculate return on investment in each firm and then make comparisons.

CAPACITY UTILIZATION

When firms are involved in the production of goods, more effective use of the manufacturing equipment that is required to produce them creates cost advantages to a firm that are indicative of higher health.

This can be observed in the case of magazine publishing companies that own printing facilities in which they produce their own publications and contract printing services to other publishers. If one company uses 60 percent of its production capacity and the other uses 85 percent of its capacity, the latter firm is spreading its fixed costs of the equipment and facilities better across its range of production.

Similar types of capacity utilization come into play in the manufacturing of recordings and videos, motion picture prints, advertising materials, and other physical communication products.

EMPLOYEE TURNOVER

The number of employees that leave and join a firm are an indicator of employee satisfaction and the ability of a firm to maintain the personnel and knowledge base that are necessary for effective operation.

A certain amount of turnover is natural as employees retire, change plans, pursue other opportunities, and move with spouses. If turnover rate is high, however, the firm loses productive ability because it must operate with persons unfamiliar with the firm and its culture, it must bear significant recruitment and training costs, and its employees must cope with natural psychological disruptions and problems caused by integrating new employees.

Although it is becoming less common for employees to spend their working lives—or the majority of it—with only one company, firms still monitor turnover rates because changes can indicate the internal problems that managers can address and because higher levels create greater training and development costs that many firms want to avoid.

Turnover rates for employees can be measured and compared over time and within and across companies. The basic turnover index is calculated as follows:

TTR = [S / N] x 100

TTR = total turnover rate

S = number of employees separated in the time period

N = average number of employees in the unit in the time period

The total turnover rate index does not provide an indication of why turnover occurred. This can be accounted for by using the same basic formula but substituting any of the following measures or other measures for S:

F = number of employees who were fired in the time period

Q = number of employees who quit in the time period

R = number of employees who retired in the time period

D = number of employees who died in the time period

PERSONNEL SKILLS AND KNOWLEDGE

The ability of personnel to carry out tasks is a critical factor in the success of companies, especially companies in rapidly changing industries. Because media firms exist in a knowledge production and technology environment, those firms whose employees have better skills in using digital and mechanical technologies and better ability to create and convey knowledge and entertainment gain competitive advantages.

Because of changing demands on the media and communications firms, retraining and development of employees becomes a managerial choice. By monitoring the skills and knowledge of different types of employees, managers can assess the overall level of their employees and develop internal training programs or send employees to external training programs that increase their ability to contribute to the firm by making them more effective or preparing them for coming changes in the industry, the firm, and their markets.

INNOVATION (R&D, NEW PRODUCTS AND SERVICES)

The degree to which a company pursues innovation affects its health by either making it a market leader or market follower. Companies that invest in research and in developing new products and services are looking toward the future health of the company by ensuring that its products and approaches are contemporary, position the company for future growth, and provide mechanisms for that growth. Innovation is important because it increases demand and profitability and helps the firm develop further.

If companies become wedded to current operations, always doing things as they have in the past, and producing the same products or services, they place themselves at risk through steady decline. This is especially true when innovations are introduced by firms outside the industry or by newcomers to the industry whose operations are not constrained by tradition and existing products. These types of innovators ultimately force other firms in an industry to change the way they operate or to face demise.

In order to protect against these possibilities and to ensure their position for the future, firms can choose to pursue internal innovation by rethinking and improving their products and services, developing new ones, and changing how they do business. In media firms content development, development of new operations, and finding new ways to benefit from content are key to innovation.

Most media firms do not have separate research and development departments as in many manufacturing and other firms, but the best firms engage in innovation by constantly researching their markets and customers, strengthening their existing publications, broadcasts, and materials. They also test and launch new publications and programs, and seek new uses for existing materials.

RESOURCE DEPENDENCE

Organizations depend upon their environment for resources because they cannot generate all the resources and functions they need to operate. Resources include such factors as capital, supplies, labor, and revenue.

An organization's structure and behavior are to a significant extent dictated by the amount and locations of resources needed and those activities that are required to acquire the resources. In order to survive, organizations must be able to obtain external resources efficiently so they enter into transactions and relationships with other organizations to acquire them.

The degrees of dependence and interdependence on specific resources and on external organizations are also an indicator of the health of a firm.

The performances of newspaper companies, for example, are dependent upon advertising income and newsprint availability and price. Television channels are also dependent upon advertising income but are highly affected by the prices for purchased programming.

A major problem of firms is uncertainty about future developments in the market and changes that may occur in the environment. This uncertainty is important, because when the environment changes, the ability to acquire resources may also change and harm a company. Because change is constant, organizations must be able to adapt to changes to solve the problems or they cannot survive.

Most companies have some form of interdependence with other organizations and providers of resources that is promoted by scarcity of resources and specialization of firms. Coordinating activities between organizations and combining organizations can alter the degree of interdependence. Coordinating activities include market segmentation, joint ventures, interlocking directorships, and the exchange of information for mutual benefit. All of these are done to stabilize markets. When interdependence is high, organizations may seek to combine through mergers, vertical integration, and diversification.

When dependency on a particular resource is high, coordination is more likely. Thus when capital is a critical resource, a firm will tend to have bankers, venture capitalists, or brokers on its board or as close advisors. If advertising is a critical resource, the firm's organization is likely to have representatives of major advertisers on a board or providing regular advice.

Organizations operating in a single product or geographic market are most vulnerable to change because they are often highly dependent upon resources in that market. Media companies that operate in more than one market are less vulnerable to change because their risk is spread and they are less dependent upon developments in any one market for survival.

Dependency on resources takes several forms. Capital dependence develops when a company becomes dependent upon one capital source, one banking firm, and so on. Revenue dependency occurs when large portions of revenue come from a single or only a few sources. Interfirm dependency develops when a single supplier provides other critical resources. This occurs, for example, when a television program producer becomes dependent upon one channel or network for sales or a newspaper becomes dependent upon one supplier for newsprint.

BENCHMARKING

Benchmarking is a managerial tool used to compare the performance of a firm against a specified level of performance or the performance of competitors. The purpose of benchmarking is to provide managers a standard against which to gauge their performance in terms of any number of operational or financial variables, including those discussed earlier in this chapter.

Benchmarking can be undertaken when a trusted entity such as an industry association or research organization is asked to measure industry-wide criteria of success by identifying processes and factors critical to success of firms in the industry. The organization then collects data on the performance of companies in the industry, permitting managers to compare their firm's performance against the average and best practices so that they can identify areas in which to seek improvement.

A magazine publisher, for example, might compare its percentage of unsold single copies against the average percentage of unsold single copies in the industry. By using the benchmark of the industry average, the publisher might find it was below the average, at the average range, or above the average.

Figure 13-6 illustrates this situation and shows that during the past year a magazine consistently has more unsold single copies than the industry average. With a 12 percent annual average of unsold copies—compared to the industry average of 11 percent—the publisher has 9 percent more unsold copies than other publishers. This difference warrants consideration of the

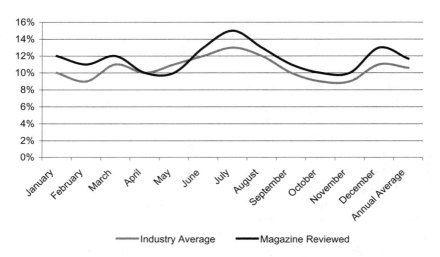

FIGURE 13-6 Example of a magazine's unsold single copies compared to the benchmark industry average

factors that may play a role to determine if changing the number of copies printed and distributed or changes in marketing may be warranted.

Benchmarking can also be used to compare performance to a set standard. A cable television system, for example, may have been experiencing problems with the reliability of their service, implemented a program to improve the service, and set a standard that there should be no more than 1 percent of customers making service calls annually. A manager can then view progress toward meeting that benchmark to determine whether the efforts are effective, as illustrated in Figure 13-7.

This type of analysis becomes even more powerful if one is able to do financial benchmarking to compare items on a company's operating statement or balance sheet. One might, for example, compare costs of borrowed capital for a radio station against the industry average. In the example shown in Table 13-1, the station's costs are lower and increasingly lower than other stations in the industry, a sign that it is carrying lower debt or obtaining capital at better rates than the average station.

Benchmarking is useful for gauging the performance of one's company, but to make it work effectively benchmarking requires managers to be willing to contribute their own data to benchmarking studies that are typically undertaken by industry associations or by researchers selected by those associations. The benchmarks improve as more companies take part in the studies and it becomes possible to break out data for different types and sizes of companies. For example, a study of newspapers might break data out by

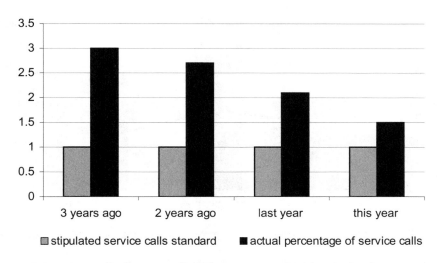

Performance of a cable company against the stipulated
benchmark of service calls

TABLE 13-1 · BENCHMARKING OF CONTRIBUTION OF BORROWED
CAPITAL TO OVERALL COSTS, IN PERCENT

	2004	2005	2006	2007	2008
Station studied	1.8	2.0	0.7	0.3	0.4
Industry average	3.3	7.4	3.8	3.5	2.0
Difference in station studied	45.5% lower	73% lower	81.6% lower	91.4% lower	80% lower

circulation categories, a study of television stations might break data out by
network-affiliated and independent stations and by population in the markets in which they operate, and a study of advertising agencies might break
out the data by the number of employees or annual billings.

Thus, a study of telecommunications costs in magazines might produce
the benchmarks shown in Figure 13-8 to which a publisher could compare
its own costs.

Even when benchmarking is not possible in an industry, a company with
multiple units of the same type of media can conduct internal benchmarking. A company owning fifteen radio stations, for example, may internally
collect and compare a wide variety of financial and operational data on
those companies to look for anomalies that need investigation and to identify best performance and practices for its other stations to emulate.

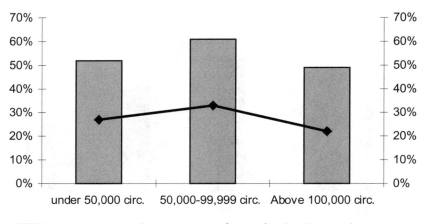

FIGURE 13-8   Benchmark example of average telecommunication costs for a magazine

SUGGESTED READINGS

Brinkerhoff, Robert O., and Dennis E. Dressler. 1990. *Productivity Measurement: A Guide for Managers and Evaluators*. London: Sage Publications.

Camp, Robert C. 1994. *Benchmarking*. München: Carl Hauser Verlag.

———. 1995. *Best Practice Benchmarking*. Milwaukee: ASQC Quality Press.

Fisher, John G. 1996. *How to Improve Performance Through Benchmarking*. London: Kogen Page.

Mendes, António Silva. 1998. *Benchmarking: Introduction and Main Principles Applied to Company Benchmarking*. Quality Series No. 7. Brussels: European Commission, Directorate-General III/Industry, Quality Policy, Certification, and Conformity Markings Unit.

Paasio, Antti, Robert G. Picard, and Timo E. Toivonen. 1994. "Measuring and Engineering Personnel Productivity in the Graphic Arts Industry," *Journal of Media Economics* 7 (2):39–53.

Picard, Robert G. 1998. "Measuring and Interpreting Productivity of Journalists," *Newspaper Research Journal* 19 (4):71–84.

Prokopenko, Joseph. 1987. *Productivity Management: A Practical Handbook*. Geneva, Switzerland: International Labour Office.

Watson, Gregory H. 1993. *The Benchmarking Workbook*. Cambridge, Mass.: Productivity Press.

GLOSSARY

accounts payable

The debt from short-term credit, typically for supplies and services. A newspaper, for example, may have received a shipment of ink for which payment has not yet been made.

accounts receivable

Debts that others owe the firm and are payable in the short term. A subscriber to a digital television service, for example, may have been billed for service but the payment not yet received.

acquisition

The purchase of another company or firm as opposed to a merger in which the firms are combined.

advertising

Paid communication by companies and individuals designed to develop interest in, understanding of, purchases of, and uses of the goods and services they offer.

alliance

An agreement made by separate, sometimes competing firms, to cooperate on specific activities for mutual benefit.

asset

Something of value owned by a firm that is shown on its financial statements. Assets include items such as cash, inventory, buildings, accounts receivable, and so on.

audience

Those persons who use a media product or service, giving it their attention and time.

audience measurement

Refers to a variety of techniques designed to measure audiences for media products or services. Typical types of measurement include demographic, psychographic, and lifestyle methods.

barriers to entry

Factors that impede the ability of new firms to enter a product or geographic market.

barriers to mobility

Factors that impede the ability of an existing firm to move into another product or geographic market.

benchmarking

The use of a standard industry measure or stipulated statistic to gain a comparison of a company with others or as progress toward a goal. The company's performance is assessed in relation to the benchmark.

brand

A name, design, sign, or other element that establishes the identity of a product or service and conveys images of its attributes and qualities to consumers.

branding

The process and techniques of establishing and developing a brand and its associated images for products or services.

business cycle

Somewhat cyclical growth and contraction in the general economy in which the fortunes of businesses improve and diminish as a result of economic changes.

business model

A description of how a product or service is offered and exchanged in the market that clarifies relationships and financial exchanges that make commerce in the product/service possible.

capacity

A term used to indicate the overall potential use of a manufacturing facility or its equipment. A CD manufacturer, for example, may have the capacity to produce as many as fifteen million copies per month.

capacity utilization

Refers to the amount of productive capacity actually used. A book printer, for example, may operate its press only for one shift (eight hours), thus using only one-third of the available capacity each day.

capital

Wealth that is accumulated and available for use.

capital availability

The extent to which desired capital is available for use by firms, entrepreneurs, and individuals.

capital expenditures

Expenditures made for items that are assets such as land, equipment, buildings, and so on.

capitalization

The wealth of a traded firm represented by the combined value of its shares in the market.

cash flow

The movement of cash through a company that can be tracked in its cash activities and accounts.

Central Bank

A nation's or region's bank that issues currency, holds the reserves of other banks, and controls monetary policies.

circulation

In print media, indicates the number of copies obtained by readers.

collateral

Assets that are used as a means of securing a debt.

competition

Rivalry in markets among suppliers and consumers.

competitive advantages

Factors that provide advantages to a firm and national industries when compared to other firms or nations. These include cost factors, skills and expertise of personnel, quality, reputation, and so on.

competitiveness

The degree to which a firm or industry can survive, sustain itself, and remain a viable competitor. There are many indicators of competitiveness but underlying the concept is the ability to generate more wealth than firms or industries in the same or similar environments.

constant currency

The value of currency adjusted for the effects of inflation.

consumers

Persons who acquire a product or service through monetary exchange.

consumer confidence

The degree to which consumers believe the coming economic period will be better or worse than the current period.

consumer expenditures

Expenditures made by individuals rather than by firms.

consumer price index

An index that measures the relative change in prices for goods and services sold to consumers. This is an indicator of inflation.

contractor

A firm or individual that receives a contract from another firm or individual to carry out work.

copyright

An exclusive right to use or distribute intellectual and artistic products belonging to those who create the works. All or part of the rights can be sold or purchased.

current asset

An asset that is liquid and available in the short term.

customer satisfaction

A measure of perception of the quality, price, or service held by persons who use or have used a product or service.

debt

Money and any rent that is due to those who have provided capital, supplies, services, and so on.

demand

Measure of the willingness of consumers to purchase or consume at a given price or availability.

dependence

Term used to indicate the degree to which firms rely upon outsiders for revenue, supplies, and other resources.

depression

A deep and prolonged downturn in the economy.

distribution

The process of moving products from a producer to a customer. Depending upon the type of product and distribution mechanism, this may include a chain of wholesale and retail transactions or may be direct distribution to the consumer.

distribution density

An indicator of the number of points of delivery that a distribution system reaches in a given geographical area. The average cost of distribution falls as density increases, so higher density is desirable for many consumer media products.

diversification

The process of changing the sources of revenue or the mix of products or services offered.

economies of integration

Declining costs that occur by integrating different activities into the same production or distribution systems. These are increasingly possible due to digitalization.

economies of scale
Declining costs that occur as output or company size increases.

economies of scope
Declining costs that occur as the scope of a company's operation enlarges.

employee
An individual who is integrated into a company as a worker and is not an independent contractor.

employee turnover
The extent to which the number of employees in a firm changes during a given period.

entrepreneur
A person who assumes risks associated with the operation of a business or creation of a product rather than merely being employed to do so.

equity
The remainder that would be left if assets were liquidated to pay for liabilities.

exchange rate
The value given to a currency when it is exchanged for another currency.

exports
Products or services that are sold or delivered outside their nation of origin.

financial flow
A description of the way that financial resources are used in a company setting.

fixed costs
Basic costs of a firm that do not change regardless of the amount of product or service produced or offered.

fluctuations in the economy
Regular changes that occur in the general economy. Sometimes called the *business cycle*.

globalization
A term used to indicate economic activity among nations worldwide.

gross domestic product
The value of all goods and services produced in a nation.

growth
Refers to increasing the size of a firm or a change either positive or negative in an economic statistic.

household penetration
Indicates the number of households within a stipulated market that have a communication technology or receive a media product or service.

imports
Goods or services produced outside a country that enter a nation.

incubator
An organization or firm designed to help spur the establishment and development of new firms.

inflation
A sustained rise in the general prices of goods and services.

innovation
The process and outcome of developing new products or services, or new features for existing products and services.

interactivity
Media and communications products and services in which action and participation by the audience or users are integral parts of the communication.

interest rates
A measure of the price paid for borrowing capital represented by the additional percentage of the total amount borrowed that must be paid for the use of the funds.

Internet
A connected system of computer networks worldwide linked to facilitate communications and data transfer.

inventory

Supplies that are held by the firm but have not yet been used. These may be items such as newsprint, television programs, or books or CDs in warehouses, and so on.

joint venture

A situation in which two or more firms invest together to provide funding for an activity of mutual interest.

liability

Value owed to others that can be claimed against the assets of a company.

life cycle

A model that describes the evolution of an industry or product from its inception to its demise. The model depicts the environment in which industries or products/services exist at different stages over time. Business analysts use these stages to locate and understand the position of the industry or product/service.

line of credit

Capital that a firm can access when desired, according to pre-agreed terms with a bank or other institution.

managerial economics

The use of economic theories and analysis tools to make knowledgeable business decisions.

management information system (MIS)

An internal computerized data management and retrieval system used by managers for operational control.

market

Term indicating the geographic area in which a firm conducts business and the persons in that area who are users of a specific type of product and service.

market share

The portion of the market, expressed in percentage, that a firm or product controls.

marketing

A variety of efforts to promote consumption or use of goods and services. Includes advertising, sales promotion, direct marketing, and a range of other activities.

merger

The joining of two firms through a pooling of their interests after which only one of the firms remains.

penetration

The extent to which a media product or service is used by a potential audience. Often manifest as a measure of penetration in households or among a particular group of persons.

product differentiation

The process of making a product different from similar types of products offered by competitors by altering its quality, features, and so on.

profit

Most often used to indicate *business profit*, that is, the funds that remain after costs are subtracted from the revenue a firm obtains during a specified period. *Economic profit* is a broader measure of profit that includes all economic costs, not merely those included on an operating statement.

Producer Price Index (PPI)

An index that measures the relative change in prices for goods and services used by producers. This is an indicator of the inflation rate for goods and services needed by producers of other goods and services.

production

The process of preparing a product for use by transforming raw and previously processed resources into the product.

productivity

A comparative measure of the value produced through the use of resources such as personnel or capital.

prosperity

A relative economic state perceived by individuals and firms because of economic growth, high employment, and increased buying power.

quality

Superior attributes in a product or service that meet or exceed characteristic and value expectations.

reach

An audience measure that includes not only those who acquire a media product or service but all those who use it. A newspaper, for example, may be received in a household and be read by more than one person.

recession
A downturn in the economy that can be caused by the business cycle or a shock to the economy.

regulation
Control over the activities of firms by governmental organizations.

reinvestment
The use of profits within a firm rather than removing it from the firm to pay owners.

rent
The price paid to use something of value such as land, labor, or capital.

research and development
Company activities designed to create and explore the potential of new products or services.

resources
Natural, human, financial, and managerial elements or factors that are harnessed and used in the operations of an enterprise.

restructure
Change in the organization and staffing of a company.

return
The overall result of operations that can be expressed as return on sales, return on investment, return on assets. The result is expressed as a percentage.

risk
Situations in which outcomes of decisions and the probability of potential outcomes cannot be fully estimated.

standards
Specifications, usually technical, for particular aspects of products or services offered by different firms. These can be mutually agreed upon or regulated by authorities.

stock or shares

Partial ownerships in companies that can be bought or sold.

stock market

An organized market in which company shares can be exchanged.

strategy

A broad plan used to guide company choices about its products, organization, operations, and use of resources.

subcontractor

A contractor working for a firm that has contracted with another firm to provide a product or service.

subscription

An agreement made between a consumer and the provider of a media product or service for future acquisition as opposed to individual purchases. Subscriptions are typically available for newspapers, magazines, and cable and satellite services.

substitutability

The ability to substitute one product for another and receive substantially the same benefits from its use.

sustainability

The degree to which a firm or industry can maintain its current operations, performance, products or services, and business models over time.

theory of the firm

A theory that argues the primary goal of firms is the maximization of the value of the company or wealth.

trade

Exchange of products or services among nations.

trade barriers

Factors that impede trade from occurring.

trade credit

Credit given by a company providing a product or service to another company.

uncertainty

A condition in which the risks of activities and choices cannot be estimated or are not identified.

value chain

A model describing the value created by different stages and processes in the workflow that makes products and services available to consumers.

variable costs

The costs of production that are affected by the amount of product produced. For example, a video company will use more blank videotapes and incur more costs if it produces additional copies.

venture capital

A form of higher-risk capital that is designed to help the development of new firms, finance management buyouts, and so on.

workflow

A description of the stages and processes required to organize and transform resources into finished products and services available in the market.

working capital

Cash available in a company to fund its daily operations.

INDEX

North American Free Trade Agreement. *See*
    NAFTA
not-for-profit corporations, 2

offensive material, 92–93
Olympic Games, 83
online advertising, 150–51
online content, 35–36, 86
online media, 55, 84, 127
online music, variable costs and, 81
online news sites, 2
online retailing, 69–70
operational characteristics, 15–22
orders, inventory and, 60
organization, content, 49
organizational forms of business, 1–2
outdoor advertising, 56, 145
over-the-counter market, 190–91
overstocking, 60
oversupply of content, 8
Ovitz, Michael, 215
ownership limits, 221, 229
ownership shares, capital and, 185
ownership structure, 92
ownership types, 2, 158, 210, 214

paid Internet model, 35–36
partnerships, 1
patterns, 12
patterns of media globalization, 231–34
Pearson, 2, 194
penetration, 131, 261
Penthouse, 77
periodicals, 2
personal portal model, 37
personnel productivity, 245
personnel skills and knowledge, 247
physical distribution, 59–60
piracy, 8
planning for profit, 14
platforms, multi-sided, 9
polarization of audience, 4, 127–28
policies, affecting trade, 226
portal model, 37
portfolios of products, 4
power of consumers, 134
power shift in communications, 4–5
PPI (Producer Price Index), 261
preferred stock, 192
Premiere League Football, 83
prescriptive regulation, 93
pressures from market, 194
print media, products and services, 26
printing, 50, 246

privatization, 194
process management, 41–42
process-oriented production, 41–42
Procter & Gamble, 142
producer's value chain, 45
product differentiation, 94, 98, 158–61, 261
product dumping, 225
product licensing, 230
product manufacturing, 41
production, 40, 261
    costs, 83–86
    flow, 41
    flow chart, 44
    methods, 7–8
    process-oriented, 41–42
    project-oriented, 42–43
    sustainability and, 57
productivity, 242–45, 261
products and services, 25–31
profit, 12–15, 261
profitability, importance of, 16
programs *versus* channels, 128
project-oriented production, 42–43
proscriptive regulation, 92–93
prosperity, 102–3, 261
protected works, 38
psychographic, audience, 124
public corporations, 2, 190, 194
public relations, 141
public service media, *versus* commercial
    media, 2
public shares, startup firms, 175
publicly traded companies, 14, 201
publishing industries, 18
    electronic, flow chart, 51
    specifics, 23
    value chains, 49–54
purchases, advertising, credit, 176–77

quality, 163, 261
Quebecor, 194

radio, 9, 26, 39, 92, 133
Random House, 65, 233
reach, 261
recession, 102–7, 262
recording artists, 223, 224
Redstone, Sumner, 201
Reed Elsevier, 209
regional trade agreements, 228–29
regulations, 191, 262
regulatory forces, 91–93, 99
reinvestment, 240, 241, 262
relationships, subscriptions, 137